D0442648

LETTERMAN

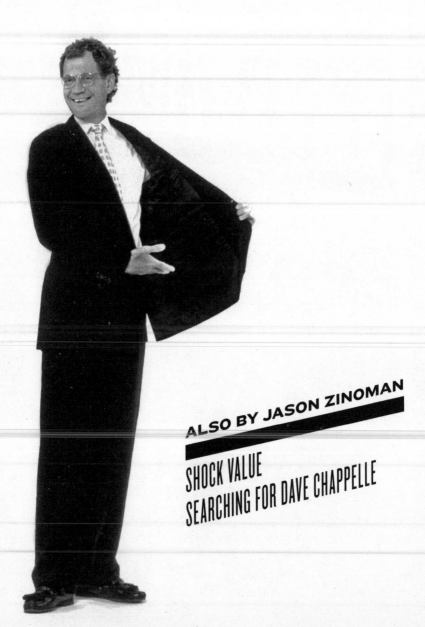

ALSO BY JASON ZINOMAN

SHOCK VALUE
SEARCHING FOR DAVE CHAPPELLE

CONTENTS

INTRODUCTION

In the summer of 1968, David Letterman's girlfriend gave him an ultimatum: Get married or break up.

Michelle Cook had just graduated from Ball State University and thought that Letterman, then working his first television job as a weekend weatherman during the summer before his last year of school, wasn't committing to the relationship. After she confronted him, he panicked. "I could not lose her," Letterman recalled. "That horrified me."

But so did the prospect of telling his parents that he was getting married. He was living at home, and he knew they would not approve. "They didn't like her," Letterman said, "but they didn't really know her."

David Letterman saw himself as stuck in an impossible situation, trapped between the demands of his girlfriend and the wishes of his parents. He settled on a solution that required the least conflict, at least in the short term: He got married in secret.

One afternoon in July, Cook's roommate, Sue Berninger, drove the couple to a house fifteen minutes from campus. Letterman had been drinking beer after beer and was buzzed by the time he was met at the door by a sober-faced justice of the peace.

"I was hitchhiking, and the next thing you know, they pick me up and we're getting married," Letterman said to the justice, introducing himself with a joke while nodding toward Cook and Berninger.

In response, the stoic man did not smile. In the course of filling out the paperwork, he asked the pair if they'd been married before. "Six times, and every one a gypsy," Letterman cracked, before answering seriously. Berninger stifled a laugh while Cook flashed Letterman a warm look of recognition.

When the time came for the traditional question of whether there was any reason they should not get married, Letterman turned his head to Berninger and joked: "This is your last chance."

Even at his own commitment ceremony, David Letterman didn't entirely commit.

David Letterman entered the national consciousness in the early 1980s, when the roiling revolutions of the Not Ready for Prime Time Players of the original *Saturday Night Live* were in transition, and the most popular comedian in America, Steve Martin, had just retired from stand-up comedy. *Late Night with David Letterman* went on the air at 12:30 a.m. when that seemed much later than it does now. Before the Internet and thousands of cable channels changed the cultural landscape, Letterman's main competition was reruns, old movies, and sleep. *Late Night* started with shots of empty New York streets followed by the camera panning up a dark skyscraper before zooming in on the one lit-up window. The opening carried a distinct message: This is the only thing on right now that matters.

Once Letterman walked onstage, standing in front of a makeshift set, he talked in a way that suggested he had a secret he wasn't telling you, a sneaky joke, implied but rarely stated. He got his point across in askance glances, deep sighs, and arched eyebrows. David Letterman hosted his talk show the same way he got married, participating in its conventions while providing mocking commentary on them at the same time. His jokes distanced him from what he was taking part in, but they also articulated a certain neurotic point of view. At the end of his many layers of ironic distance, Letterman could be hard to read, but what made him so fascinating was that something seemed to be bubbling underneath the surface, a tortured personality with a self-lacerating streak.

I became a devoted David Letterman fan not long after I first turned on a television. Outside of cartoons, the shows I liked best as a child were sitcoms scored to laugh tracks. Talk shows seemed grown-up and boring—until I saw *Late Night*. Along with its dark, unfinished design and intimate nightclub mood—it didn't sound like any other comedy on television—what struck me most was how aggressively disinterested the host seemed, as if he thought everything around him was absurd or phony or both. His attitude was that of an irreverent kid who refused to take anything seriously.

Letterman represented a version of New York cool that seemed more accessible than punk singers in ripped shirts or dapper sophisticates on Broadway. He wore white sneakers, unkempt hair, and a conspiratorial expression. His smirking tone was so consistently knowing that he seemed as if he must know something.

In the 1980s and early '90s, during the first comedy boom, when clubs sprouted across the country and stand-up became one of the quickest routes to sitcom stardom, Letterman inspired an entire generation of comedians. He created a blueprint that was followed by almost every late-night show with an adventurous bent, and helped define a sensibility that changed the entire culture. At a time when talk shows were still trafficking in the chummy sensibility of the celebrity roast, David Letterman brought a certain kind of knowing, ironic, and elusive voice into the mainstream.

Letterman wasn't the first late-night talk-show host or the most popular or powerful one. But he was the most influential. Letterman didn't just create two new network television franchises and produce some of the funniest, most innovative comedy in the history of television, in a career that spanned more than six thousand hours of performance. He created a new comic vocabulary that expanded our cultural sense of humor and made a persuasive case for the daily talk show as an ambitious art form.

By the time he retired, there were more talk shows than ever before, and yet they were radically different from the shows that were on when *Late Night with David Letterman* first aired. The proliferation of entertainment options has fragmented the culture and changed the way we watch these shows. You don't need to stay up anymore to see late-night television, and going viral matters almost as much as ratings. Talk shows have become collections of parts as much as unified wholes, and they are more likely to reach niches than mass audiences. The late-night talk show still looms large, but Letterman is its last giant.

How did a repressed Indiana weatherman who dreamed of hosting *The Tonight Show* put on a distinctly New York show that was a rejection of the conventional show business world? What enabled this quintessentially detached ironist to become the most emotionally galvanizing entertainer on television in the wake of September 11? Letterman the man was guarded, shy, and fiercely private, and yet he spent decades revealing his changing mood to millions of people every night. His contradictions only make him more compelling, not just to his audience but to his peers. "He's like our Bigfoot," Judd Apatow said of Letterman's reputation among comedians.

A talk-show host who didn't always seem to enjoy talking to people, a reserved man who spoke to millions of people every night, one of the most trusted entertainers of his time, whose ironic style kept emphasizing his own insincerity, David Letterman is one of the most famous entertainers in the world, and yet he remains an unlikely and enigmatic figure.

This book is the result of a lifetime of television watching and three years of reporting, including many hundreds of interviews with those who knew and worked most closely with David Letterman. It covers his entire career, from his childhood and his broadcasting roots in Indiana to his final years on the air, but it focuses on his most fertile era and the foundation of his artistic reputation: his years at NBC, when he did his most significant work. This spectacularly creative period featured three great eras of broadcasting with distinct aesthetic styles. In the early 1980s, Letterman was a fairly traditional host putting on an often experimental show that was literate, daring, and often baffling. His persistent target was television itself and, more specifically, the talk show, scrambling its conventions, shifting perspectives, and blurring the line between real and fake. By the middle of the decade, Letterman's performance had become more confidently theatrical, and *Late Night* had evolved, marked by extravagant stunts, an absurdist streak, and show-length parodies.

In these two periods, Letterman leaned heavily on a writing staff that was critical to his success. His greatness has always been the result of collaboration, an argument against the common wisdom about judging talk shows that is often attributed to Johnny Carson: It's all about the man behind the desk. To truly understand the art of David Letterman, you must look beyond the desk. "This show has always been somebody else's voice," Letterman said in 1997. "I still have ultimate veto, but I haven't had an idea since I was eleven, really. My viability as a creative voice is limited."

His most important creative partner was Merrill Markoe, who met him when he was a comic in Los Angeles. They started dating and working together, eventually collaborating on *Late Night with David Letterman,* where she was its first head writer, as important as anyone in establishing its distinctive aesthetic. Their tumultuous romance gave birth to the acerbic, adventurous late-night show. After a decade, they broke up, and Letterman's third great era had begun, one in which the writers became increasingly marginalized and the focus shifted away from scripted comedy and more toward the irritable personality of its host. While early *Late Night* was about an ordinary guy in a mad world, this new period turned into its mirror image: an eccentric surrounded by a more conventional talk show. This transformation culminated in a late-night war when Jay Leno was picked to host *The Tonight Show,* which led to Letterman's moving to CBS and starting the *Late Show* to compete with his old network.

It was the summer before I left home for college, and the rivalry between Jay Leno and David Letterman had become one of the dominant storylines of the entertainment press. It's hard to exaggerate, and a little embarrassing, how much this contrast mattered to me. It was a litmus test of whether or not you were the kind of person worth talking to. In the second week of the *Late Show,* I traveled to New York to see the show in person for the first time. When I arrived at the Ed Sullivan Theater, inflamed by the cult-like fervor of a die-hard fan, I approached a member of the *Late Show* staff patrolling the line and asked him if I could get an autograph from the host. He told me he would get one if I could find a can of Spam.

This put me in a difficult position. The doors were opening in fifteen minutes. Could I find Spam in Times Square in time? Missing the show would have been heartbreaking, but the possibility of getting an autograph from David Letterman was irresistible. Along with a friend, I dashed out the door, charging from store to store, receiving shaking heads and blank stares until finally I found one that carried Spam. We raced the several blocks back to the theater minutes before showtime and handed the can to the staffer before being seated.

When David Letterman first walked onto the bright blue stage, dwarfed by the towering ceiling of the historic theater where teenagers screamed at the Beatles, he looked different from the man I had been watching for many years. He was energetic, stylishly dressed, larger than life, but also somehow smaller than he was on television. Letterman masterfully played to the camera, but in person it was hard to read the shifts in his expression. His irritation seemed broader, more overt.

On the old show, Letterman was often pointing out the fakery around him, smirking at the artifice. So it was strange to see a staffer waving his arms after jokes, encouraging big laughs. Paul Shaffer's band sounded much louder live than on television. Primed with anticipation, in part because of a massive amount of press about the late-night war, the audience roared at every joke. So did I.

Afterward, I waited in front of the theater for the staffer. Once the crowd filed out, he came by and handed me my can of Spam. On the back was David Letterman's signature, next to a note: I LOVES MY SPAM. I was thrilled. I took the Spam to college and kept it on my desk for years.

Two decades later, I saw Letterman again, this time inside a restaurant just a few blocks from the Ed Sullivan Theater, nearly nine months after he retired from his job. Letterman is different from the guy he played on television, but he shares many qualities with him, including knee-jerk irreverence and an ironic attitude that keeps him at a distance from what he's saying. His defining quality, the one that scores of colleagues and friends describe again and again, is a fierce and persistent critical eye about his own flaws that frequently verges on self-flagellation. When I asked those who worked with David Letterman to recall his happiest moments, they tended to take a long pause.

Letterman discussed his career with the bemusement of someone looking back on a former life. Dressed casually, he had grown a Lincoln-like beard that hung down his face in an unruly mess. His wife didn't like it. Neither did his son. "The more people protest," he said, with a smile, "the longer it stays."

Letterman was sober, thoughtful, and understated throughout the interview, with no trace of the showmanship he displayed hosting a late-night talk show. One exception was when I brought up seeing him during his second week at CBS. I was curious to know whether the autographed Spam was an oddball tradition. But when I started explaining what had happened, Letterman's face dropped, his head shaking. There's no way, he said, with melancholy eyes, that he signed the can. Someone on his staff must have faked the signature.

That I got a phony autograph changed a story I had been telling for decades, although it didn't exactly end my innocence. Yet Letterman kept apologizing, even after I told him it was not necessary. Perhaps he thought it made him look phony or that he had let down his audience, but he aggressively dramatized his anguish and flamboyantly exaggerated his transgression. The mood darkened for an instant, creating the kind of gloomy moment I had heard about from many of those who worked closely with him.

For Letterman, self-criticism was almost reflexive. During our conversation, he expressed regret about the way he'd treated guests, network executives, and his wife. He regretted his own fear of failure and his tendency to be cautious. He even regretted his own tendency to regret. After apologizing over the signed can of meat, he looked nearly apocalyptic. "I feel like I've let everyone down," he said.

In less than a minute, he had turned an old story about a can of Spam into his own operatic tragedy. It was ridiculous, heartfelt, and also strangely funny. Only when he started lashing himself did David Letterman look most vividly like himself.

PART I

EDUCATION OF A TALK-SHOW HOST

1947–1979

Did you hear McDonald's is now serving breakfast?
Now there's a dream come true.

—David Letterman, stand-up act in the late 1970s

SHOCK JOCK

When David Letterman was twelve years old, two disasters struck. His father, Harry Joe Letterman, suffered a heart attack, and, while he was recovering, his business partner decided to sell his share of the flower shop they ran together. The family suddenly had hefty medical bills to pay, so he couldn't afford to buy him out. "From that point on, everything started to go away," David Letterman said. "It was awful."

The seeds of David Letterman's anxiety were planted in his childhood home, a modest single-story house built after World War II in the quiet Indianapolis neighborhood of Broad Ripple. His parents were children of the Depression who didn't benefit from a safety net. Money and health worries were a constant. It was not Harry Letterman's first heart attack, or his last. Yet he was garrulous and outgoing, with a boisterous sense of humor, while his wife, Dorothy, was quieter, exacting and stingy about doling out approval. She worked as a church secretary and raised David and his two older sisters.

When Letterman was born, in 1947, his family didn't own a television, so his first memories of broadcasting were not from sitcoms or network talk shows. Radio was and remained his first love, even when a television arrived in the house when he had just begun elementary school. Harry Letterman loved the comedy of Jack Benny and Jack E. Leonard, a wry insult comic predecessor to Don Rickles. When the show *Monitor* was on the radio during weekends, Letterman and his father laughed at Bob and Ray, the team of Bob Elliott and Ray Goulding, whose low-key deadpan routines parodied the media and turned the most mundane situations into delirious absurdity. "It was the first time our sense of humor overlapped," he said of the show he discovered around the age of six. "We both got it."

Asked what radio shows his mom liked to listen to, Letterman recalled with a laugh: "You know, for some reason, we didn't care what Mom liked." She liked soap operas and some talk shows. Letterman mostly remembers her as withholding, often telling the story of how she got irritated when Ed Sullivan would ask his audience to applaud for music acts before they had even performed. "She thought you should get applause on merit," he said.

David Letterman, a soft-spoken kid with a gap between his teeth, remembers his father as a smoker and a drinker with painful dental problems. A tumor even forced him to have his teeth pulled. "I remember him on the floor, writhing in pain," Letterman said, shaking his head. "It was like 'Oh, Dad, what have you done?' He was always self-conscious about his teeth." Letterman described this scene of his father in pain from half a century ago in vivid detail, and anxiety about his own health (including different kinds of tumors) would haunt him throughout his life.

To a young Letterman, his father's problem was not just bad luck with his health and a shaky business career. Even at an early age, Letterman could tell his father had other dreams that he ignored out of duty. Harry Joe Letterman's real passions were artistic. He read music and played the organ, stopping by the church to deliver flowers on Saturday and sitting down to play for a few minutes. He also had literary aspirations. *Parade* magazine had a contest called the Great American Writer Test, where you filled out a survey and were sent a pamphlet to test whether you were a great writer. He was accepted into the program but couldn't afford to sign up. "It broke my heart," Letterman recalled, "because even as a kid I knew this is not how you get to be a writer."

To his son, Harry Letterman seemed most at home when he was serving as the emcee of a church potluck dinner or hosting a meeting at the Indiana Flower Association, where he would tell jokes. "He loved doing that more than his actual job," Letterman said. "My dad's life did not work out the way he wanted it to."

This made a distinct impression. Letterman cites his parents when asked about his own prickliness or lack of warmth. His mother could look tight-lipped and uneasy, he said, but when you asked her if anything was wrong, she would shout: "I'm fine!" Letterman inherited her stoicism, repression, and belief in hard work. He worked bagging groceries at a supermarket throughout high school.

In high school, Letterman did not excel academically or socially. He wasn't a jock or a theater kid. He preferred poking fun at groups to joining them, but he was not a nerd and even displayed a mildly subversive sense of humor that his peers enjoyed. As a joke, he once wore a jacket and tie along with Bermuda shorts and knee-high socks to a school dance. According to friends, Letterman made an effort to dress cool, adopting a preppy look, wearing a madras shirt. But friends also recall his insecure streak. Every day, Letterman rode with a few boys to school. Once, when he was picked up in a '39 Chevy at his home, a kid made a crack about his shirt. Letterman immediately went back to the house to get a new shirt, without saying a word.

Early on, though, Letterman showed an interest in radio and television. In middle school, he and a friend recorded shows on a reel-to-reel recorder, doing parodies of *Leave It to Beaver* and *The Adventures of Ozzie & Harriet.* He also made a mock talk show, in the style of Steve Allen, whose occasional juvenile prankishness sparked his imagination. "[Letterman] emulated him," said Fred Stark about his middle school friend. "We sat in my basement and made a fake talk show set out of a toilet paper tube and a cigar box. He would sit behind the desk. I was his Paul Shaffer."

But Letterman's comedic sensibility was apparent even earlier. At seven he collected four friends in the parking lot outside of his elementary school to put on a spoof of *Winnie the Pooh.* Besides coming up with the story, Letterman cast the roles, gave his friends lines on the spot, and told each of them where to stand. Then the show started and Letterman stood back, arms crossed, and laughed at everybody who took part in it. "That was part of his charm," said Stark, who played Eeyore. "People hung around to see who would get zinged."

David Letterman's broadcasting career began almost as soon as he left home for college. He attended Ball State University in the mid- to late 1960s, when campuses all across the country were hotbeds of tumult and protest. Ball State, located in Muncie, Indiana, was hardly Berkeley, and Letterman was far from a wild-eyed activist. His social scene revolved around the Sigma Chi fraternity, a boys' club whose alumni included John Wayne and Barry Goldwater. Letterman was never particularly interested in politics. Instead of joining the ranks for or against Vietnam, he incorporated news about the war into a prank on the saleswoman at the campus bookstore, asking her with a straight face if she sold napalm. "It's a gelatinous substance that burns on anything. The U.S. armed forces used it in Vietnam," he explained blankly as his friends nearby cracked up.

Letterman grew a long, shaggy beard that he sometimes paired with a long trench coat that could fit nicely into the folk scene. His fraternity brothers described him as shy and uncomfortable with new people. "Dave didn't let people close to him," said Jeff Lewis, a fellow Sigma Chi. "I asked him about it and he said, 'If they got to know me, they wouldn't like me.'" Lewis recalls him being concerned about the social events: "He said, 'Listen, don't be upset if I don't go to the parties.'"

At rush events, Letterman displayed an aggressively teasing charisma, selling underclassmen on the fraternity by mocking the neighboring fraternity. "He said, 'If you don't like girls, go next door,'" said Mike Little, a fraternity brother whose nickname, "Fatty No Neck," was given to him by Letterman, who assumed the role of the pledge trainer, or "magister," supervising the new class of members and organizing the pranks. "It was an instant confidence booster for me," Letterman told the Sigma Chi magazine in 1984. Today he mostly recalls fraternity life as an excuse to drink as much beer as possible.

In the tumultuous 1960s, Letterman cared more about partying with friends than political activism, but he became a campus radical of another sort, coming down clearly on one side of the generation gap as a polarizing figure in university radio. In many ways, his experience clashing with the head of his college radio station would set him on the path to being an irreverent performer and anticipate later battles with television executives.

The first person to give David Letterman a broadcasting job was Dr. William Tomlinson, who ran the Center for Radio and Television, as well as the school radio station, WBST. Tomlinson, who had worked as an audio engineer for CBS, had a formal manner, was a stickler for the rules, and spoke with a news anchor's portentousness. "I am convinced he would have worn cap and gown to class given the opportunity," said Mike Rogers, one of Letterman's classmates.

Tomlinson insisted that the disc jockeys on his station be clean-shaven and not smoke. Cursing was frowned upon. The shows had to be about the music or the news, not personality. And as for rock 'n' roll, he kept it off the air. In a story in the Ball State newspaper, Tomlinson took pains to point out that they played "good music," which he explained euphemistically as that "whose popularity would last for years."

Tomlinson hired Letterman to work at the radio station, but from the start, they were on a collision course. Tomlinson's cultural references were classical music and *Playhouse 90*, while Letterman liked Steve Allen and swaggering deejays with big voices and colorful personalities. He listened to rock 'n' roll and comedy on the radio, on a large console that broadcast stations from all around the country. Along with Bob and Ray, he liked the deejay Rich King, who started his freewheeling afternoon show out of Cincinnati the same year Letterman began college. King made up stories about fake baseball teams or nude beaches and passed them off as news. "When I first heard Dave," said Chuck Crumbo, a classmate, "I thought, 'This is Richard King all over again.'"

Such stunts were not on the curriculum of Tomlinson's announcing class that Letterman took. Instead, students were required to pronounce the names of famous composers. Letterman couldn't care less about classical music, and decided to launch a protest with his friends. "I remember going to see the dean to call out the head of the department, hoping he would get fired," Letterman remembered, shaking his head at the futility of the gesture. "I was a cocky kid."

WBST aired classical music, historical documentaries, and occasionally some middle-of-the-road pop music that wasn't too square to alienate students. Andy Williams and Frank Sinatra were standards. Some Elvis. They also had news. Letterman wanted the format to be more flexible, to draw more students to the station. Short of that, he found more creative ways to shake up the station.

LETTERMAN

Letterman hosted a music show where his job was to write and read the copy that would explain the background of the pieces and biographies of the composers. The disc jockeys would get the information from record jackets and books that were loaned to them by the School of Music. Letterman followed the script at first, but eventually started making up stories. When introducing Claude Debussy's "Claire de Lune," he said, "You know the de Lune sisters. There was Claire, there was Mabel."

A music teacher called the station manager to complain, and Letterman was fired—for the first time.

That Tomlinson was working at CBS when Orson Welles read *The War of the Worlds*, the H. G. Wells story of an alien invasion that many took as a genuine news report, might have made him more sensitive to blurring the lines between fact and fiction. Letterman saw it differently. "He was in the control booth when they were pulling a huge hoax on America," he said, "and yet he couldn't put up with my nonsense?"

WBST was short-staffed and couldn't afford to lose popular disc jockeys. So Letterman was brought back, though it didn't take long for him to get into trouble again. "He hatched an idea to play rock 'n' roll after midnight," said Al Rent, the student manager of the station. "I printed flyers saying 'Listen to David Letterman at midnight.'" They sneaked onto the air after midnight to play rock records on a show called *Make It or Break It,* inspired by a local radio show of the same name, starring a pompadour-wearing Brooklyn-born disc jockey named Dick Sumner, who broadcast from a glass booth at the top of a drive-in hamburger restaurant not far from Broad Ripple. Letterman asked listeners to call in and say whether they liked a song. If not, he broke the record in half and crushed it with his hands, the vinyl crackling on air. At the end, he tabulated the votes and said he would give away a record of the winning song to the first person who came to the radio station office the next morning. The next day, there was a line down the hallway greeting Tomlinson. Letterman didn't show up, and there were no free records.

"Dave didn't worry about the consequences. I did," Rent said. In a desperate move, Rent came up with the idea to move Letterman from music to the news, reading the stories from the AP and UPI wire services from around the world. "In hindsight, what was I thinking?" he said. "Like he wouldn't embellish the news?"

On the afternoon show, Letterman delivered periodic updates on scores for the "International Fungo Ball League," a fake sport where a point was scored when one team pushed a cast iron ball out of the stadium and onto the opposing team's bus. Letterman delivered these descriptions in a news anchor's voice full of stentorian authority. He also wrote fake stories, infuriating Tomlinson, who would call up Rent and demand, "Are you listening to your station? Did you hear what Letterman said?"

In one newscast, Letterman and a friend introduced themselves as Barry Budweiser and Mike Michelob. Tomlinson took Letterman off the air again. This tension between Tomlinson and his renegade host continued, coming to a head in the winter of 1968, during a field trip to New York—Letterman's first visit to the city. Tomlinson took fifteen broadcasting students by train. While there, Letterman got his first look at a national television studio and sat in the audience of *Match Game*, whose guests that day were Steve Allen and Jayne Meadows.

New York's drinking age was eighteen, and Letterman took advantage of it. He left the tour of CBS and walked to the bar at the Hotel Edison. Later, he and his friends headed uptown to check out the Sigma Chi house at Columbia University.

On their last day, Letterman and two friends went to a bar to watch a Rangers hockey game, got drunk, and lost track of time. When they checked the clock and realized their train was about to leave, they rushed to Penn Station, late. They hadn't packed their bags, so Tomlinson had to send someone to the hotel. When they returned to Ball State, Tomlinson called them into the office and said they could be expelled for their behavior.

Darrell Wible, a professor at Ball State who saw potential in Letterman, said that the student deejay was "in the department doghouse from that point on." In a book about his time at school, he recounted an argument he had with Tomlinson about Letterman, in which the head of the department stated bluntly, "As far as I'm concerned Letterman is stupid."

A divide opened up on campus about Letterman. Some saw his small rebellions as hilarious; others found him insufferable. He inspired devotion as easily as he did annoyance. Making up stories about composers or the news is the kind of humor that some people get, and others do not. It's not even a joke, really, because there's no punch line, no clear place where the tension is released. It's more like an elaborate prank. If you don't get it, the effect can just be confusing and, once you realize you've been had, even embarrassing.

Letterman didn't adopt the countercultural poses of young comedians of that era when it came to drugs or sex or politics. What he shared with the sixties youth culture was irreverence in the face of authority and an aggression that didn't mind if it was alienating. When it came to his humor, he didn't pander. You got it or you didn't—and he was willing to live with either result.

Letterman's quintessential joke was the benign lie, and it was one he stuck with his entire career. He was inventive in working fictions into the news. He didn't just make up stories—he committed to them. This was what he had done when he told the justice of the peace that he picked up a few girls on the way to the wedding. And it was what he did on the radio in college.

Lying opens up a vast amount of creative running room. It's at the root of every work of fiction, and there's an art to a good lie, one plausible enough to not dismiss out of hand but still ridiculous enough to signal its falsity. Letterman would sprinkle his fabrications with concrete details and technical terms to give them veracity. His lies were dumb mischief, anarchic fun for a small audience. "I was playing exactly to my friends, calculating what would make them laugh," he said. "It was very inside. It was that more than anything else."

For some students, Letterman's shaky status with the station represented larger problems about the school's student radio. They saw WBST as stodgy and out of touch with the rock 'n' roll revolution. Three students left WBST and started their own, more rambunctious radio station, based out of Wagoner Hall, an all-male dorm of four hundred students. WAGO was set up in a twelve-by-six-foot janitor's closet, and its broadcasts didn't reach outside the dorm. It went on the air on Valentine's Day with the Buckinghams' "Kind of a Drag," a bubblegum song about getting dumped, and by 1968 WAGO had become the one campus station that broadcast all rock, with some raunchy comedy mixed in.

The Wagoner Hall revolt, as one student called it, gave the university an alternative to WBST, which was going defiantly in the opposite direction. In the fall of 1968, Tomlinson introduced a new, rebranded station that would emphasize "fine arts broadcasting," which meant almost exclusively classical music. WBST increased its programming hours and added more airtime on weekends, during which they would play opera. Tomlinson brought in a new manager. Some balked at having to play even more classical music. Many quit.

"It was a very tense time. Everything took on an us-versus-them quality," said Thomas Watson, the student program director, who had to navigate between the administration and the talent who filled up twelve hours a day of programing.

Letterman didn't leave the station. He may have been the disc jockey who flouted the rules most often, but he remained willing to work within the system. He stuck with WBST and even helped out by staying around on weekends during the summer to run a show that played opera broadcasts from New York.

The station, meanwhile, tried to rein him in by putting another student, John Gall, in charge of the board and microphone during his show. Letterman quickly co-opted Gall. Between records, he would announce that he had a guest in the studio and start interviewing Gall, who was forced into playing a member of the mob or an Indian ambassador. "It was thought I could keep control of the situation, since I had control of the mic and the equipment," Gall said. "It was like hiring a fox to guard the chicken coop."

On February 6, 1969, Tomlinson sent a memo to Letterman: "I am informed of several infractions that have been evidenced by you as a student member of radio station WBST. Because of the serious nature of these infractions, it is not deemed advisable for you to be retained by us as a future member of the radio station."

Letterman had been taken off the air before. But this was different. Watson was in a tough position. "Letterman became a cause célèbre," Watson said. "I tried to keep the peace in the family by giving Letterman plenty of room, but this only created discipline problems with the other staff announcers. Why did they have to walk the straight and narrow if David didn't?"

Watson turned to Wible for advice. The professor, a veteran broadcaster who had covered local events like the Indianapolis 500, had long been a supporter of Letterman's, encouraging him in classes and at the station. But he didn't back him up this time. Wible advised Watson to take action. When he was fired for the last time, Letterman was upset. "We were kids, but he saw this more seriously," Watson said. "It was painful for him."

When David Letterman got dismissed from his campus radio station, it was the first time he had gotten on the wrong side of an employer, become a cult sensation, and left for a bigger stage. But it would not be the last. This time, he went to the commercial station WERK. Letterman also started doing a comedy show on WAGO, called *The David Letterman Show.*

Letterman performed the show with an upbeat rat-a-tat-tat energetic patter that was a parody of the distinctive cadence of the Top 40 style called Boss Radio popular among AM disc jockeys in the 1960s. He adopted a highly affected voice interrupted by whistles, squeaks, and other hyperactive sound effects. As soon as he left a classical station for a rock outlet, he immediately made fun of the kind of voices who appeared on rock stations. Letterman was not an advocate for one side of a culture war. His comedic instinct was to mock and belittle whatever world he inhabited.

In one episode, he called a groggy, bothered waitress on campus named Lila Whip, who was recovering from her late-night shift at the local diner. She sounded as if she had just woken up. "Lila Whip, this must be your magic and enchanted evening, because this is David Letterman, fun seeker of the radio." Letterman delighted in unusual words and names and also in mocking hype and promotion. And even in his fast-talking radio voice, he made "magic and enchanted" sound like empty slogans. She mumbled something about her boyfriend, and Letterman made lascivious noises.

On this station, Letterman sounded slightly outside his comfort zone: high-energy, playing a character, and going for dirty jokes. Unlike at the campus radio station, where by fabricating stories he transformed a music show into a joke, here he sounded like he was trying to fit in. At the same time, his gift for unusual turns of phrase was evident. After playing a clanging sound effect, he asked her to guess it. "It sort of sounds like horse dentures falling into rusted Howitzer shell casings." Letterman replied enthusiastically and said that, for getting the answer right, she had won a poisonous hunting arrow. "Maims first time every time," he touted.

The woman playing Lila Whip was Michelle Cook, his girlfriend, the first of several whom he also worked with. Letterman and Cook shared a sharp, contentious sense of humor. Cook, statuesque and reserved, belonged to a conservative sorority, Alpha Chi, which had tossed a member out for spending the night at a hotel with her boyfriend. To some sisters, she seemed more interested in her boyfriend than in sorority events. "Her goal in life was to marry him," said Pat Wiehle, a sorority sister.

She succeeded, though married life didn't at first go as planned. After they returned from the justice of the peace, Cook insisted that Letterman go home and tell his parents. Worried about their disapproval, he once again pushed off a confrontation, avoiding conflict at all cost. He told Cook he would tell them, but when she went back to her home in Fort Wayne, Letterman returned to his parents' house in Broad Ripple and said nothing. She waited and waited. But Letterman couldn't bring himself to do it. "I lived in terror that my parents would find out," he said, adding exasperatedly, "You can't keep things like that hushed up."

Weeks passed. Cook warned him that if he didn't tell his parents, she would. She kept her word.

One night, Letterman returned home to find his parents waiting for him. They were shocked and upset. His mother thought the reason they had gotten married was that Cook was pregnant. They pressed him with questions about their plans. "I walked right into a shit storm," he said. "My parents were horrified and depressed. They were angry. Why and how and what was going to happen and on and on. They were really hurt, deeply hurt. And they had every right to be."

After he graduated, Letterman moved in with Cook in Broad Ripple, only a few blocks away from his family. His mother was initially cool toward Cook, who came to the house for Thanksgiving the year after they were married. "When she got back, Michelle said it was awful," said Jeff Lewis, who knew them both. "She said the only thing

Dorothy said to her was when she turned in the car and asked, 'Are you cold?'"

But they grew closer. Cook got a job as a buyer at a department store and brought in a steady income, providing a solid baseline of support for her husband as he got his start in local television.

His first appearance on television was a summer job as a booth operator at the Indianapolis branch of WLW, a midwestern media powerhouse that produced a slate of local shows on radio and television. Created by an experimental permit granted by Franklin D. Roosevelt in the 1930s, WLW, which had a bustling operation airing in four cities, was known as "the Nation's Station."

Letterman logged all the shows and signed off at night. He would keep track of the time. To pass the time, he would toss pencils at the ceiling or build a giant ball of tape. "The office manager finally cracked down and made rules that prevented him from raiding office supplies," said Rick Posson, the general manager of the station. His first major exposure was as weekend weatherman. He quickly attracted attention by doing the same thing he was getting punished for at the college radio station: making up white lies in the middle of forecasts. With a deadpan delivery, he said the "higher-ups" had removed the border between Indiana and Ohio to make one giant state. "Personally," he said, "I'm against it."

But whereas he had been fired for making up stories at the campus radio station at Ball State, he was encouraged at WLW. At the time, local news all across the country was embracing an amiable, informal style of broadcasting known as "happy talk," where the anchors cracked jokes, ad-libbed, and generally acted like they were snapping towels in the locker room. Letterman was seen as Indiana's version, comparing hailstones to cans of ham. "Everyone was like, 'God, how about that,'" Letterman remembered. "So what I did worked for me. They said, 'Keep doing it.'"

This made him something of a local star. When Channel 13 did a survey to figure out its most popular on-air personalities, Letterman came in second. He got the chance to host a children's show, *Clover Power*, and a late-night movie show, *Freeze Dried Movies*, where he did sketches that included an interview with the governor of Indiana. In his second week, he had a ten-year anniversary show—a send-up of the self-congratulatory nature of these shows that would have fit in perfectly in the early years of *Late Night with David Letterman*. "I was dying to be funny," he said. "Any opportunity I had to be funny, I had to seize it."

But his popularity never grew beyond being a cult favorite, and his success did not last long. His movie show was canceled, and when the station announced a search for a full-time weatherman, Letterman did not get the job. Being funny was fine for the weekend weatherman, but for the full-time position, they wanted a performer with gravitas. The fact that Letterman had become a cult favorite for his jokes didn't matter, and his options around town seemed limited. He was extremely frustrated.

Letterman was starting to think more seriously about show business. Tom Cochrun, another former college classmate, spent many evenings with Letterman and Michelle around this time, during which they would have dinner, sit in the living room, and watch television. He recalls watching *The Tonight Show* with Letterman one night when Johnny Carson did Carnac the Magnificent, a fortuneteller with a gaudy turban who responded to setups by Carson's sidekick, Ed McMahon, with concise punch lines. It was a hokey conceit designed as a delivery system for one-liners. Watching the show, Letterman started talking back to the screen, making up alternate jokes. "Letterman started saying jokes that were funnier than Johnny's," Cochrun remembered. "That struck me: He wanted to do this."

Having failed to advance in television, Letterman returned to radio. With a smaller audience, he flourished, writing comedy segments for programs on WNAP, a small sister station of the behemoth in the city, WIBC. Tom Cochrun did the news and hired a team of funny personalities to present short satirical sketches. The Letterman on these shows, of which a few recordings survive, has a more refined voice than the one in college. He isn't riffing. He's making carefully crafted comedy, taking aim at news anchors by adopting the mock stentorian authority in their voices.

Letterman specialized in skewering salesmen and self-promoters of all kinds, including publicists, spiritual gurus, and psychics. His sketches were parodies, but of a very narrow range of types, most of whom were pompous and assured confidence men and authority figures who spoke in the trumped-up language of show business. An ad promising to protect you from bullies promised to teach the "ancient and mysterious art of origami guacamole, the most deadly of the martial arts."

In one that seemed to poke fun at rigid teachers like Tomlinson, Letterman did a mock ad pitching the "Dingle Academy of Big-Time Broadcasting," wherein a foolish huckster named Willard Monroe Dingle teaches you how to achieve fame and fortune in television. What stands out in these sketches is that their humor comes not from jokes but from amusing descriptions, strange turns of phrase, and cutting sarcasm. But there's also a clear point of view, a vision of the world that sees phonies everywhere.

When Letterman was twenty-five, his mother told him that she and his father were getting a divorce. He was stunned. She said his father's drinking had become too much for her. She ended up not leaving but calling Alcoholics Anonymous, and two men came over and became his father's sponsors. He quit drinking and started hosting events. "He wanted me to come to one of the meetings," Letterman said. "And I did, and by God, he had taken over. He would write jokes. It was like the Friars Club. He just liked being the center of attention." Harry Letterman never got a platform like the one his son would have, but in this room, performing for a group of people struggling with alcoholism, he seemed happy.

Not longer after, Harry Letterman suffered another heart attack and died. "I just felt like he never quite got to do what he wanted to do," Letterman reflected. "So that was a very strong observation for me. I really wanted to make good on my personal commitment, because I know it was probably the same as my father's personal commitment, but he just never had the opportunity or the pathway to fulfill it."

Soon after his father died, Letterman made the most difficult decision of his young life, concluding he needed to move out of Indiana if he was going to pursue a career in television. The prospect of leaving home, where he had jobs and a reputation as a talented and charming, if occasionally difficult, broadcaster, for a big city where he would be completely unknown terrified him. He had turned down out-of-town offers before, including a weather job in Minneapolis. But he was tired of being a booth announcer and didn't want to report on the weather anymore.

His father's death presented a cautionary tale on the dangers of waiting too long to take a big risk with your life. But even after he decided to head to the West Coast, he wasn't entirely ready. First, considering the worst-case scenario, Letterman decided he needed to save enough money so he and Cook could survive if he couldn't find work for half a year.

He worked a drive-time slot at a sleepy station called WNTS, a third-tier country station reinvented as the first all-talk station in the area. It had an older, conservative audience. As with his stint on local television and student radio, Letterman developed a devoted young following but also a lot of complaints. He had a midday show that included call-ins from listeners who often wanted to talk about Vietnam and Watergate, and he handled them brusquely, at best. When a man called saying that the town of Carmel was overrun with Communists, Letterman leveled with him in a deadpan: "You have to give them Carmel. The stores are overpriced and the football team is horrible. Give them Carmel and hold the line at Norwich." The caller contacted the general manager and complained. "Now, twenty-five-year-old guys are on the floor," said his boss, Jeff Smulyan, "but seventy-year-old guys think this guy is a Bolshevik. We had that every day."

Letterman also, predictably, made up stories that had fun with respected institutions. At one point he suggested that the island of Guam had bought the Soldiers and Sailors Monument, a statue in Indianapolis that pays tribute to veterans. The most important spectator event in Indiana was the Indianapolis 500, so of course Letterman took aim, announcing that the race was being moved to an interstate. But this job was a poor fit for Letterman. It was a call-in show where people didn't want to banter or joke around so much as chat about politics. Letterman never saw himself as a pundit or a newsmaker. He felt his limitations and was often reminded of them. After telling a caller he didn't know who the deputy mayor of Indianapolis was, a local newspaper columnist took him to task, writing that if he didn't know who was running the city, he shouldn't be in charge of a topical show.

Letterman saw a potential escape route when Allen Ludden, a veteran game show host, and Betty White came through town and appeared on his show. Letterman gently poked fun, reporting that the newest tourist attraction in town was the Allen Ludden Wax Museum. Ludden found Letterman funny and told him that if he moved to Hollywood, he should contact him, implying that he could help him get some work. Letterman had saved some money, and now he had his first real Hollywood contact. "That was huge," he said. He was ready to make the move.

The day before Letterman left town, Tom Cochrun and his wife invited him to their home in southern Indiana. Letterman brought his pickup truck, fully loaded. He was wearing a soccer jersey and talked soberly about their plans in Los Angeles. He seemed unsure about the prospects, but Cook was far more enthusiastic and positive. "She was the principal cheerleader for this move," Cochrun said.

Cochran and his wife could sense the anxiety and offered support and encouragement. "If Dorothy [Letterman] was unsure about his comedy, Michelle was the antithesis. She was supportive. They had a plan."

Letterman said that leaving home was petrifying and that Cook's confidence was critical. "I don't know if I could have done it without her," he said.

By the time he left, in 1975, Letterman was a broadcasting veteran with nearly a decade of work, albeit one whom few outside of Indiana had seen. He had not done any stand-up or much in the way of talk shows, but he was not green. He had experienced his share of failure and logged hundreds of hours on the air. He had hosted several radio shows, a late-night movie showcase, and a show for kids. He'd covered sports and the weather, and had even done political chat. Letterman didn't leave Indiana to become an entertainer. He already was one. But that didn't mean he could make a living at it.

"If it doesn't work out," Letterman told his friend Tom Cochrun, "I'll work at a gas station."

WHEN DAVID MET MERRILL

Not long after moving to Hollywood, Merrill Markoe made herself an orange T-shirt that read, in black letters, IMPORTANT WRITER.

That no important writer would wear it was only part of the joke. So was the preposterous idea that any aspiring writer for television and the movies could be important. Markoe arrived in town with almost no show business experience and a few scripts she couldn't sell. But she was no fool. With the shirt, she skewered self-promotion while engaging in a bit of it herself. "It got attention at parties," she said.

Markoe had left behind a six-year relationship with an artist in San Francisco and given up a career as a fine arts professor at USC. She was a painter, but after auditing a few screenwriting classes, she'd decided to try comedy. Between asthma attacks, she worked hard to write spec scripts for sitcoms that she didn't like that much. Markoe was highly self-aware and hostile to any trace of bullshit, which included, to her eyes, most of television. When the head writer of *Welcome Back, Kotter* asked her if she liked the show, she didn't know what to say, because, she thought, what intelligent person possibly would?

Markoe was raised in a turbulent Jewish household that was often on the move. She was born in New York and lived in Englewood, New Jersey, until her father's plastics business (inherited from her grandfather) went bankrupt and the family relocated to Miami, where he worked as a building contractor. Her mother, who scrupulously marked up her daughter's papers for school, was briefly a copy editor for *Time* magazine during World War II and got her master's degree in librarianship.

"My mom didn't work," Markoe said. "She preferred to use her time perfecting her rage. She did a lot of seething."

Like many funny kids growing up in the 1950s and '60s, Markoe found escape in *Mad* magazine, as well as the jokey horror fanzine *Famous Monsters of Filmland*. As she got older, her comedy taste leaned more toward the literary. Markoe adored the arch style and wordplay of Robert Benchley, whose Algonquin Round Table wit operated at a frequency that was easy to miss. At the same time, Markoe was smart enough to have no hang-ups about dopey jokes. In a scene from a screenplay she wrote about a singles complex called Hidden Valley, one of the bachelors sold a song about cheese that featured this lyric: "Whether you call it fromage or queso, / If you love cheese, just stand up and say so."

Markoe didn't like most of what was on television, but there were exceptions. *Saturday Night Live* made a huge impact. "It was the first show I saw that made fun of TV as a form," Markoe said. "Before that, TV didn't really see itself."

While that is an overstatement—Jack Benny and Ernie Kovacs pioneered a self-aware style at the dawn of television—the medium's fourth wall was indeed much sturdier in the 1970s than it is today. The few shows that drew attention to their own conventions, and spoofed themselves, appealed to Markoe. Norman Lear's *Mary Hartman, Mary Hartman* was another revelation. It placed an average American housewife, a prototypical soap opera audience member, inside a surreal melodrama and watched her steadily go mad. The title poked fun at how soap opera characters often said things twice. When Markoe got to Los Angeles, one of the first people she called was its head writer, Ann Marcus, who hired her as a researcher, which led to a job writing jokes on a new revamp of *Laugh-In*. When she couldn't get any jokes on the air, she went down to the Comedy Store, on Sunset Boulevard, to try them out. It was March 1978 when she first saw a laid-back comic there named David Letterman.

They were both represented by William Morris, which they talked about backstage at the Store. Markoe, who had been casually seeing another comic for a few months, thought this hilariously Hollywood. "How did this happen?" she thought to herself. "I'm discussing *agents* with a guy?"

Once Markoe started talking to him, one thing became clear: David Letterman was not her type. Her last boyfriend had been a painter, and this guy, dressed casually in sneakers, seemed like a frat guy. "He was the kind of person I would have never been friends with," Markoe said. "But he was cute."

Letterman had also struggled to find work as a writer, so he tried stand-up comedy. When he saw Markoe onstage for the first time, he was immediately impressed. "She looked—the term used to be 'preppy,'" he said. "I was very attracted to her. She looked like she was from the East Coast, and her jokes were very heady, much smarter than what you were getting at open-mic night."

In the late 1970s, the Comedy Store was a fairly new institution, one that didn't even pay its artists, and while there were many hotels or nightclubs where you could tell jokes, few venues showcased only stand-up. It was a place to perform but also to meet young people who told jokes for a living and possibly be seen by a booker from *The Tonight Show*, which could immediately launch your career. Jay Leno was a regular. Richard Pryor and Robin Williams would drop by. Andy Kaufman was often there, trying out his latest stunts. Among these performers, Letterman seemed square. He had gone from being the only bearded guy in a fraternity house to being the most clean-cut stand-up in a hip comedy club. He was shy and socialized little, although among female comics he was developing a reputation as a ladies' man.

Letterman, who went onstage because he thought it would lead to television work, was new to stand-up, but his many years of experience in broadcasting proved to be an asset. Onstage, he displayed an easy charm, particularly when bantering with the crowd spontaneously. His prepared jokes weren't particularly conceptual, adopting a wry, observational take on fast food, local news, and commercials. His stage persona projected an ordinary midwestern guy struggling to get by in the big city. One of his most dependable jokes was about how he used dried-up toothpaste as dinner mints. Despite not being an outlandish personality like Pryor or Williams, Letterman stood out because of his attitude—sarcastic, knowing, occasionally harsh but in a way that kept the audience on his side. He also favored quirky language just unusual enough to get your attention.

"I remember noticing the way he turned a phrase," Jay Leno said about seeing him onstage for the first time, recalling with particular admiration Letterman's joke about editorials on the local eyewitness news. Observing how anchors were forced to take stands—albeit uncontroversial ones—on political positions, Letterman imitated a blowhard newsman with a $4 suit and an $8 toupee made of the same material. "We here at Channel 13," he began, naming the actual station he worked at in Indiana, "would like to take this opportunity to say that we are diametrically opposed to the practice of using orphans as yardage markers in driving ranges."

It was a characteristic flourish for Letterman, mocking the hollow authority of a news anchor, but with an unexpected image ("orphans") that turned the satire toward the ridiculous and slightly cruel. Leno saw that this was someone who understood how the right word choice could juice an ordinary joke into something funnier. "I went up to him and said, 'What a clever way to phrase that [punch line],'" Leno recalled about meeting his future rival, while adding pointedly that Letterman's joke writing remained raw. "He wasn't a comedian, though. I think he learned some of that from me, and I learned his use of language."

Among comics at the Store, Letterman started to seem like a rising star when he signed up with the heavyweight management firm Rollins Joffe Morra & Brezner. They had shepherded the careers of Mike Nichols and Elaine May and Allan Sherman in the 1960s and, later, Robin Williams and, most critically, Woody Allen. "Rollins and Joffe were comedy gods," said Robert Morton, who was then a page at the Ed Sullivan Theater but would go on to produce Letterman's show for more than eight years. "They were the credibility that every comic wanted. They had the ear of every network, every studio."

Stu Smiley, who had worked for the agency, described them as sophisticated types, but the kind who could close a deal. "They used to say Charles [Joffe] had the balls of a thief," Smiley said. "These guys had pedigree. Every day, Jack Rollins wore a suit."

Buddy Morra, Charles H. Joffe, and Larry Brezner (Rollins, who would go on to produce Letterman's talk shows, was based out of New York) first saw the future talk-show host doing stand-up at the Westwood outpost of the Comedy Store while looking for actors for a new sitcom in development about comedians. They were all impressed. His set was just fine, but it was the commanding way he handled the crowd that caught their attention. Letterman had none of the jittery anxiety of other young stand-ups. He was relaxed, and between jokes he would crack his neck or whistle with his two hands, charming the crowd.

But even as his career took off, his marriage suffered. Michelle Cook got a job at the May department store and supported his comedy career, financially and emotionally. Still, the economic anxiety that had marked his childhood home haunted him. Club work did not pay, and he had no day job. Comedy scouts from *The Tonight Show* had seen him at the Store several times without giving him a television spot. "My wife was working while I was in the playground shooting baskets, feeling like a bum," said Letterman. But he started to see a regular income when Jimmie Walker, a comic who had become a star on the show *Good Times*, hired him to write jokes for $100 a week. Walker had a team of young comics helping him out, including Leno, Elayne Boosler, and Paul Mooney.

With Cook working in the day, and him at night, they saw each other much less than they had in Indiana, and they soon became distant. Cook and Letterman had little experience with serious relationships. While Cook had pushed Letterman to go to Hollywood, their marriage didn't survive the trip. "He said that his first wife, Michelle, was constantly complaining they lost every friend they had because Dave would drink and start making jokes about what's wrong with them," said Steve O'Donnell, one of the most critical writers during Letterman's late-night career.

Letterman's longtime director Hal Gurnee felt that Dave couldn't stand that she ironed and folded his underwear and socks. "It would be so middle class," Gurnee said. "It would be like people you'd expect to work in an insurance agency. He wanted to be a comic. Comics don't have their underwear ironed."

Letterman later described what went wrong with Michelle Cook as entirely his fault: "I went a little nuts and misbehaved and it came apart, but I think that it's my own doing—or my own undoing."

They separated and eventually divorced.

Letterman and Merrill Markoe started as friends when he was married. "I wasn't the bridge," Markoe said. The day after meeting Letterman at the Comedy Store, she went to the Rollins Joffe office (she wasn't represented by them) to talk about a pilot, "Stranger Than Fact," that she was writing with Ed Bluestone, the *National Lampoon* writer who had come up with the famous cover line "If you don't buy this magazine, we'll kill this dog." "Stranger Than Fact" was a comedic spin on *The Twilight Zone.* At the meeting, Buddy Morra mentioned that his client David Letterman had just said nice things about her. Markoe pressed him on what. "That he thought you were sort of special," Morra replied.

When she got home, she called the Comedy Store, found out that Letterman was doing a set at 12:20 a.m., and headed out at midnight, worried that it would look like she was trying too hard. She saw Letterman in the main room and exchanged hellos right before he went onstage. Finding a stool in the corner to sit on, she watched his set. Letterman did very well, left the stage, and suddenly appeared by her side. They sat quietly next to each other watching Robin Williams tell jokes. When she got home, Markoe described the scene in her diary:

He pretended nonchalance. He was quiet. He didn't talk. I got nervous so I pretended that I didn't care who sat where. Then I started to get uptight that he would think I was there to be picked up. So after Robin's set was over I said, "Listen, good luck at the Roxy tomorrow night." And I left. Now I am wishing that one of us would have said something. Maybe there was something I was supposed to do. But I have no idea what it was. When I was driving away down Sunset I noticed him crossing the street alone. I honked and waved. He entered the apartment building across the street and I saw him push the elevator button. But by then I was worried. Why was I so cold?

Why was he? Not my fault, I don't think. I wish he would have responded to me. Or maybe he did and I was supposed to do something? No idea.

Not long after, Letterman asked her on a date. He took Markoe to a filming of a game show, *Liar's Club*, hosted by Allen Ludden, in which he was the celebrity guest. Letterman wore a striped hockey shirt, white-and-green Adidas sneakers, and white cotton pants with drawstrings, which he called his "date pants." Markoe brought a liter of Perrier.

"This was before everyone had bottled water," Letterman said. "I thought: Wow. But later it may have turned out she had a urinary tract infection." Markoe confirmed this was true.

On *Liar's Club*, celebrities told true and false stories to contestants who had to guess who was telling the truth. Letterman was at ease in this format, crafting elaborate lies that showed off his playful use of language, his unusual syntax, and his sense of the absurd. On one episode that may have been the first date, he riffed about pirates. "Number one enemy of pirates is mildew," he said, setting up a punch line. "Mildew scuttles more missions."

There is a comic eloquence to this line—every word necessary and surprising, ending with an alliterative flourish. This kind of word-drunk humor also appealed to Markoe. Who used the word "scuttles," anyway? "The first thing I was attracted to about Dave was his noun choices," she said. They also shared a towel-snapping sense of humor. On the way to the studio, Markoe asked Letterman, "Don't you have to be a famous person to be a celebrity?"

After walking into her place for the first time, Letterman cracked a joke about her furniture: "Ahh, good, the last of the aluminum couches." She had bought it in a thrift store and thought it was cool. "I came from a family that made fun of me constantly," she explained. So I thought someone making fun of me is someone who understood me."

They shared a silly sense of humor. After he received a piece of junk mail that got his name wrong, she called him Don, in a move that was both needling and affectionate. He returned the favor by sometimes calling her Dorothy. They were not sentimental, and in public they had the affectionate repartee of best friends rather than young lovers. "They were absurd together," said Gerard Mulligan, Markoe's friend from the Bay Area. "I remember going to a restaurant [with them]," Mulligan said, "and the waiter coming over and Dave said, 'So I'd like you to bring us an assortment of foods, and at the end we'd be very happy to pay you. Does that work out all right?' And the guy said, 'Yeah.' Eye roll."

Markoe had a restless, analytical mind given to brooding. She could be as insecure as any aspiring comedy writer raised in a neurotic home. She wrote in a childhood diary: "I'm never getting married. I'm never having kids. I'm never getting married. I'm never having kids." A resistance to matrimony stuck with her, even after her father told her on his deathbed that his proudest accomplishment was his marriage. She didn't believe him.

After his relationship with Cook ended, Letterman was in no rush to get married. Markoe recalls going with him to pick up his stuff from his wife's house in North Hollywood. All his possessions had price tags—the ones he didn't want were ready to be sold. Letterman picked up a hockey stick; it had a sticker on it for twenty-five cents. Markoe offered to keep one of their dogs, Bob, but she got a second one, just in case the relationship didn't last. They started spending nights together, trading lines for jokes, working on the same club bills, collaborating on scripts.

From very early, Letterman's managers saw him as a potential talk-show host. He fit the profile, which in the late 1970s meant something specific: clean-cut, midwestern, no noticeable ethnicity. Jack Paar was from Michigan, and Dick Cavett grew up in Nebraska, as did Johnny Carson, who was born in Iowa but moved when he was eight. These stars had no trace of either coast in their voice. "Why are no talk-show hosts Jewish?" Albert Brooks once asked. "Because no one wants to go to bed with a Jew?"

Talk-show hosts were also wry, light, and glib. Letterman ignored religion and race and any other hot-button political subjects. "He was edgy, but he looked clean-cut and accessible. That's unusual. Do you know what you can get away with looking like that?" said Buddy Morra, who didn't think Letterman was much of a stand-up, but perfect for television. He soon started getting regular television work.

Markoe helped him with pitches for many shows, including a proto–reality show called "Dumb Guys in Action" and "Travels with Dave," a spoof of Charles Kuralt's "On the Road." They also wrote a several-page pitch for "Have a Nice Day" that now reads like a blueprint for the filmed comedy on Letterman's talk shows: "We seek to cover local events of no particular significance as though they were of great national importance."

One of their more bizarre projects was the movie screenplay "Son of Santa," in which Santa's disgruntled elf foreman Winky shoots his boss, leaving Santa's sons—a drunk, Johnny, and a gay design student, Kenny—in charge. Kenny switches the traditional Christmas dinner to soy-and-nut loaf, and the holiday colors from red and green to rose and mist. After the rebranding flops (kids do not take kindly to receiving carrot sticks and sushi in their stockings), some business and religious leaders create their own holiday. Buddy Morra read the script and was not impressed.

Markoe wrote for Letterman's stand-up act as well, helping him with jokes that he would use on television and onstage to start his career. They were an odd couple. Letterman had an assured persona, honed after a decade of broadcasting, but not that much material; his collection of jokes was thin. Markoe, a prolific writer with a ferocious work ethic, was far more confident in her material than in her onstage

LETTERMAN

character. "She had very sharp writing but was reticent to really sell it," said the comic Rich Hall.

Letterman thought Johnny Carson looked like the uncle you really wanted to make laugh. She thought he looked like he'd ignore her at a party. Markoe's range of comedic influences was much wider than Letterman's, which he quickly realized. "She was a great education for me," Letterman said.

It was well known around the Comedy Store that its owner, Mitzi Shore, liked Letterman. Markoe's reputation was less established. "Her writing was smart and original," recalls Sandra Bernhard, who was one of the few successful female comics at the Store. "But it was still like 'That's who Letterman is dating?' She was kind of androgynous, a guys' girl, which maybe that's what he liked about her."

The most prominent women in comedy, like Phyllis Diller and Joan Rivers, were doing jokes about their husbands and the dreariness of their own lives. Markoe did not relate. The first joke she wrote for her stand-up revealed her typically askew sensibility: "A little bit about me," she began. "Not many people are aware I'm the inventor of a great sport known as Giant Golf. Whole families spend the entire day pushing a twelve-ton golf ball into a trench." Even when she told a self-deprecating joke about her love life, it spiraled into the weird flourish rather than the confession. "I didn't have a date for the senior prom at my high school, so my father made my brother take me" was the premise of one of her jokes, which led to this twist: "Pretty sad, but it worked out okay. My brother and I are getting married. We got a house in the Valley. We're going to settle down and raise mutants."

In the late 1970s, getting booked on *The Tonight Show* was the goal of every ambitious young stand-up comic. It was the quickest path to stardom. So when Johnny Carson told *Rolling Stone* in 1979 that female comics "are a little aggressive for my taste," it put women who wanted to make a living in comedy in a bind: To succeed in stand-up, you needed to have a strong point of view; but to get on *The Tonight Show*, you couldn't be too aggressive, either.

"I was having a hard time figuring out who I was allowed to be," Markoe said about her stand-up persona. "I knew how to write jokes, and I knew what I thought was funny, but I didn't know what I could get away with as a woman."

While she struggled as a stand-up, Markoe devoted much of her comedic energy to writing and helped push forward Letterman's career. Their comedic skill sets complemented each other. Letterman liked bantering with the crowd, while she preferred mapping out a joke on paper. He had a confidently sarcastic delivery but thin material, while she had sharp conceptual jokes but trouble finding the right persona with which to deliver them. Letterman was a powerful comic weapon. Markoe supplied the bullets.

When David Letterman first moved to Hollywood, he called Allen Ludden, who had offered to help him if he moved out west. With his help, he started getting steady work. He had shown a quick wit as a guest on *The $25,000 Pyramid* and *Liar's Club*. (Letterman had even been a panelist on *The Gong Show*.) He had less luck selling scripts to Hollywood or getting a show off the ground for television. A scout for *The Tonight Show* even passed on him. And he was removed from a satire of *60 Minutes*, called *Peeping Times*, after a test audience didn't like him. By the beginning of 1978, it was easy to look at what Letterman had done in show business and conclude that his future was in game shows.

It's tempting to imagine an alternative history of the game show genre with David Letterman as its signal star. Would he have created an irreverent deconstruction of its tropes that revitalized the form? The best guess we can make is to look at his first job hosting a national television program, *The Riddlers*, produced by Bob Stewart, the impresario who created *The Price Is Right* and *Password*.

Stewart had been impressed with Letterman's humor from other game shows.

"I have mixed emotions about it," Letterman said on a Canadian talk show after shooting the pilot. "If it goes on the air, I think it will be a lot of fun. But then again, game shows are often dismissed as wasted time on the network." And back then, before channels proliferated, network time was precious.

The Riddlers pitted panels of ordinary people against celebrities answering riddles, in a format that mirrored *Family Feud*. Its mood was aggressively peppy, marked by candy-colored set design and circus music. Waiting backstage with the guests during the pilot, the actress Jo Anne Worley turned to Letterman right before his introduction and said, "Well, from this moment on, you'll be known as a game show host."

Letterman's heart sank. As he walked onstage, holding a microphone and an unsmiling expression, he presented a stark juxtaposition. Instead of adjusting his sensibility to suit this game, Letterman became more contemptuous, referring to the celebrity guest Michael McKean as "this brain trust over here." When another actor attempted a joke, Letterman made him pay for it. "Oh, there's comedy everywhere," he said, as if to brush off anyone trying to steal the focus. At one point, he made an incongruous crack about his loneliness. When he found out a female contestant was from Indiana, he made a creepy joke about how he had spent time staring through her window. Letterman grimaced, rolled his eyes, and even leered. When an actress said the riddle was "You're the part of my body that says 'hooray,'" Letterman interjected, "I would have said the brain, because it had the day off."

Like a virus, he planted himself and attacked the show from within, making everything around him look idiotic while keeping his distance. In a skeptical look, he communicated indifference that made you wonder who he was and what he was really thinking about.

"You were the first game show host I ever saw who knew it was crap," McKean told the host on a *Late Night* appearance in 1990.

The pilot unsurprisingly did not get picked up but it did circulate around the network and actually boosted Letterman's reputation. Dave Feldman, a consultant to the programming department for NBC, sat in with a focus group and two executives from daytime programming to watch the pilot. People laughed at Letterman's jokes, but when asked to judge his performance, they said they were taken aback by his sarcasm. Feldman later talked to several executives including Paul Klein, head of programming, and said that "as copies of the pilot circulated around 30 Rock, Letterman's stock went up rather than down."

M errill Markoe was thrilled when she got offered a job writing on a new variety show starring Mary Tyler Moore, called *Mary*. The day after spending the night with Letterman, she went to work on the show for the first time. At the writers' meeting, she checked out the list of cast members and was shocked to see Letterman's name. Even though they were spending most nights together, he had never mentioned he was working on the same show. She later learned he had known she was up for the job. Looking back, Markoe said this was "a portent of many things to come."

In a cast that included Michael Keaton, Letterman saw the benefit of having an ally on staff who knew his voice. But how his sarcastic charm fit into a program that mixed singing, dancing, and comedy was a challenge. *Mary* had young performers with a foot in the counterculture shoehorned into an old-school variety format that was all smiles and jazz hands. Markoe did bond with a fellow comedian, Valri Bromfield, and smuggled in a few funny bits.

She wrote one piece where Letterman held a chart explaining how a magician pulled a rabbit out of a hat—the kind of bit a talk-show host might deliver after a monologue. Playing off the fact that the secrets behind magic tricks are notoriously disappointing and simple (part of the reason magicians never tell them), Letterman explained, in a solemn scientific tone, with much technology and jargon, the endless complications of the trick. The elements of the joke reveal the intersection of Markoe's and Letterman's humor: the shared enjoyment of comic inventions, the silly snatches of language (the rabbit was transported to the Stanford Linear Accelerator), and the wry attitude toward anything show business. Poking fun at the sober voice of authority, they delighted in taking the magic out of the magic trick. This was a tactic they would return to again and again.

That was not, however, the perspective of the show, which would interrupt a comedy sketch with earnest song-and-dance numbers. Markoe and Letterman conspired to get him out of these bits to avoid humiliation. Letterman did not like confrontation. "I became his secret agent on the staff," she recalled. But she could accomplish only so much, especially when Letterman was called upon to play an anchorman named Carmen Meringue, wearing makeup, earrings, and a tower of fruit on his head. When he participated in a dance number, he looked horribly ill at ease. Instead of plowing through, he became stiff-backed and wry, looking miserable. "The hard part was that I had to sing and dance and dress up in costumes," he said. "That was tough. I knew my limitations, but this really brought them home."

If *Mary* taught him that he couldn't sing or dance, his cameo role on *Mork & Mindy* was a lesson in the dangers of acting. Letterman was cast as an obnoxious motivational speaker who kept telling his followers to sit down and shut up, and bragged about his Rolls-Royce. The casting agent probably thought that Letterman's stage persona would make him a natural for this superior jerk. But in a villain role that required him to commit, he looked as uncomfortable as he did in a chorus line.

In an era of entertainers who did a little bit of everything—singing, dancing, and a few jokes—Letterman was a specialist. And while his early experiences were failures, they helped him understand his limitations. Wil Shriner, a fellow stand-up comic and friend, recalled how miserable he was on the drive to the studio to shoot *Mork & Mindy*. On the way home, Letterman said, "I will never do that again."

More roles came his way, however, and his management team encouraged him to take them. The most promising, and the one that could have sent his career in a radically different direction, was for the movie *Airplane!* He was offered the lead in this trailblazing comedy, playing Ted Striker, for whom his arched-eyebrow sensibility could have fit in nicely. When he tested for the part, the directors, Jim Abrahams and David and Jerry Zucker, could sense that was why he was there. When Letterman didn't get the part, Jerry Zucker called to tell him. "I've never seen an actor so happy to be told they didn't get the role," he recalled.

Even though it was filled with flops and misfires, Letterman's brief stint struggling to build a career in Hollywood had taught him the valuable lesson of what not to do. His management booked him on a variety show that was a summer replacement featuring the Starland Vocal Band, on which he wrote, did sketches, and made wisecracks. He also shot a talk show called *Leave It to Dave*, another clash in styles, in which he made his entrance coming down a slide. It never aired.

Letterman's career didn't take off until he finally got booked on *The Tonight Show.* On November 24, 1978, Johnny Carson introduced him as a regular at the Comedy Store who had appeared on *Mary* and was about to host the Rose Bowl Parade. Letterman entered through the curtain, fiddled with his belt, and rubbed his hands. Dressed in a suit and short tie, he did not let his nervousness invade his pacing or delivery. Unlike in his other television appearances, where he seemed at war with the format, he confidently delivered a wry stand-up set with pitch-perfect timing and quirky phrasing. Less than two minutes into his set, he described heading to an airplane bathroom, which he called "the lavatory of the aircraft," and observing a sign on the wall that read, "Do not place metal or glass objects in the toilet." Letterman took a long pause, put his hands in his pockets, and relaxed his shoulders, then said, "That always ruins the trip for me."

The difference between Letterman and so many observational comics is that he doesn't hammer home the pointlessness of that common sign. He doesn't ask, "Who does this?!" Taking a more indirect approach, he instead imagines himself as the one person who thinks of putting metal and glass in the toilet. The audience laughed quietly at first, then louder, and finally came what any comic would have recognized as the most beautiful sound in the world: the booming laughter of Johnny Carson. Letterman's face lit up before he delivered his punch line: "I like to go back there, wash a load of dishes . . ."

In the set, Letterman's persona was resolutely that of a financially strapped and ordinary Indiana everyman, and in his longer set pieces he positioned himself as the acerbic voice of reason facing some form of lunacy. While he remained slightly aloof, there was a note of self-conscious hipness that would be absent in his later work. He did one marijuana joke whose punch line involved a joint rolled with Pampers. Letterman came off as being as mainstream and relatable as Carson, but from the other side of the generation gap.

When he finished, the band started playing, and for a moment he froze, looking unsure of what to do, before Carson called him over to the desk. "Rolling a joint in Pampers," Carson said, tickled by this new comic. "I like that."

Letterman glanced away, smoothing his pants. Over the course of the interview, he shoehorned jokes into his answers, asking questions of the unseen audience, as if he were doing crowd work at the Comedy Store.

After saying he was from Indiana (which earned some applause), Carson asked if he had worked in radio there. Letterman didn't answer the question. "I know we have some folks from South Bend," he said instead, to applause, before muttering, with an oddly nasty note of sarcasm, "Beautiful there, what a town." Carson appeared surprised and delighted by this unnecessary crack. Why would he sneer at the crowd or that town? Then Letterman moved into his joke: "The one thing I'll always remember as long as I live, growing up in Indiana, is Dad teasing me with the power tools."

Letterman may have been an amiable Indiana comic, but his material about his home state did not indulge in sentimental cliché. His first appearance made clear that his all-American exterior masked a darker, more off-kilter sensibility. Ever sensitive to what worked for a broad national audience, Carson could see that Letterman's performance had just the right amount of hipness to appeal to his crowd without alienating anyone.

When Letterman closed with his reliable joke about "being diametrically opposed to the practice of using orphans as yardage markers in driving ranges," the crowd did more than laugh. They gave the sign of true success on *The Tonight Show*: a round of applause. "I have a feeling after your shot today, you're going to be working a lot outside the Comedy Store," Carson said. "I hope you come back with us."

Five weeks later, Letterman did just that. After doing well again with the audience, he was asked back the next month. Letterman now had a problem: He had used most of his best material. Merrill Markoe helped him out with a new supply of jokes.

One of them was about a dog food commercial's slogan: "All beef—not a speck of cereal." Letterman paused. "My dog spends the day rooting through the garbage and drinking out of the toilet," he said, sarcasm rising. "Chances are he's not going to mind a speck of cereal." The crowd's laughter moved into an applause break. Later, during a commercial break, *Tonight Show* producer Fred de Cordova came over to Letterman and said, "Have your people call me about hosting."

Letterman was lucky in his timing. He began appearing on *The Tonight Show* around the time when its host was shifting from working four days a week to three, along with taking fifteen weeks of vacation. That meant national exposure for a steady stream of guest hosts, including Joan Rivers, John Davidson, Bob Newhart, and David Brenner (all of whom hosted seventy times or more). Letterman not only performed well on the show in his three appearances, but he seemed a good fit. He was clever, but not in a way that showed off. He was handsome, but not so much as to be intimidating. It didn't hurt that he had a profile similar to Carson's: studied broadcasting in college, worked in radio, game shows, and the weather. But as soon as he started guest-hosting in March 1979, Letterman felt deeply out of place and fearful. "I recall getting a call from Pasadena at 11 p.m. from him," said his agent, Deborah Miller. "'I don't have a monologue. It's not right. It's not working. Come out.' And it was working fine. He just was not a secure guy."

A month after Letterman guest-hosted *The Tonight Show* for the first time, Johnny Carson shook up the entire television landscape by telling the network he was going to leave the show. This was the culmination of a simmering battle with the then-flagging network over how often its signature star took time off. NBC president Fred Silverman, who saw the ratings decline with guest hosts, told *Newsweek* he wished Carson would return to doing the show four days a week.

This irritated Carson, who not only ran the most reliable hit on the network but had become a figure comparable in late-night stature to what Walter Cronkite was for the nightly news. And while he seemed the picture of calm on the air, Carson was a fierce competitor, insistent on control. In response, Carson told Silverman he would do even less, and said that once his contract was up, in a year, he was done. This had two major effects on the future of David Letterman: It increased Carson's clout at NBC (not to mention his bargaining power), and it started a rumor mill about which comic would replace Carson.

The names floated in trade publications included David Brenner, Chevy Chase, and the most recent new guest host, David Letterman. It helped that Letterman had signed an exclusive deal with NBC in May 1979. Now he was an NBC employee with no show at a time when it seemed possible that, after seventeen years on the job, Johnny Carson could leave *The Tonight Show*. Only a few years after moving from Indiana, Letterman was already being talked about as the host of the most powerful and popular talk show on television. It was a remarkable turn of events.

Carson, of course, did not leave *The Tonight Show*. But his threat put the network on the defensive and helped him negotiate a generous deal in which he got exactly what he wanted: a massive contract of $5 million a year, a shorter show (cut from ninety minutes to an hour), and ownership of the program in the time slot after his, which at that time was the *Tomorrow* show with Tom Snyder. The news made clear who the most powerful person at NBC was.

Carson was enthusiastic about Letterman, and so was Silverman, who had looked around at alternatives. He had seen Letterman charm an audience at a benefit in his honor and liked his folksy affect. "He was a little caustic," Silverman said, "but I thought he could improve our demographic."

Silverman offered Letterman a show in the morning. Daytime was dominated by older viewers, and with the network in last place, he was willing to take a chance. "There are only so many hemorrhoid advertisers," the exec later told *Rolling Stone*.

So, only a month after Carson signed his deal, *The David Letterman Show* premiered, replacing three game shows, including *Hollywood*

Squares. NBC's advertising campaign paired a photo of Letterman with the slogan "A face every mother could love." Fred Silverman imagined Letterman as an extension of the *Today* show, mixing chat with stars with some jokes and news segments read by an anchorman. In an early meeting, Silverman told Letterman that they should create a family of performers to help him fill out the show.

The model for the show, explained Silverman, was *The Arthur Godfrey Show.* Godfrey was a titan of broadcasting who ran the most popular radio show of the postwar era, simulcast on television. He was a folksy host, more of a conduit to entertainers than a performer, the kind of star Bob and Ray would spoof and Letterman's mother liked. He became notorious in the press for firing one of his stars on the air, right around the time Letterman started watching television. It was the first talk-show scandal that the young Letterman knew about, and his response was that of many viewers: "I liked Godfrey," he explained, "until he started firing people on the air."

Letterman was flabbergasted at this directive. Arthur Godfrey was far from the cool, modern entertainer that Dave aspired to be. Silverman recalls Letterman repeating Godfrey's name over and over again in the meeting. "He said, 'Arthur Godfrey?! Godfrey? Godfrey?'" he said. "He couldn't get over it. 'Godfrey?'"

In 1980, network television was at a turning point. The old variety shows were passé, remnants of an era when Las Vegas was the height of show biz. But Silverman remained a believer and was willing to take a risk, programming comedy on network television in the morning for the first time in years. *The David Letterman Show* was conceived as a kind of hybrid of talk, music, and sketch comedy, based in New York, with Letterman as the ringleader. Silverman wanted a daily gossip report with the Hollywood columnist Shirley Eder and service-minded segments about makeovers and beauty tips. He also wanted a nineteen-year-old banjo player from Alabama to perform on every show.

Letterman had no interest in any of this. Instead he hired Markoe as the head writer, and they got to work putting together comedy that their friends would like. The couple spent one of their first days in New York City in 1980 with a real estate agent who drove them around the tristate area. Letterman introduced himself as Merrill, and Markoe as Donna. They settled on a place uptown but spent most of their time in Rockefeller Center, working.

Since he knew him from *The Riddlers*, Letterman asked Bob Stewart to produce the show. He thought Stewart was savvy about the business, and they got along, but their friendship (they played squash together) perhaps blinded them to how different their sensibilities were. The sixty-five-year-old Stewart, short, stocky, and bald, had achieved success with game shows rooted in banter between guests and hosts, which was quite different from a talk show rooted in comedy.

Stewart liked the cheerful irreverence of David Letterman, but he didn't want to build a whole show around it. Not in daytime. He had made several hits in morning television and felt he knew what an audience wanted. He envisioned Letterman doing comedy along with cooking segments and chat with celebrity guests.

Stewart hired jazz pianist Frank Owens as musical director, the second African American ever to be given that role on a network talk show (Billy Taylor, the music director on *The David Frost Show*, was the first), and gave him a gentle Michael McDonald–penned theme song. Owens, who had worked with Chubby Checker and Johnny Mathis, was encouraged by the producer to play mainstream pop songs. R&B was nixed. The goal was to not shake things up, but play some comforting standards. "I could have gotten an all-black band, but I wanted to be cool," Owens recalled. "So I got two of them, two of us."

Bob Stewart brought along his regular game show crew from the *Pyramid*, including longtime employees like Jude Brennan, who handled the booking, direction, and production side. Markoe saw Stewart as distinctly old-fashioned, hiring people who were out of touch with the kind of bold comedy she wanted to put on the air. "My first clue of what Bob Stewart was like to work for came when I noticed that his loyal long time employees were all mousy and quiet and non-assertive, scared to say anything," Markoe wrote in her diary. "They reminded me of residents of The Village of the Damned."

While Stewart handled the production side, Markoe was responsible for the writers and talent. She hired the comics she knew from the comedy scene around Los Angeles, casting her friend from *Mary*, Valri Bromfield, and Edie McClurg, one of the early stars from the Groundlings troupe, as well as her friend Gerard Mulligan. West Coast stand-up comics like Wil Shriner and Bob Sarlatte joined up. And after seeing him perform at a club in New York, Letterman hired the comic Rich Hall to write for television for the first time.

Once they began taping test shows in June, it was clear that Stewart's and Markoe's different visions would clash. Markoe balked at the old-fashioned segments Stewart suggested, like giving $50 to audience members who had certain things in their pockets. He insisted on a rigid structure of twelve segments in every show, and during the sketches he sighed loudly with displeasure. One of the writers, Ed Subitzky, a veteran of *National Lampoon* magazine, remembered a disconcerting conversation in the men's room with Stewart. Standing next to him at a urinal, Stewart blurted out, "You know what's wrong with this show?" Subitzky said he didn't. "It has no substance," Stewart replied, then flushed.

Stewart did not think the comedy produced by the writers was working, and according to the director, Bruce Burmester, who had worked with him on the *Pyramid*, he also didn't like being told what to do by a woman. "He was a male chauvinist pig," Burmester said. "He didn't respect her. Part of that was she was a woman."

Before the show even premiered, it was riven with turf wars. Stewart controlled the bookers, whom he called "people getters," led by his wife, Anne-Marie, who signed up a robot named Nutro to give on-air nutritional advice (voiced by a person off to the side). "Isn't he darling?" Mrs. Stewart said to Markoe before a test show. Markoe and Letterman were horrified.

Stewart's displeasure escalated, and weeks before the premiere he told Letterman that the problem was the comedy—the characters and sketches. He wanted more Nutro. Markoe balked and asked Stewart not to make disparaging remarks during the test shows, because, as she put it in her diary later, "the negative vibes were inhibiting attempts at constructive rewrites."

On June 12, two weeks before the premiere, Stewart quit. David Letterman's shot at television stardom was imminent, and its producer, who also happened to have more television experience than anyone in the room, had already pronounced it a failure. His talk-show career began with no one in charge.

PART II

THE ANTI-TALK SHOW

1980–1984

If I was unable to do this show, the proper succession goes: David Letterman, General Alexander Haig. Or is it Letterman, Tip O'Neill, then Alexander Haig?

—Johnny Carson, *The Tonight Show*, April 8, 1981

THE ART OF STUPID

O n his fourth day as the host of his own talk show, David Letterman walked onstage and was greeted by a colorful sign blaring his name. It was 9 a.m. He rubbed his hands, looking embarrassed, waved his arms like a referee signaling a missed field goal, and implored the crowd to stop applauding. "Stop it. Stop it," he said.

Letterman awkwardly backtracked behind a table on a set that looked like a poorly maintained knickknack store. When he sat down, his legs shook back and forth. At the same time, his friend Bob Sarlatte leaned into the screen, with no introduction. He was sitting on a couch by a table, playing the sidekick. Sarlatte began telling a joke about San Francisco baseball when Letterman stopped him with an acerbic put-down: "This means nothing to anyone but you, you know?"

Sarlatte flashed a look of irritation, then plowed ahead with his doomed joke, earning a few muffled laughs. Things became more tense several segments later when Letterman introduced Edie Mc-Clurg. Sitting on a stage adjacent to the table, she performed a monologue in a plastic mask, as a 105-year-old version of herself, that felt more like performance art than comedy. She concluded by saying that she lived in the David Letterman Home for the Perplexed, and then fell asleep. McClurg opened her eyes, now out of character, walked over to Letterman, sat down, and took off her mask.

Letterman asked her how she was able to play an older woman, and McClurg responded in a self-serious tone that as an actor, she felt like she was all ages. Letterman could not feign interest, but instead of changing the subject, he dismissively imitated a theremin from a 1950s science fiction movie. "You've dumbfounded me," Letterman said, digging the knife deeper.

The David Letterman Show went on the air with no producer, a shoestring budget, and a collection of disparate performers jostling for attention. It was a disaster. "Nobody really knew what they were doing," said Rich Hall. "Merrill was the one keeping it together."

Only three years after teaching painting, Merrill Markoe became the de facto producer of a live television show. Each evening, she sat in the cramped offices on the tenth floor of Rockefeller Center, staving off panic, counting the minutes in each segment on her fingers. How long, she wondered, would she need for the opening monologue? Considering that Letterman liked to ad-lib, should she schedule four or six minutes? Then there's a commercial. How much time do they need for a guest? Markoe knew nothing about managing a show. She had no helpful system for mapping out the comedy and the guests. She sometimes guessed wrong on the timing of segments, and Letterman would need to banter with the audience to fill the ninety-minute show. "My life has never been worse," Markoe wrote in her diary during the show. "Dave would be upset and yell at me all night and all day I would dodge machine gun bullets."

But it was on this first week on the air that she made one of her greatest contributions to the history of television. In the final fifteen minutes, Letterman introduced a new segment, not with enthusiasm but with something closer to his heart: extravagant lying. "It's going to be unbelievable," he said, a tiny grin emerging. "The Smithsonian has already phoned and already said they want a copy of the tape for the time capsule. Have the folks stay home from work, and keep the kids home from school. History is being made."

It was the birth of Stupid Pet Tricks—the brainchild of Markoe, who was inspired by one night in college when she and a few friends turned putting socks on a Doberman pinscher into an evening of entertainment. The network suggested she use trained animals, but she refused, launching one of television's most enduring bits, with 135 segments over the course of three shows and thirty-four years. Sean the Dog, who performed the original stupid pet trick, walked onto the set, turned around, and closed a door with his paw. Then he answered a phone, knocking it off the receiver. Like a sportscaster analyzing a game-winning shot, Letterman showed it again in slow motion. "We paid for the instant replay," he told the audience. "We may as well use it until you're bored silly."

Markoe and Letterman loved dogs—they owned two, and found any excuse they could to put them in a comedy sketch. But what made this conceit work was that it bridged traditional entertainment with Letterman's caustic sense of humor. It was the grand crowd-pleasing tradition of animal acts but from a new perspective, starting with its name: blunt, snarky, and impertinent. "If they didn't call it Stupid Pet Tricks, it's Pet Tricks," said the comic Steve Martin. "I don't know if I want to see Pet Tricks."

To Letterman, the word "stupid" also meant something delightfully bizarre. It became a kind of shorthand on the show. "Dave or Merrill would always say, 'That's so stupid,' which was a compliment," said Edd Hall, who worked on graphics.

Of course, every bored kid knows that being stupid has its pleasures. But the context of Stupid Pet Tricks mattered. "His idea was, we have this multimillion-dollar operation and we're showing a dog closing a door," said Gerard Mulligan, who wrote for Letterman for more than two decades. He further explained the idea: "I am just wasting your time and mine, telling pointless anecdotes, just making stuff up here. And yet you're watching. Who's the fool?"

In 1980, when David Letterman's morning show went on the air, seven out of the ten highest-grossing movies were comedies, including sharply crafted hits like *9 to 5, The Blues Brothers, Stir Crazy,* and *Airplane!* Comedy on television, however, was less impressive. Network lineups included well-made sitcoms like *M*A*S*H* and *Laverne & Shirley,* effective entertainments that traded on warm nostalgia (*Happy Days*), and farcical physical comedy (*Three's Company*). But most popular comedies were not as adventurous as what was going on in live stand-up from George Carlin, Robin Williams, or Richard Pryor. Lorne Michaels and the original lineup at *Saturday Night Live* left the show that year, and, like many, Letterman and Markoe thought that without them the quality of the sketch show had fallen.

ABC tried to capitalize by launching *Fridays,* an overt rip-off that admitted as much in its first sketch when the cast dressed up as the Coneheads, Killer Bees, and other characters from *SNL.* The show, starring Larry David and Michael Richards, premiered two months before Letterman's morning show and even shared some of the same talent, such as Rich Hall and Andy Kaufman, who staged a fake fight on *Fridays* two years before he did it on *Late Night with David Letterman.*

Fridays aired at a time when television was considered by many to be a cultural wasteland filled with pleasing diversions at best, brainrotting ephemera at worst. In 1978, an advertising executive named

Jerry Mander wrote a book called *Four Arguments for the Elimination of Television*. It was an alarmist polemic that argued that television was irredeemable. But it was taken seriously. The idea that television might be bad for you was reflected in one sketch on *Fridays* in which Michael Richards played the parent of a young girl who asked if the tooth fairy was real. He told her it was not, which led to more hard truths, including that he was merely an actor, and she was sleeping not on a bed in her house but on a stage set. Richards then broke the news about the medium they were on: "Television sucks."

This common assumption was the essential context of the start of David Letterman's talk-show career. *The David Letterman Show* may have been a chaotic and cluttered mess, but, unlike everything else on the air in the morning, it had a skeptical take on television that seemed necessary and vital. Many of the comedians who grew up watching sitcoms from the 1960s and talk shows where the hosts did their own advertisements were now building stand-up routines on making fun of commercials and the stupidity of sitcoms and blow-dried anchormen on local news. Letterman brought this adversarial attitude to daytime television.

In one episode, he rolled a television onstage and announced that he was going to see what was on the other channels. Then he poked fun at those other shows while treating his own as secondary. Letterman took a sharply cynical attitude toward the disposability and superficiality of television.

Only a week after the premiere of Letterman's new show, *The John Davidson Show* replaced *The Mike Douglas Show*, signaling a move in talk shows to cast younger talent. When the *New York Times* ran a story on "the new generation" of talk-show hosts aiming for a younger demographic, its critic John O'Connor lumped Letterman and Davidson together. Davidson, like Letterman, was a frequent guest host on *The Tonight Show*, and his vehicle was another ninety-minute chat show. Of course, Davidson couldn't have been more different—he looked delighted to be on TV and had the kind of sunny personality that might easily break out in song or shake his hips with a dance exercise teacher. In an essay from 1980 about the art of guest hosting for *The Tonight Show*, Kurt Andersen described Davidson as "peppy, bland, cute and sincere in just the right measure to seem as though he'd be good at it."

Newsweek gave Letterman's morning show a mostly positive review, comparing its best moments to Martin Mull's satire of television talk shows, *America 2-Night*. "Both Carson and Letterman possess the same effortless wit, but David seems closer to his audience," the critic Harry F. Waters wrote. "Roaming the house with his mic last week, he playfully asked a burly visitor from Texas to go out for some coffee. Sure enough, one hour later, the guy happily returned with a full tray, receiving applause and a tip from Letterman."

The David Letterman Show was less popular with audiences, earning a fraction of the viewers who'd watched the game shows it replaced. Many affiliates, including those in key markets like Detroit, Boston, and San Francisco, dropped the show, replacing it with syndicated versions of *Three's Company* and other sitcoms. On August 4, NBC cut the show from ninety minutes to an hour. Carson sent Letterman a telegram saying, "Congratulations. It only took you a few weeks. It took me 22 years."

It didn't help that Letterman was not a natural promoter. Three months before his show premiered, he visited Indianapolis to see the NCAA basketball tournament and signed up to appear at a raffle at a hotel run by shopping-mall magnate Mel Simon, who was one of the richest men in the country. Once he arrived, Letterman decided he didn't want to perform. Instead of calling to cancel, he made his old Ball State fraternity brother Jeff Lewis do it. "Nothing he hates more than direct conflict," Lewis said.

For audiences who associated morning television with soap operas, game shows, and friendly talk, *The David Letterman Show* was a jarring change of pace. Conan O'Brien stumbled on the show as a high school senior. He described the disorienting experience of seeing Letterman for the first time:

> His hair resembled an ill-fitting vintage leather motorcycle helmet. His front teeth had a massive gap that looked almost painted-on as a joke. He was wearing the requisite broadcaster's tie, but khaki pants and Adidas sneakers. His set looked wrong, as if he had thrown it together minutes before the show—strange photos of dogs decorated the wall behind him. And then there was his manner. His smile was not ingratiating, but mischievous and ever so slightly malevolent. He was not comfortable in his own skin at a time when everyone on television, by definition, was comfortable in their own skin. And on top of it all, he was doing a comedy show in the morning. What the hell? Who does a comedy show in the morning? What's wrong with this guy? Who let this happen?

The morning show featured many elements that would later form the backbone of *Late Night*—and the most inventive ideas came from Markoe. Rich Hall said she was the one who shaped its sensibility: "She liked goofy, off-the-wall humor, sublime stuff, and not just joke-joke-joke," he said. "The prevailing attitude was: 'It's daytime, no one's watching, so let's do something different.'"

Right from the start, Markoe, taking advantage of Letterman's experience as a radio show host, had him call people from his desk. Letterman also did a bit where he offered to make a difficult call for an audience member who wanted to let his parents know he wasn't coming home or to break some bad news. This took advantage of his skills at crowd work, riffing with strangers, while also dramatizing his fear of confrontation.

Just as she wrote jokes for his stand-up act, Markoe developed ideas for the show that would eventually become standards in late night. Along with Stupid Pet Tricks, Markoe started Small Town News, a "desk piece" in which Letterman would poke fun at articles from local papers. She also came up with probably the most artistically fertile segment in the history of the show: Viewer Mail, which she conceived as a parody of *60 Minutes*. "Their mail was always intelligent and well considered," she said. "When we got on the air and I started reading our mail, I quickly realized it was mainly insane people. So I thought it would be funny to just present *our* viewers: irrational, insane, illiterate."

Markoe produced and edited filmed videos (called remotes by the staff) on the streets of New York. She had Letterman visit the home of the first airline stewardess. For another, they dressed someone up in a cotton suit and headed over to the Cotton Exchange. These segments hinged on the spontaneous response of New Yorkers on the street and relied on open-ended premises.

Markoe and Letterman opened a show with a monologue by NBC's air-conditioning repairman, whose thick New York accent and stilted line reading could only have come from a real person. She was drawn to the eccentric and the ordinary, verging on the dull. In one remote piece, they simply set up the camera on a busy street, called it a fashion show, and had Letterman make funny comments to passersby. He did a version of that bit again when Steve Allen, the original host of *The Tonight Show*, was a guest and they cracked jokes watching a video feed of strangers walking down Sixth Avenue. "I always thought this would make great late-night TV," Letterman said to Allen as the screen showed pedestrian traffic. "You just let this thing go."

The audience laughed, but Allen understood that Letterman was not completely joking. Allen had pioneered man-on-the-street comedy, although he worked with actors playing characters in these bits, not just pedestrians. Letterman had less interest in mixing the real and the fake. He understood that street life could be funny enough if seen with the right perspective. Letterman and Allen watched people walk by like voyeurs camped out in a Times Square bar, and it was very funny.

"We were working with reality as an element, instead of the wholly created fantasy of sketch comedy," Markoe said. They wanted the stars to be ordinary people. "Famous people were on *The Tonight Show* and *Merv Griffin*," Letterman said. "We wanted real people." At the time, this was a radical idea.

It also represented the major difference between the sensibility of *Saturday Night Live* and that of David Letterman. From the very beginning, Letterman and Markoe knew that they wanted to make comedy out of the raw materials of the world, transported to a show business context. It was something they had talked about for years, ever since they developed their early pitches for television shows that never got off the ground.

But it also had a practical motivation. Writing funny sketches every day was difficult, and Letterman was not a particularly good actor. He certainly didn't like doing it and would often talk about his disdain for the fake surprise of show business, as well as the talk-show convention of doing characters with cheap, silly costumes. Johnny Carson's recurring characters on *The Tonight Show*, like Aunt Blabby and Floyd R. Turbo, were examples of what Letterman and Markoe were trying to avoid. That's not to say they didn't create their own, but they tended to be ones that played with their own fakery.

Markoe wrote a character called the Impostor that became one of the early running gags of both the morning show and *Late Night with David Letterman*. Letterman would introduce a surprise guest who was famous, but wasn't necessarily someone everyone would be able to recognize. (A respected novelist was perfect.) Then Ed Subitzky, the bespectacled, bald, and extremely mild-mannered former *National*

Lampoon writer, walked out and sat down to talk to Letterman. He answered a question, then paused, confessed that he was a fake, and ran out of the studio, apologizing to everyone in the audience. Letterman was left onstage looking surprised. His advice to Subitzky the first time he played this character was simple: "What we are looking to achieve here is stupid."

Letterman understood that this was never going to be an easy sell for a morning audience used to game shows and cooking demonstrations. "You could look at that Ed Subitzky bit and say there's no substance," he said. "But we didn't feel that way. He was not the kind of guy you generally see on TV, especially at ten in the morning." To Markoe, the Impostor character both poked fun at the *Tonight Show* convention of the contrived surprise celebrity drop-in and also added the tension of something going wrong and the host not knowing what to do.

The most important element of the morning show to the future talk shows of David Letterman may have been that it was not taped but filmed live, with no editing to fix mistakes. When he moved to late night, he would almost never stop tape. No matter how badly things went wrong, the cameras kept rolling. It was the morning show that established that bedrock principle, even against the host's better instincts.

This helped prevent Letterman from pandering to the tastes of the audience. There was no rehearsal audience on which to test a joke with a crowd. What went on the air was what Markoe and Letterman thought was funny. The morning show was raw, amateurish, and often surprising, and it evolved into something accomplished and funny. But first Letterman needed to clean house.

There were too many kinds of entertainment packed into the hour to get a clear sense of the host's voice. The episodes were crowded and muddled with sketches, stand-up, news breaks with musical acts. Fred Silverman's concept of a family of performers never entirely worked. NBC anchor Edwin Newman proved an odd fit with the sketch performers, who made Letterman look uncomfortable. Dave also never developed chemistry with his musical director, Frank Owens. The host once asked him if he had anything to say. "I should have said something personal," Owens recalled. "Instead I said something like 'I'm just glad to be here.'"

What the show needed was a producer to replace Bob Stewart who could streamline this production. Letterman and Markoe had gone through a laundry list of names, including Roger Ailes, who had produced *The Mike Douglas Show*. Letterman's agent, Deborah Miller, called Ailes, but after considering the job, he turned it down. Buddy Morra knew of a producer who worked with Robert Klein, and he came in for an interview.

Barry Sand, a Brooklyn native with an economics degree from the Wharton School, had a mane of white hair that evoked the Hollywood boss in *The Godfather* who ended up with a horse's head in his bed. He, too, had worked for *The Mike Douglas Show* and as a writer for *A.M. New York*, a local daytime show on ABC (a predecessor to *Good Morning America*) hosted by John Bartholomew Tucker, who had been one of the last hosts of the radio show *Monitor,* which Letterman listened to as a kid. Sand had the gruff demeanor of someone who had spent years hitting daily television deadlines. To Markoe, he seemed pure old school, just like Bob Stewart.

As a result, she was wary, even hostile, during the interview: "How do I know you're not going to fuck us over?" she asked, still feeling burned by Stewart. Sand, whose mouth was filled with cotton wads from gum surgery, was taken aback. "Merrill went at me," he recalled. "She was not accommodating from the get-go. But she became nice."

After being hired, Sand quickly started cleaning house. He could see that the show was a chaotic mess: The scheduling was confused and the planning haphazard. He couldn't believe there was no board in the office that announced the schedule and what was slated to be on the show. "What did we know about a board?" Markoe said.

Sand also realized that the staff needed an overhaul. From the directors to the cameramen, no one knew how to put on a daily talk show. "They were game show people," he said. "On a game show, it's rigid. If there's a gag and it didn't get in the range of the camera, it didn't get on." There were also too many people competing for attention, too many characters in the way of the star. Letterman recognized these problems, but when things went wrong, he retreated. So when Bob Sarlatte didn't work out, he didn't say anything. He didn't fire him. He just went cold. Letterman needed a bad cop. Sand, a television veteran who wasn't afraid to yell to get his point across, filled the role perfectly.

"It was total chaos, like Normandy," Sand said. "The show had no direction or personality, and Letterman was buried. He was a straight man, and he's not one. He had all these funny people around that I had to fire."

Sand started work on a Friday about a month into the run and held a meeting with all the department heads. He then fired the performer Valri Bromfield, who left the show without much drama, and Edie McClurg, who went on to have a long career in movies like *Ferris Bueller's Day Off* and television shows like *Small Wonder*. "Edie was more vocal and hurt," recalled stage manager Dency Nelson, who said McClurg expressed her anger off camera through one of the characters she performed on the show. "Edie held up a picture of Dave and said, 'This guy fucked me.'"

Perhaps most consequentially, Sand decided they needed a new director who understood how to shoot live comedy. So he fired Burmester and went looking for someone with more experience in talk shows. Television talk-show directors did not have a high profile, nor were they terribly ambitious in the early 1980s. *The Tonight Show* had a staid format, with camerawork that swiveled like clockwork from the curtain to the desk. There was little improvisation and a limited amount to do in staging a show. Directors often cued takes between cameras by snapping their fingers.

Stu Smiley, who worked with Jack Rollins, happened to bump into a seasoned director named Hal Gurnee on the street. He had worked for years with Jack Paar on *The Tonight Show* and, though he had left television, he was looking to renovate a new home. Still, he was willing to entertain a meeting to make a little money. Gurnee met with Letterman and Sand for about half an hour. For most of that time, Gurnee and Letterman talked about losing their fathers (Gurnee's father left home when he was seven and returned to see him only once).

Letterman respected Gurnee's experience in talk shows and also recognized a fellow wiseass. Sand thought he would be too old, but after a meeting, Letterman said to hire him. "One of the reasons why all of this worked was I was getting on in years, and honestly I didn't give a shit," Gurnee said. "I didn't care whether I would be fired. I didn't need this. I did it because it was fun to do."

Gurnee helped David Letterman understand the possibilities of the medium. He proposed ending a show with the host walking up a ladder and exiting from the top of a screen, and then opening a new one the next day by climbing down. Letterman tried it out. He took another bit for a cold open from Charlie Chaplin, in which he started on a close-up of Letterman and then opened wider to show him hanging upside down.

The new director saw mishaps as opportunities. Talk shows did have scripts, but Gurnee kept his eyes on the action, waiting for something to happen that he could adjust. The chaos on the morning show wasn't something to eliminate, but to exploit. So when Judy Collins started a song and her microphone didn't work, Gurnee used his microphone to talk to Letterman.

"We don't have sound, but let's try it again," Gurnee said. Then Letterman entered the picture. "You know, ladies and gentlemen, what you have just witnessed is a screw-up." Collins looked thrilled at the excitement of this accident. And instead of getting angry, Letterman came across as light on his feet. Gurnee said little in this exchange, but by establishing this relationship, he took the viewer backstage without moving the camera off the star. It broke the fourth wall by adding an element of self-awareness. It also set a precedent. Gurnee and Letterman would find some of the show's greatest comedy through their interplay.

On one late-August episode, the show incorporated a marriage anniversary party for an actual middle-aged couple, Sam and Betty Kotinoff, onstage. Letterman brought out a band and a cake, and the Kotinoffs held sparklers right before the credits rolled and papier-mâché rose petals and confetti fell. But when the confetti hit the sparklers, they burst into flames.

Letterman was thanking his guests on the air when the fire began, quickly spreading. Before the host knew what had happened, Mr. Kotinoff started stomping on the ground, but from the viewer's perspective it was unclear why. Gurnee noticed, however, and panned down to discover several small fires heating up right under the feet of the couple, who were surrounded by about fifty of their friends and family. Letterman now realized what was happening and started stomping as well. A stage manager with a fire extinguisher rushed onto the stage. The crowd scattered. In the midst of this chaos, Gurnee shifted from an overhead shot to a wide one back to Letterman's anxious face. Instead of downplaying the disaster, Gurnee turned it into an action film.

Gurnee ended with almost a close-up of Letterman, looking at the floor. The singer crooned. The band played. The show went to black, and *Wheel of Fortune* began. Downstairs, *Tomorrow* host Tom Snyder was watching Letterman's show on the monitor with Stu Smiley, and remarked that the show was not going to be on the air for long. He wasn't the only one. Letterman despaired. Gurnee, by contrast, was elated.

"What he perceived as good for the show and what I perceived sometimes didn't always jibe," Gurnee said. "It just doesn't. I love when things screw up. I don't like to see people made a fool of. But life is that way. That's what you're looking for. You're looking for things that you wouldn't even think of doing."

The David Letterman Show started evolving after the staff overhaul, becoming more focused on its host, and also more unpredictable and strange. The fire was an accident, but many of the oddest moments were not. Markoe would play pranks on Letterman during the show. In one interview, a man dressed in a parka and wearing skis randomly walked right across the stage. Letterman didn't like these surprises, but his irritations became good television. One of the most elaborate stunts Markoe pulled on the host was on the morning of October 15. Letterman was backstage before the show began, listening to his announcer, Bill Wendell, offer up his off-kilter introduction in his booming voice: "And now . . . Davvvvvvid Letterman." But when Letterman grabbed the doorknob and tugged, it didn't open. The show was going to start without him. He bounced on one leg and looked for help. Someone on the staff said, "Try the guest entrance." Dave tried another door, but it was also locked.

High above him was a tiny camera placed on the top of the set by Hal Gurnee, who was filming this scene (a trick he had learned from working on football and baseball games for NBC with Roone Arledge). With Letterman scrambling to find a door to enter, the scene was wonderful farce, anticipating a similar scene in *This Is Spinal Tap* in which the heavy metal band couldn't find the stage.

The sound of laughter became audible backstage, but Letterman did not look amused. "That's it for me," he said. "No point in doing the show. I'm not going out there now." He took his jacket off and unzipped his pants before someone on the crew finally opened the door. Gurnee moved to a shot from the front of the stage as the crowd roared, Letterman walking out holding his jacket in his arms. "Kind of a little surprise on your friend Dave, here," he said, his temper building. Merrill Markoe was standing to the side of the stage, wearing her "Important Writer" shirt.

Without so many characters to write for, Markoe had more freedom to work on material for Letterman. Viewer Mail evolved. It was no longer simply the host reading letters and assuming the audience saw the humor. Now he added insulting quips that became known on the show as Snappies. For instance, one letter from a fourteen-year-old kid announced randomly that he could read backward. "Gee," Letterman said. "What an annoying kid." Then the phrase STUFF IT came on the screen backward.

Viewer Mail had turned from being about the stupidity of the letters to the cutting wit of the host. As a result, the bit became more satirical, because who else on television was treating an audience this way?

David Letterman had a built-in trust with Merrill Markoe and Hal Gurnee. They understood his sensibility and knew how to exploit it. But there was also a healthy tension. Markoe favored conceptual comedy more than Letterman did. Gurnee delighted in improvisation and spontaneity in a way that Letterman did not—you don't get *The Tonight Show* doing that kind of stuff. In their own ways, Gurnee and Markoe pushed him away from that dream and toward something more daring. But their work wasn't enough to save the show.

Prompted by bad ratings, NBC announced on September 26 that the show was being canceled. When the next episode aired, three days later, the host addressed the news by accident when Tom Snyder was a guest, talking about the difficulty of being a host for as long as he had. Letterman made a face like he had eaten something sour, and Snyder recognized he had stumbled onto a sore spot. "I know you hadn't said this," Snyder told him, "but I am sorry this program is going to disappear."

LETTERMAN

The crowd moaned in disapproval. Snyder praised Letterman for trying something adventurous, then went on to blame the network, in the grave tone of a crusading journalist on a soapbox. "With this show not being in this building, a little bit of television in New York is going to die, and we'll all be the poorer for that, and unfortunately there are some people down the hall on this floor who don't recognize that."

Letterman looked devastated, cringing while quickly moving to change the subject. He had long seen failure where others saw success, but this time there was no arguing the point. He'd gotten his shot at a talk show, his dream had come true, and, four months of dismal ratings later, he was being yanked off the air and replaced by two game shows.

They still had several weeks before the final show, and the news of its demise actually had a liberating effect on Letterman and his team. What did they have to lose? In October, they shot an entire show in a stranger's home in Cresco, Iowa, and dedicated another to a farmer named Floyd Stiles, who flew in from Missouri. Letterman took the elderly man out to Sixth Avenue, introducing him to people as if he were a movie star.

In his final episode, Letterman thanked Barry Sand for putting the show together, briefly mentioned Hal Gurnee, and started chuckling when he came to his girlfriend. "This show is a lot fun to do, because it was peculiar on some days," he said at one point, adding decisively, "The person responsible for that feeling is the head writer, Merrill Markoe."

Letterman soon returned to his previous life in Los Angeles. He opened for Helen Reddy at the Garden State Arts Center, in New Jersey, an outdoor venue not friendly to comedy. On the ride home with Stu Smiley and Wil Shriner, he didn't say a word. This was a long fall from a network talk show. He played Harrah's in Lake

Tahoe with Dionne Warwick. Waiting backstage before the show, he called his mother. She answered but told him that she was busy and couldn't talk, since she was going out with her new boyfriend (whom she would later marry). Letterman hung up and threw the phone across the room.

Letterman could have stumbled into a movie career or perhaps returned to doing stand-up full-time. There was yet another opportunity to reinvent the game show when Merv Griffin was looking for a host. "Merv called us one day and said, 'What about David Letterman hosting this game show?'" said agent Deborah Miller about the prospect of his replacing Chuck Woolery as host of *Wheel of Fortune.* "I said, 'It's not exactly what we have in mind.'" The job went to Pat Sajak.

Losing his show seemed like a disaster to David Letterman, but it would turn out to be another fortunate break. New opportunities would soon arise, and it proved an asset to have fewer commitments. While his show had poor ratings, he had received good reviews and developed a cult following that included many in show business. Martin Scorsese (in the midst of cutting *Raging Bull*) had fallen in love with the show and sent Letterman a fan note. Most in the press and the industry blamed his poor showing on his time slot. You couldn't put a sarcastic comedian on in the morning, opposite game shows and cheery chat.

Only a few months after the show went off the air, Johnny Carson, who also lived in Malibu, invited Letterman to once again guest-host *The Tonight Show.* Letterman hosted for a week in December 1980 and one day in January. *The David Letterman Show* won a Daytime Emmy, which raised his stock even more and cemented the idea that the problem with the show was not the star but the time slot. But winning an Emmy was small solace to Letterman.

"It was the most somber afternoon of our life," Barry Sand said of winning the Emmy. "There was a big party after the awards and he wants to go home. I'm thinking, 'I want to have fun.' But no. He had no joy. There was no joy in his life."

The ending of his show had also wreaked havoc on his relationship with Markoe. They fought. As they were preparing to return to California, they got into an argument outside their apartment on West Eighty-second Street over what had happened with the show. "If it wasn't for you and your crazy ideas," he said angrily, "I'd still have a talk show like John Davidson."

NOT TONIGHT

Jay Leno was riding his motorcycle through Malibu with his friend and fellow comic Wil Shriner when he suggested they drop by David Letterman's house. Shriner thought it a bad idea to surprise him so soon after his show had been canceled. But Leno persisted.

Letterman's one-floor home was tucked away in a quiet part of the neighborhood, behind a yard several minutes from the beach. His red pickup truck was in the driveway. When the two comics arrived, Leno rolled his wheel up to the front of the house. Letterman opened the door, and as soon as Shriner saw him, he knew he should have trusted his instincts. Upon entering Letterman's home, Leno immediately started cracking jokes about the sparse decoration. "Were you robbed? What happened?"

Leno walked down the hall and looked out the window. "No pool?" he said with mock condescension. Letterman thought to himself, "Jay had to see what I had done with my money."

Merrill Markoe was there as well, and Shriner got the sense that they had walked in on a fight. Letterman didn't offer a drink or food or suggest they sit down. "What are you doing here?" Letterman asked brusquely. Leno finally got the hint. Letterman just stood there, waiting for the two comics to leave. Shriner told Leno they should go. On the way out, Letterman put his hand on Shriner's shoulder and whispered sarcastically, "Bring *all* your friends by."

Markoe and Letterman went from embattled co-workers hashing out problems at work to a couple with time on their hands back in Los Angeles. Not long after their move back to the West Coast, they broke up. Markoe moved out and rented a new home in Pacific Palisades.

But among those who worked on the morning show, the prevailing attitude was that the network had plans for David Letterman, which meant possible opportunities to work on another show. The comic Rich Hall, in his mid-twenties, thought he had a future with the next Letterman project—and with good reason. He'd had as much success as any writer getting jokes on the morning show. It was his first television job—he would go on to star on *Saturday Night Live* and have a long, successful career in stand-up—and he appeared on camera often, doing satirical movie reviews with overt product placement (on *Dressed to Kill*: "One of the most horrifying scenes in the movie is the shower scene, when Angie Dickinson is attacked while lathering up with Happy Pelican soap") and mock news reports like one from the grassy median on Park Avenue, in the style of a National Geographic dispatch from the wilds of nature.

Merrill Markoe thought Hall was funny, and that he was one of the few people on the original staff whose aggressive, sarcastic style was a perfect match for Letterman. "Rich Hall and I wrote most of that show," Markoe said.

After the cancellation, Hall visited Los Angeles and looked up Markoe, whom he saw as something of a mentor. The split with Letterman was still on her mind. "She told me how crazy Letterman was acting," Hall said. Before long, Hall heard from his manager, Deborah Miller, that Letterman (whom she also represented) was upset he was spending time with Markoe. When asked if they had dated, Markoe said she "did spend time with Mr. Hall after I moved out [from Letterman's house]. It didn't last long."

Hall hadn't anticipated getting stuck in the middle of the relationship of the two people he had worked for only months before. While waiting to go onstage at the Improv, Hall was informed by Miller that Letterman was outside, waiting to talk to him in the parking lot. "She was hysterical," Hall recalled. Once he left the club, he got into Letterman's car and settled into the passenger seat, with Dave behind the wheel and Miller in the backseat. The atmosphere was tense. "What's going on with you and Merrill?" Letterman asked, not angrily, but in a serious tone. Hall told him he had nothing to worry about, that he wasn't dating her. "I was a young guy," Hall told me. "But I told him, 'You better get yourself together and protect what you have, because she's the one who made that show good.'"

Miller wanted to hide underneath the seat. "Dave wasn't saying he wanted to fight him," she said, "but I wasn't sure it didn't have the potential to get physical." After ten minutes of strained talk, they said their goodbyes and Hall returned to the club to do a set, pondering what he had just done. "I thought, 'Did I just dress down David Letterman?'" he recalled. "He was my boss."

Weeks later, Letterman and Markoe got back together. "We had a very emotional reunion," Markoe said. "Definitely the most intense emotion of the entire relationship." She moved back in but kept the rental, just in case.

Westinghouse Broadcasting Company had quickly contacted David Letterman about setting up another show for syndication. But NBC's president, Fred Silverman, decided to act fast to keep

Letterman in the fold, offering a generous holding deal to him and Hal Gurnee. "It was a defensive move," Silverman said.

Yet even as he signed him to a deal, Silverman didn't know exactly what to do with Letterman. Carson was locked in on *The Tonight Show*, and Silverman wanted to replace Tom Snyder with Steve Allen in the following time slot. For a network executive with a sense of history, it made perfect sense. Allen provided a nice change of pace for late night—someone as renowned for experimentation and innovation as Carson was for effortless charm. They would make a natural pair. There was only one problem: Johnny Carson had negotiated control of the time slot after *The Tonight Show* and nixed it.

With Allen rejected for the 12:30 a.m. time slot, David Letterman seemed like an appealing alternative. Critics liked his morning show, which had a mischievous streak. He could be a Steve Allen for a new generation. Letterman was already costing the network money with Silverman's expensive holding deal, and by winning the Emmy, his reputation at the network as a talent who only needed the right vehicle had grown. NBC offered him the job.

Letterman was just thirty-two years old when he started working as a late-night host, guesting on *The Tonight Show*, but he had the track record of a grizzled veteran. He had been fired from his first radio show when he was a teenager. His Indiana late-night movie show was canceled. He didn't get the local weatherman position he wanted. Political talk radio proved a poor fit. His game show pilot didn't get picked up, and he was terrible at sitcoms. His variety show premiere was a bust. And his morning show was canceled.

From an outsider's perspective, his career may have seemed like a quick rise, but to Letterman, this was his last shot. In an interview right after he started preparing for *Late Night with David Letterman*, in 1981, he described show business with a weary cynicism: "It's crap and it's annoying and it can wear you down."

Whereas his father had needed the threat of divorce to stop him from drinking, Letterman gave up alcohol right before starting his late-night show. His high school and college friends don't recall his being a bad or destructive drunk, but it had gotten him into trouble before and he needed to focus. Choosing television over beer was a critical decision for Letterman. It's notable that in retirement, when asked if he missed the adrenaline rush of doing the show, he nodded and said, "Oh, yeah. It's why I used to drink."

Letterman said he had no interest in replacing Johnny Carson and added that popularity and acceptance in television was not that much of a goal for him; doing something different was. "To me, nothing would be greater than to have a regular print outlet on a magazine or a newspaper," he said. "Authors like Robert Benchley and S. J. Perelman are still with us although they are long gone. Tell me who produced *Bosom Buddies* last week."

Letterman, who referred to this period as his "years of indoctrination with Merrill," learned about Benchley from her. She was the one in the relationship who was more skeptical about television, less interested in putting on a show that resembled *The Tonight Show*. They had worked together for years now—in stand-up, on *Mary*, and on the morning show. They had built a shorthand.

Late Night was required to work under conditions established by *The Tonight Show* that aimed to make the shows distinct: no monologue, no big band. *Late Night* needed to send a list of guests to *Tonight* to see if they were acceptable. If they regularly appeared on *Tonight*, there were rejected. Of course, Markoe had no interest in doing a show like Carson's anyway. "Oh, well, I thought," she said. "I guess that just leaves us with every single other thing in the world."

But these rules formalized and clarified the mission of *Late Night with David Letterman*: to be different. And in 1982, when the late-night talk-show landscape was relatively unpopulated, that meant different from *The Tonight Show*.

Letterman and Markoe wanted the show to have none of the artifice of Johnny Carson's Burbank production. Instead of elaborate set design, they built a New York studio with bare walls and transparent scrims that allowed viewers to see backstage. The set had the look of a rehearsal room, a sharp contrast to the polished decor of *The Tonight Show*. The distinctions extended to the jargon used on the show. Letterman didn't do a monologue; he gave "opening remarks." His desk appeared on the right of the stage, with his band to the viewer's left, the reverse of *The Tonight Show*.

Letterman had a list of possible titles, and the one he went with—*Late Night with David Letterman*—he would, characteristically, grow to regret. "*Late Night* is like calling Coke 'brown fizzy soda,'" he said, looking back, and added that they should have kept the name *Tomorrow* from Tom Snyder's show. "*Late Night* is like 'men's room.' It's nothing but serviceable."

Letterman brought back most of the staff from the morning show, including Merrill Markoe, Hal Gurnee, and Barry Sand. Rich Hall was one of the few regulars who did not get invited back. "Maybe [Letterman] was uncomfortable having me on the show. I don't know," Hall said, adding that any awkwardness didn't last long, since Letterman invited him back many times as a guest. The bandleader Frank Owens also did not return.

"Frank [Owens] was really straight, too conventional," Barry Sand told me about the piano player from the morning show. When Letterman called with the bad news, Owens made a show of pretending not to care, faking blubbering tears. "They wanted to go with a personality," he said. "But you've also got to consider the racial element. There were hardly any black musicians in theater or television then."

Letterman wanted to move in a different direction aesthetically. *The Tonight Show* rarely booked rock bands, and its orchestra had a big-band sound. Just as he had on his college radio station, Letterman was looking for someone who played music from his generation. Sand proposed Paul Shaffer, a Canadian musician who had been doing studio work since leaving *Saturday Night Live* in 1980. He was popular among the cast of *SCTV*, where Sand had worked, and loved rock 'n' roll. Letterman knew and liked Shaffer from his *Saturday Night Live* appearances accompanying Bill Murray's cheesy lounge singer "Nick."

Shaffer had been impressed with the morning show, and met with Letterman and Sand during the Christmas holidays in 1981, then Sand for a second time. "Barry Sand always asked the same things," Shaffer recalled. "How much lead time do you need? Could you play the foil?" As soon as he heard these questions, Shaffer knew he was perfect for this job.

Paul Shaffer fell in love with show business at an early age, singing Broadway standards before he could read and staying up late to watch Ed McMahon banter with Jerry Lewis on his telethons. Riveted by the seemingly sincere way these performers talked to each other, trading flattery while dropping words like "marvelous" and "cat," Shaffer wanted to be part of this foreign world. But while he grew up listening to Broadway and Las Vegas entertainers, his heart belonged to rock music. He loved Elvis and Motown. He started a band in school. His father, a lawyer who preferred Frank Sinatra, encouraged his son's interest in music. Shaffer wanted to play in rock bands, but his most critical artistic and professional experience came in a musical.

After accompanying his girlfriend on a 1972 audition for the Toronto revival of *Godspell*, a rock musical by Stephen Schwartz that had become a New York hit, Shaffer was hired as the musical director, even though he couldn't read music. He was a quick study, picking up the songs by listening to the cast album. It was his luck that this Canadian production proved to be almost as much of a 1970s magnet for elite comedy talent as the Comedy Store in Los Angeles. Shaffer met many aspiring comedians in the cast, including Martin Short, Gilda Radner, Dave Thomas, and Andrea Martin. Every Friday, they would hang out with friends, including John Candy and Eugene Levy, and improvise comedy bits and songs in what they called Friday Night Services. Their prayer book, Shaffer said, was *People* magazine, a new publication that was their connection to American show business. They were all obsessed with it.

Martin Short said that Shaffer loved coming up with premises for jokes for the others to play, but that he was also a perfect complementary player, because of his memory for songs. "He was a computer about music, even though he couldn't read it," Short said, recalling their parties as joyful variety shows for themselves. "We would improvise songs and lyrics all the time. I have a tape of Paul and I at Dave Thomas's house in July of '73. We are performing full-out. I'm doing Tony Bennett, we're doing songs for [the musical *You're a Good Man*] *Charlie Brown.* Dave comes in and says, 'Breakfast is ready.'"

Paul Shaffer points to these comedic and musical jam sessions as his show business education. "Hanging out with them changed my life," said Shaffer, who would be the usher at Short's wedding. He learned comic timing from all these comedians, but their attitude toward show business stuck with him as well. Martin Short did a Sinatra impression that poked fun at the singer while also betraying a sincere affection. "I loved Sinatra but didn't want to admit it," Shaffer said. "That was my father's generation. Marty opened my eyes to appreciating it."

Shaffer brought that sensibility to *Late Night.* That he didn't read music was a source of insecurity during his early years, but it proved to be great training for the show, because it forced him to commit many songs to memory. He hired a four-piece band that could adjust on the fly, nimbly moving into the songs after a few notes, adding musical jokes throughout the show, often in response to something that would happen.

Its ethos was a distinct shift from Doc Severinsen's band on *The Tonight Show,* reflected even in the name. While Frank Owens directed the David Letterman Symphony Orchestra, Paul Shaffer led what became known as the World's Most Dangerous Band, a nickname taken from Dick the Bruiser, the "World's Most Dangerous Wrestler," who was popular during Letterman's childhood.

Shaffer put together a group of performers he knew well, recruiting three musicians from the 24th Street Band—guitarist Hiram Bullock, the bassist Will Lee, and the drummer Steve Jordan—whose second album he produced in 1980. He had also worked with Jordan on *Saturday Night Live*. The band aimed for an intimate, driving sound. Unlike other shows, which introduced guests with a loud song, Shaffer went against the grain, playing nothing when movie stars entered, though he and the band did introduce stand-up acts with music. The only sound was the applause of the crowd. This was not a show that was going to manipulate you with a booming, triumphant sound track. It was more low-key, cooler. "Dave never wanted to pretend for the audience that anything was other than it is," Shaffer said. "He was very particular about being honest with the audience, even if it was setting up a bit."

Since he understood how to support comedians in a joke, Shaffer was a better match for Letterman than Owens was. What was less clear at the time was how his wry sensibility would complement and clarify the attitude of the host, turning their relationship into a bedrock of the show.

Shaffer said nothing in the first few episodes, in part because his microphone wasn't on. "The engineers said, 'I don't think they want it on,'" Shaffer said, referring to the production staff. "So I had to go back to Barry [Sand]." They put it on, and sure enough, by the second week, after Letterman introduced the band, Paul Shaffer spoke his first words on *Late Night*. "We are going to swing tonight," Shaffer said. "I want to tell you, David Letterman."

Wearing a conservative brown jacket, Shaffer spoke this Vegas-style slang tentatively. Looking startled at this turn of events, Letterman bent over laughing. "Why, thank you very much," he said. "That was Paul doing a little talking over there."

Letterman encouraged Shaffer to interject more on the show, which resulted, in the first year, in a fairly limited but integral comedic role for Shaffer. After Dave finished his opening jokes and walked to his desk, Paul would always say a sentence or two in the language of a Las Vegas hipster. "We're in a cuckoo, groovy mood," he might say. Or "You are wild, David, that's why I love you." To which Letterman would respond with highly enunciated diction: "Thank you, Paul." And that would be the extent of their interaction, give or take another sentence or two.

Shaffer would sometimes explicitly mention casinos or reference how his hoarse voice was due to a case of "Vegas throat." That he was heading up a rock band in New York made this Las Vegas character illogical, but that didn't matter. Shaffer's humor was rooted in language, the jargon of a previous generation's idea of cool, and a wry attitude toward show business, both of which Letterman enjoyed. In response to the daily quip from Shaffer, he would often pause and cackle merrily before repeating it.

At times Shaffer seemed to be mocking the flattery Ed McMahon regularly doled out to his host on *The Tonight Show*. "You are my music, David, you are my sun," he would say, and Letterman would wait just long enough to register the inanity of the comment, then move on. But he wasn't singling out one person so much as a type of entertainer. In the early shows, Shaffer was essentially playing a one-note caricature. "It became a character, a fugitive from Las Vegas," he said.

Shaffer's cartoonish character set the tone for the show. His overt phoniness represented a brand of dated show business, the nearly obsolete Las Vegas style that Steve Martin had also been sending up. Letterman was at his best when he had a focus for his sarcasm, and Shaffer gave him his first really rich target. Dave would roll his eyes at him and express bewilderment at his hackneyed lines. Always good-spirited, Shaffer could take an insult with a smile. He took a lot of them.

LETTERMAN

"Paul's temperament is easygoing," Martin Short said. "He's not confrontational and doesn't storm out. Even people who are prickly, Paul can get along with them."

It was a helpful quality working with Letterman, whose inclination was to mock and insult whatever was nearby. For him, such scoffing was knee-jerk. In the first few years of *Late Night*, Shaffer became a punching bag standing in for a certain kind of entertainment figure. But Shaffer imbued his character with affection. "You parody what you love," he said, adding that he also became what he mocked.

David Letterman didn't see it exactly the same way. His (and Merrill Markoe's) comedy always maintained a distance between himself and the thing he was mocking, and he had no affection for the chummy lingo and false emotionalism of the personalities that Shaffer was sending up. Letterman was the hero of his show, but unlike on *The Tonight Show*, the sidekick didn't merely fill the role of a television pal. Shaffer was that, but he also proved to be a foil. And he wasn't the only one.

The first person to appear onscreen on *Late Night with David Letterman* was not the host or his bandleader, but a short, white-haired man walking toward the camera, followed by a looming shadow. Striding through a cavernous, dark room, he wore a suit and glasses, looking like a dotty old English teacher from a 1950s high school yearbook. Footsteps echoed eerily as he walked toward the camera, his face illuminated in spotlight: "Good eeeeevening." In the style of a spooky narrator from a gothic horror movie, he read the script from the opening of the classic Universal movie *Frankenstein*, explaining that David Letterman was a mad scientist, creating a show "in his own image."

The man was Calvert DeForest, a struggling actor from Brooklyn who had worked as a receptionist at a methadone clinic. After multiple appearances, he would come to be known as Larry "Bud" Melman, a name given him by Markoe and Letterman. His performance was the first sign that *Late Night with David Letterman* was going to be something really odd and often even confusing. What stood out was not what he was saying, but how ineptly he said it. His voice was thin, inexpressive, and oddly flat, and his facial expressions numbered not much more than one. If he was there to conjure the spirit of Boris Karloff, it was the version directed by Ed Wood. When the time came for him to shift gears from cautioning the audience to a passive-aggressive joke, the camera moved in to a tight close-up. "Well," he said limply. "We warned you."

His awkwardness undermined the spooky mood, turning it into something ridiculous. But it also had an alienating effect, drawing attention to itself. No one had ever seen this man, and there were no jokes, so it was decidedly not funny in a traditional way, even though one might detect a vague parody of horror. But this monologue didn't commit to that, either, since what stood out most was how uncomfortable DeForest was. Was his amateurishness the joke? It didn't seem so. Most shows introduce themselves warmly, courting the audience with some of their best jokes. This was a welcome that seemed designed to baffle. It looked as if something had gone awry.

Markoe had spotted DeForest in a NYU short film made by Karl Tiedemann and Stephen Winer, whom she hired as writers on the show. "King of the 'Z's" was a comedy-savvy satire about Vespucci Pictures, a cut-rate fictional studio in the golden age of Hollywood that made westerns in which cowboys emerged out of subway trains. DeForest played a bumbling, Dr. Frankenstein–like figure in the short film, sending up old movie styles, a part not unlike the one he played at the start of *Late Night*.

Markoe met with Tiedemann and Winer, and at the end of the interview she said, "We're looking for somebody like that little guy in your movie." Winer responded, "You're not looking for somebody like that guy. That's the guy you're looking for."

Originally the opening was not designed to use the exact words from *Frankenstein*. But once Markoe saw that version, she said she wanted the actual language from the movie. She didn't want satire; she was looking for something weirder than that. It was a small decision, but one that reflected the core aesthetic of the show: *Late Night* didn't invent something out of nothing. It took what was already in the world and made you see it in a new way. The point was not to mock *Frankenstein* so much as appropriate it. At rehearsal, Tiedemann asked Letterman if he was bothered that few would get the nod to the movie, that he would start his late-night show by confusing a large proportion of his audience.

Letterman replied, "For me, anytime you can fill up network time with something like that, I put it in the win column."

Years later, Letterman would describe this as arrogance. "We thought we had all the answers," he said. "We thought television had made a huge mistake and we would fix it."

Late Night with David Letterman didn't just look cheaper than other shows on television. Its characters emphasized its own terribleness, which veered into kitsch. DeForest was an awful actor, and Shaffer played the role of a hokey, out-of-touch bandleader. They made *Late Night with David Letterman* seem less like a talk show than a parody of one.

This provided a ripe context for the snarky sensibility of the host, making his knee-jerk sarcasm seem pointed, with more serious intent than he actually had. Letterman had always been irreverent, but Shaffer and Melman presented him with certain targets. In his opening remarks, what other shows called the monologue, David Letterman spent an inordinate amount of time sarcastically hyping and effusively praising the show. "What a power-packed, historic extravaganza we've assembled for you tonight," he said at the top of one show.

Letterman told his audience how great the show was going to be, but he didn't look like he believed it. He incessantly talked about the magic of whatever mundane thing was happening in that moment. His opening remarks featured few jokes, often just one. He could become jittery and distracted, looking offscreen, referring obliquely to jokes. As a new late-night host, Letterman could be wooden in his movements and vocal inflections—traces of the TV weatherman remained in his delivery. His performance was far more tentative than the show, which was boldly unconventional and aggressively experimental.

Mostly, Letterman projected indifference verging on boredom. A common phrase on the show occurred when Letterman would stop in the middle of a boast and say, "If that's not enough—and by gosh, don't you think it ought to be?"

Letterman also regularly said, with a deadpan that could look positively morose, that he was "having more fun than humans should be allowed to have." In his first year, the central joke of Letterman's performance was a preposterous celebration of just how incredible this awful-looking show appeared to be.

In the second week, *Late Night* began an episode with a familiar talk-show vignette: the desk and a microphone. But there was something different here. The host was absent, and in his place was a dog sipping a glass of milk, which went on for a full minute, a seemingly endless span of time for television comedy, before the glass toppled over, the milk spilling. Cue the start of the show. The artist William Wegman, who owned the dog, appeared later on the show and talked to Letterman about surrealism, but the dog's presence was never explained. Merrill Markoe's background as an art professor was making its way onto late-night television.

A leading candidate for the most flamboyantly strange comedy bit in the history of *Late Night with David Letterman* was buried in the final minutes of a show in the middle of the first year. After an interview with a guest, the show returned from the last commercial to Letterman in a pirate hat, surrounded by chaos, smoke billowing through the studio, the furniture upended. A nurse ushered a woman up the aisle, a column cut through the host's desk. There was no explanation for the random nonsense onscreen, nothing to prepare you for this tumult. "Oh, well," Letterman said, his tie loose. "Something you have never seen before on network television." Then the credits rolled.

Markoe loved this comedic non sequitur, excitedly telling the staff the next day, "We baffled all of America! Nobody knows what the hell we were doing!"

Letterman was more ambivalent about such conceptual tricks, but Markoe encouraged and fought for them. "She had an endless enthusiasm for formal innovation," said Randy Cohen, who wrote for *Late Night* for six years. "And I believe Dave in his heart of hearts had none. He would have been perfectly happy to do the Carson show."

Markoe pushed for these shifts in perspective, and in the show's first few weeks, she kept the camera on the move. In one episode, *Late Night* began from the point of view of the host in his dressing room, walking down the hall and onto the stage, so that instead of seeing Letterman, the image was of the audience. In another, the audience saw the show from the perspective of a guy in the back row, complaining. Letterman was barely visible, but we heard a running commentary about what was wrong with the show.

Markoe also filmed and edited a series of video pieces from the point of view of a dog, showing us legs and grass and an entire world from below, not unlike how *Peanuts* cartoons relegated adults to mumbling afterthoughts. These perspective shifts subverted expectations of what a talk show was supposed to look like and were a sharp contrast to *The Tonight Show*, with its fixed camera. In one recurring bit, called "Limited Perspective," which originated as Markoe's attempt to satirize the kind of movie review that obsessed over the credibility of an event in a movie, Letterman invited people to review a film from a ludicrously narrow point of view. A driving instructor, for instance, found fault in the Mel Gibson action film *The Road Warrior* because the post-apocalyptic motorcycle drivers didn't wear safety helmets.

Markoe's greatest contributions were the filmed remote pieces, which she wrote, edited, and produced. They were short absurdist videos starring Letterman as the sensible, sarcastic man in a city full of eccentrics and fools. She directed and cut these pieces for the first four years of the show, establishing a template. The comic films were created out of real parts of New York: storefronts, tourists, neighborhood restaurants. This was not the first time a talk show had taken cameras out on the street, but for late-night television, Markoe launched a new comic style, one that mixed scripted and improvisational work and used the city as a studio set to exploit playful juxtapositions and build silly alternative histories.

Most of these films were conceived by Merrill Markoe scouring the telephone book, looking for local businesses that could provide grist for a premise. "I looked for language, misspellings, weird names of places," she said. "I looked for stuff you never saw on TV. I remember a tour of Paris based on a bunch of places I found that had Paris in the title."

The second one was called "Alan Alda: The Man and His Chinese Food." Letterman began on the street, holding a microphone, speaking in a sober journalistic voice: "In the last several years, much has been said of Alan Alda the TV star, the film star, the writer, the humanitarian, the champion of minority causes, but it's surprising we don't know much about Alan Alda the lover of Chinese food." In the style of *60 Minutes*, the film then cut to Letterman asking probing questions of Chinese restaurant employees: How does Alan Alda eat his food? What kind of food does he like? Is he good with the utensils?

Part of the comedy came from a cheap joke about the accents of the immigrant owners of the restaurants. But it was also a deft satire about celebrity and the idiocy of entertainment journalism, treating celebrity taste in takeout food with immense gravity. Some of the first reviews of *Late Night with David Letterman* singled out this Alan Alda film and praised these man-on-the-street bits. The *New York Times*' critic praised the host's "gift for getting great mileage out of apparently trivial situations."

In its first few months, *Late Night with David Letterman* received mostly positive reviews, but that didn't provide comfort to the host, who fixated on never-high-enough ratings. Still stung by the loss of his last show, he constantly feared cancellation. To those on staff, he often seemed unhappy and frustrated with the show.

At the end of a typical episode, David Letterman would rush away from his desk, rip his jacket off, push the studio doors open, and then head to his dressing room and slam the door. Then he examined with Markoe, in detail, what an absolutely miserable job he had done.

Letterman fixated on technical problems or what he saw was an error in booking or a botched punch line. He never enjoyed the successes and scrutinized every failure, musing darkly about the implications and pivoting from self-criticism to despair in a blink. His temper built, but it always circled back to himself. There were dents in his refrigerator from his taking out his anger at himself. "He would become very depressed and enter into a cyclone of unhappiness and anger about how his show-biz career was totally over," Markoe explained. "He was always like this, but I was under the impression that once the show was launched and was going well, this would level off." It did not.

In the first year, Letterman hung around the office and traded ideas with the writers on staff. But his standards for comedy were high and hard to read. He rejected 80 or 90 percent of the ideas, and, early on, *Late Night* stuck closely to the same formula as the morning show. Letterman didn't show this harshly self-critical side of his personality on television, instead coming off as tightly wound and repressed, a guy who didn't show his emotions. His onscreen persona was carefully controlled, a buttoned-up and straitlaced ordinary midwestern guy rolling his eyes at the world. At his best, he looked like he was barely trying, a leading man who didn't really care what you thought of him.

He was much darker in magazine profiles during that period. "If you have any sense, you'll adopt the view of life that if the bucket of shit can explode, it will explode," he told *Rolling Stone*, whose writer sounded surprised by the star's offstage anxiety four months after his premiere: "For an upcoming captain of show biz, he's kind of a worry-wart."

Letterman could be extremely thin-skinned, his anxiety emerging at unexpected moments. "You can hurt his feelings real easy," Barry Sand said, adding that this didn't mean he would pull punches. "He would always hurt someone's feelings and be like, 'I should never say that.' He was always trying to take back what he said. Complicated guy."

Barbara Gaines, a production assistant who came over from the morning show, said the office had a locker room atmosphere, with everyone ribbing each other, but she learned that the host could be wounded easily. "We would joke around and he would call me an asshole, but if I called him an asshole, he would be like, 'Why did you do that?'" she said. "He was very sensitive. He didn't like it if anyone didn't like him."

Early on, as *Late Night with David Letterman* struggled to book big stars, the show made a virtue of a limitation by creating its own, using a small pool of regulars who had informal deals to return to the show often. Letterman was most at ease with broadcasters or fellow comedians, none more so than the stand-up comedian Jay Leno.

Leno got his first sustained national exposure doing dozens of guest spots on *Late Night*. He was one of the most popular guests in the show's history, and the two comics, while competitive off-camera, had chemistry onscreen.

Leno felt comfortable with Letterman in a way he never did with Carson. "I could say, 'Nice tie, Dave.' I couldn't say that to Johnny," Leno said, explaining that Letterman was a peer. "I was like Rickles to Dave's Johnny."

Leno understood the style of comedy Letterman favored from their years working at the Comedy Store. When Dave interrupted him by echoing something he said, Leno didn't race through to get to the punch line. He knew that Letterman adored funny phrases, and that they were critical to the joke. "Dave always laughed on the way to a joke," Leno said. "On the show, I would never get to the punch line, so I would try to make him chuckle with an odd phrase."

Many younger comics who couldn't get on *The Tonight Show* found a home on *Late Night*. The stand-up comic Carol Leifer said she knew that she could get away with more inside jokes with Letterman. "It was the hipper kid brother of *The Tonight Show*," she said. Martin Short started doing *Late Night* when he was a performer on *SCTV* and would prepare rigorously for every appearance, presenting twenty to thirty pages of material from which the talent coordinator chose before every segment. "I structured it like I would a movie shoot," Short said. After several virtuosic guest spots, packed with songs, impressions, and explosive jokes, *The Tonight Show* invited him to be a guest and he turned it down, preferring to stick with what he considered the cooler show.

Late Night pursued guests who were more on the cultural margins. Brother Theodore, a singular German monologist who delivered enraged rants off-Broadway, regularly brought the energy of performance art to *Late Night*. Dressed in black and wearing a stern expression, he came off as a parody of an intellectual saying very important things. His laments about the culture were epic. The locution of his philosophic tirades echoed that of old Hitler speeches, making him seem the model of the dangers of believing things too deeply.

Paul Reubens was another inspired weirdo who found national attention and an artistic home on *Late Night*. A cult performer in Los Angeles, he developed the character Pee-wee Herman, a giddy juvenile in a suit and bow tie, with the irreverent innocence of a character cut from a 1950s sitcom. Reubens had heard from an agent that Johnny Carson was "uncomfortable with the Pee-wee character," but he proved popular with David Letterman, appearing frequently in long segments filled with silly jokes, prop humor, and quips designed to throw the host off guard.

"He made fun of me, but he really did seem to genuinely like me as well," Reubens said. "The other person who he had a similar relationship with was—I hate to say it—Richard Simmons."

These appearances earned Reubens a manager who set him up on a theater tour that eventually led to his own movie, *Pee-wee's Big Adventure*, and television series, *Pee-wee's Playhouse*. In the same way that an appearance on *The Tonight Show* could jump-start the career of a stand-up, *Late Night* became a launching pad for more eccentric performers, the place to find challenging, uncomfortable, even annoying work. "I think it's important to have guests who annoy the public," Letterman once said in an interview. "It feels good to scream at the TV once in a while, to go to work and tell everyone how annoyed you are."

As with Shaffer and Melman, Letterman excelled at playing off eccentricity, situating himself as the relatable figure the audience could identify with. The actress and comic Sandra Bernhard was peculiarly gifted at rattling the host. Her first appearance was promoting *The King of Comedy*, a Scorsese movie in which she plays an obsessed fan stalking a talk-show host, and her dozens of guest spots carried a similar vibe. While she was more aggressive and flamboyant than Letterman, her humor was tuned at a similar frequency: perpetually ironic and cynical about show business.

Bernhard regularly turned her spots into caricatures of seduction, declaring her mad crushes on Letterman, kissing him, and at one point even coming on the air with a padded stomach and saying she was pregnant. In the middle of the bit, she said her water had broken, and Letterman handed her a *Late Night with David Letterman* sponge. When she reached down to her crotch, he stood up and walked out of the studio. Bernhard took his seat and did a Letterman impression. It was dynamic television. "I found him sexy and flirted with him, and it was obvious I could make him uncomfortable, which I found interesting," Bernhard said. "I hadn't seen that on talk shows, with the exception of flirting between Angie Dickinson and Johnny. So I played that up."

Unlike Short, Bernhard frequently went off-script, which caused tension at times, including with the bit about the fake pregnancy. "But that was their thing: pranks, but they didn't like it when you did it back to them," Bernhard said.

No guest did more to define the unpredictable early years of *Late Night* than Andy Kaufman. He had become famous from starring in the sitcom *Taxi*, but his stand-up pioneered an experimental comedy that made audiences wonder if he was acting or not. As a guest on Letterman's morning show, Kaufman appeared glassy-eyed and meek, looking distraught, snot running down his nose. Letterman looked unsure what to say, stammering. Kaufman said he was not working, was finished with *Taxi*, and appeared to have trouble finishing a sentence. Then he asked if he could do a bit, and walked over to a stool to tell a story about how his wife had divorced him and taken the kids. He asked the crowd to stop laughing. Then he walked into the crowd with his hand out, asking for money.

His melancholy performance had none of the artifice of the carefully glib and cheerful stories you expect on talk shows. It was in the style of heartbreaking realism, even if, like most of what Kaufman did, it was an elaborate put-on he would never publicly acknowledge. His original concept had been to end this segment by taking a gun out and shooting himself. Markoe rejected the idea.

Kaufman became a frequent guest on *Late Night* and appeared in the most famous episode of the first year of the show. He had been working in professional wrestling, a contrived sport that at that time was covered by sports reporters as if it were real. Kaufman appeared on *Late Night* several times in the first year, talking about his wrestling rivalry with Jerry Lawler, a beefy 240-pound wrestler from Tennessee. After they did in fact wrestle, Kaufman returned to *Late Night*, along with Lawler. This time Kaufman was wearing a neck brace.

After the two men got into a heated argument, Kaufman confronted Lawler, who responded by slapping him. Following the commercial break, Kaufman returned to the stage and grabbed a cup on Letterman's desk. He cursed and tossed the coffee at Lawler, then ran away. Letterman looked stunned at this explosive turn of events but demonstrated why he was such a talent, keeping his poise and taking control of the situation with the perfectly timed quip.

"I think you can use some of those words on TV," Letterman said, then added, in a deadpan, "but what you can't do is throw coffee." At the start of the following night's show, Letterman apologized for the outbreak of violence and insisted that he had no idea that the fight would break out. This was true, although Lawler later admitted that he and Kaufman had planned it in advance. Letterman then told the audience not to look to him to break up fights. "Under this eight-dollar suit," Letterman said, "beats the heart of a wimp, ladies and gentlemen."

I n early reviews of *Late Night,* one thing on which the critics agreed was that David Letterman was a terrible interviewer. As some of the staff writers would joke, he was a talk-show host who didn't like to talk to people. That wasn't really true, but his interviews could make it seem that way. He had no interest in actors or acting. "I never met anyone in show business with less of an interest in meeting celebrities," Jim Downey, a *Saturday Night Live* writer who went to work at *Late Night* at the end of the first year, said of Letterman.

Celebrities are how a talk show gets attention, not to mention ratings. Early on, there was tension with the network over the star power of the bookings. NBC wanted more famous people; Letterman resisted. David Letterman usually did not visit with guests before the show. They saw him for the first time on the air, and when the interview was over he shifted his focus back to his staffers. Letterman was so inept at feigning interest in his guests' new projects that he seemed to be doing it on purpose. He regularly got the titles of the television shows or movies they were promoting wrong. He did not ingratiate or play nice. The tone was set from the first question he ever asked a guest on his late-night show: "This may not be of interest to anyone, and it's barely of interest to me," Letterman said to Bill Murray, who had come onstage distracted and drunk.

He insulted a movie star and the talk-show interview in one sentence. And he did it without any righteousness. In the first few months of *Late Night,* Letterman could be cautious, slow to interrupt, and tentative in engaging in debate. He did display a few consistent obsessions. He had a sensitive ear for phoniness and canned talking points and loved asking about money and authenticity. He pressed the famous trial lawyer Gerry Spence, "I've always wanted to ask a lawyer, 'Can you manipulate a jury?'"

When Carl Reiner came on the show and praised Letterman, calling him subtle and brilliant before saying that he hoped the network understood how good he was, Letterman flashed a flamboyantly skeptical face. "That's bullshit, isn't it?" he said, his curse edited out. Reiner doubled over in laughter, looking lost about how to respond: "How do you handle that?"

Unsurprisingly, not all actors responded well to this kind of interview. Letterman asked Harrison Ford if he got paid for the sale of Indiana Jones merchandise. "Let's not talk about money," a clearly irritated Ford responded. Yet Letterman could also display a surprisingly naive side. When Christopher Reeve introduced a clip of his new movie, *Deathtrap,* by saying, tongue in cheek, that it was the "crass commercial" reason he was there, Letterman looked genuinely surprised: "Wait a minute. You would have come on anyways, wouldn't you?" Reeve said simply, "No." Letterman folded his arms, hurt.

In Hollywood, Letterman developed a reputation as cold and unhelpful at best, mean at worst. The press, NBC executives, and his own staff all agreed that Letterman's interviewing was a weak spot to be worked on. The host himself said he was terrible.

Everyone was wrong.

Letterman's interviews elevated a segment typically used for promotion dressed up with show business stories into something unpredictable, dramatic, and potentially exciting. You wanted to see how Letterman would get along with a certain celebrity. His hostility in front of the famous helped define the populist style of the show and established him as more blunt and honest than the usual smiling host. His awkwardness *seemed* purposeful, a comment on the absurdity of flattering actors.

In a show business version of triangulation, Letterman established a connection with the audience by distancing himself from his guest. Scott Aukerman, who hosts one satirical talk show, *Comedy Bang! Bang!,* and produces another, *Between Two Ferns,* recalled being mesmerized by these interviews as a kid. "Just the fact he would interview people and seem to not care what the other person was saying and using them as springboard for jokes, I was like, 'Finally,'" Aukerman told me. "It didn't matter who Letterman was interviewing, because he was fascinating."

For his part, Letterman never saw himself as doing anything different from other talk-show hosts. "For me, it was just an extension of high school or college," he said. "You're running around with your buddies making fun of each other."

THE HARVARD TAKEOVER

O n his first day as a writer on *Late Night with David Letterman*, Tom Gammill took a piece of paper, wrote FUCK EXXON on it, and taped it to his window, sending a message to the offices of the oil giant across the street. His writing partner and office mate Max Pross chuckled. Minutes later, to their surprise, a security guard knocked and told them to take the sign down. "I wasn't radical or anything," Gammill said. "It just seemed like something you do for a laugh."

Gammill, then twenty-four, had the lanky and bespectacled look of an op-ed writer for the *New York Times*. Shorter and fairer, Pross, also twenty-four, projected a similarly cerebral style. They had grown up in the Northeast, met at Harvard, and started writing as a team at *Saturday Night Live* right out of college in the late 1970s, before getting a job working for David Letterman.

They were not intimidated or, at first, particularly impressed by

Letterman. He was a guy from Indiana who hosted a daytime talk show, while they had worked at the hippest comedy on television. Many of their friends from *SNL* thought Letterman was bland. "The Bobby Darin of comedy," one called him.

Both shows were shot in Rockefeller Center, but the difference in atmosphere was dramatic. At *Saturday Night Live*, the refrigerator was packed with Budweiser and everyone stayed late brainstorming ideas. At *Late Night*, everyone seemed sober and left for home by the early evening. "*Saturday Night Live* felt like another year of college," said Pross. "*Late Night* was like an insurance office."

Pross and Gammill were the first two of a small army of *Late Night* writers who had cut their teeth at *The Harvard Lampoon*, a college humor magazine that had a major impact on the show and on pop culture at large. Championing scathing and literate parody, the magazine started getting national exposure in the 1960s, spoofing *Mademoiselle* and *Playboy*, then gave birth to *National Lampoon*, a satirical magazine that reached millions of subscribers. Its writers helped define the first years of *Saturday Night Live*, but they would have an even greater impact on *Late Night with David Letterman*.

As soon as they were hired, Gammill and Pross lobbied Merrill Markoe to hire their friend George Meyer, a twenty-five-year-old former president of the *Harvard Lampoon*. Inflamed by the righteousness of youth, Meyer was a ferocious critic of any joke that seemed played out or pandering. He traced the evolution of his superior sensibility to the office conversations at the *Lampoon*. "It was nasty, adolescent, cutting, and occasionally erudite," he reflected. "We sometimes had highfalutin references. But the tone was usually disparaging. The tone was to denigrate and demolish something."

These three *Lampoon* writers arrived at *Late Night* with swagger. "We would sit around saying, 'Monty Python was *pretty* good,'" Gammill recalled.

Letterman did not at first embrace their ideas, thinking them too esoteric for network television. "They had a much broader view of television comedy than I did," Letterman said. "I worked in night-clubs where you had to get laughs, so I thought anything conceptual was hard to sign on to."

But the *Lampoon* clique quickly recognized an ally in Markoe. "Merrill was sly and playful, while Dave's [sensibility] was generally more joke-oriented," Meyer said. "A lot of the time, Merrill was going for more a mood and a tone. She liked to create a loopy three minutes that was essentially silly or a fool's errand." Gammill recalled that they would pitch Markoe ideas, hoping she could convince Letterman of them.

The *Lampoon* writers intimidated others on the staff. "Tom and Max had *Saturday Night Live* credits, and I was just in awe of them," said Andy Breckman, another of the original writers. "They hated people," recalled Richard Morris, one of the few stand-ups on the writing staff. "They always wanted to be over you. To win. They were sarcastic. They had to get the upper hand. Maybe I wasn't strong enough to withstand that sarcasm and competitive pressure."

One major early divide on the staff was over Larry "Bud" Melman, whose bumbling appearances earned bigger laughs than just about any-thing else on the first year of the show. Offstage, Calvert DeForest was not that different from how he was on the show: earnest, innocent, a little slow. He loved the theater, and many on the staff assumed he was gay or asexual. But unlike with Paul Shaffer, the way the show used Melman carried a hint of cruelty, since DeForest did not seem to be in on the joke. In one notorious bit, DeForest was supposed to read "'Twas the Night Before Christmas" to a group of children in a holiday-themed episode (that took place during the summer). The book handed to him by the prop department was in French (the staffer later insisted this was an accident), leaving DeForest in an impossible situation on the air. He tried to recite the poem by memory, making things up as Hal

Gurnee panned over the faces of the baffled children. Backstage, the writers roared laughing at the poor man panicked over what to do. And they replayed it on the show the following day, followed by Letterman saying, "It was magic, wasn't it?"

This was the kind of mistake the morning show had turned into freewheeling comedy, but now it was at the expense of a slow man clearly suffering. "I could see how grown-ups would argue that we were taking advantage of this poor guy, but we weren't grown-ups," said Breckman. "Now I would feel uncomfortable using someone like that. He clearly was challenged. It was kids running amok after the grown-ups went to bed."

The *Lampoon* writers laughed, too, and they didn't necessarily have any moral qualms about it, but they did think leaning on Melman was easy and even hackneyed. "I remember thinking he was a comedy crutch," Gammill said. "What are we going to do next? Just throw garbage at Larry 'Bud' Melman?"

The writers Stephen Winer and Karl Tiedemann, the ones who'd discovered DeForest, saw it differently. A competing contingent from NYU, they were smart, ambitious comedy nerds without the caustic slant of the *Lampoon* writers. Tiedemann, who dressed retro, with Buddy Holly glasses and a suit and tie in an office where jeans and a T-shirt were more common, viewed Melman in the tradition of fools like Private Duane Doberman, from the 1950s sitcom *The Phil Silvers Show*, a slovenly dim bulb played by an actor, Maurice Gosfield, famous for stumbling over his lines. Winer thought he tapped the humor of a guy gamely trying despite inevitable limitations. "That was the big split," said Winer, describing the divide on the staff over Larry "Bud" Melman. "Some of the writers wouldn't write for him."

While Winer and Tiedemann got many Melman sketches on the air—including an homage to *The Honeymooners* called "The Honeymelmans"—the *Harvard Lampoon* contingent was increasingly frustrated during the first year at the show. *Police Squad!*, a show by the Zucker brothers, had recently premiered, bringing a giddy satirical style to television that they admired more than a lot of the more earthbound desk pieces on *Late Night*. Letterman was a fan of *Police Squad!*, but when Pross discussed doing parody like that on the show, the response was not enthusiastic. "The impression I got from him is 'We can't do that here,'" Pross said, adding, "Dave wanted the show to be more like the Carson show than we did."

Pross and Gammill were restless, but not as much as George Meyer. Bearded and intense, Meyer hated doing the same bit twice— known on the show as a refillable. Stupid Pet Tricks was great, but doing it again? What's the point? Repeating a joke was pandering to the audience. "George was always sulky and contentious," Markoe said.

Meyer thought the show settled too often, and he even quit on one occasion because an idea of his was botched in the execution. The bit was called "Crowd Pleasers," and when asked why it bothered Meyer, Markoe joked, "It pleased the crowd."

Merrill Markoe was unhappy in a different way. She thought they were putting on a good show and took particular pride in the remote video segments she produced. But Letterman's anxiety did not subside, and Markoe feared that work was damaging her personal life. Over the summer, she rented a house in the Hamptons so she and Letterman could get away from the show, but even on vacation Letterman brooded over press attention and ratings. There was no television reception at the house, so he went to work rigging a series of wires and pieces of aluminum foil to the antennae. He strung them out the window and hung them into the driveway, fixing the set so he could watch the Jerry Lewis telethon.

"We are spending 10–12 hours a day at work consistently," Markoe wrote in her diary about the vacation in the Hamptons. "Other than moments from our weekends at the beach, it would be difficult to prove there was a summer."

Throughout 1982, Letterman was chronically, persistently, and occasionally loudly unhappy. Part of the head writer's job was to take a steady stream of rejection from the host, who in this case added his own cranky pessimism. "It was a daylong fistfight," Letterman said about the first year on the show. "You get up in the morning and you go at it, then you go at it all day, and then you go at it at home. And you go to bed."

Letterman attacked his performance every night, and while he directed most of his anger and sense of failure at himself, it didn't always feel that way to Markoe. As she wrote in her diary in late 1982:

> The last ten months have included a nightly discussion about what a failure we are. Sometimes it is just Dave blowing off steam, working out his insecurities but often I am the wrong recipient of this info because it includes an attack on the work I have been doing all day. I remember specifically one time, right before air, when Dave (in a fit of nerves) leaned over and said: "The show tonight is laugh free." As it turned out, the pieces all went very well but as I watched them being performed my blood pressure was soaring and I literally felt light headed and faint with nervous fear that I had given him inadequate material that would adversely affect his career.

In front of the writers, Markoe tried to keep her unhappiness to herself, but this became increasingly difficult. Gammill recalled her quipping to the other writers, "*You* sleep with him."

Markoe considered quitting, but she loved her work. She decided on a compromise: to resign as head writer but stay with the show. It was a wrenching decision, but she felt she had to do something to save the relationship. Letterman was not surprised. "I think we were both relieved," he said. "It was getting bloodthirsty." Markoe still regularly shot remotes and acted as an informal adviser to the rest of the staff. She took half of her previous salary.

Once she'd decided to stand down as head writer, Markoe sought a suitable replacement. She needed someone diplomatic and steady, who could handle the moods of the host and the disparate personalities on staff. Markoe thought Andy Breckman made the most sense and settled on him. He was smart, funny, diligent, and a few years older than most of the staff, so he seemed like he could be the adult in the room. Once the other writers found out that Breckman had gotten the job, however, some were not pleased.

Breckman was immediately pelted with questions by the other writers: How exactly would this work? What would the procedures be every day? How would we submit stuff to you? Are you going be talking to Dave alone? "I didn't have any of the answers," Breckman recalls. "I was off-balance and surprised. And I could tell they were very skeptical."

Tom Gammill started asking the other writers what they thought about the decision. Meyer was the most vocal critic. "As a paranoid young man, I thought that was an indication they wanted to go to a more joke-oriented—I don't want to say mainstream—a less Harvardy direction," he said. "I bristled at that." He shook his head recalling his reaction. "I was a screwed-up young man," he added.

Breckman called all the writers together and began brainstorming a new dial-it-services bit, a desk piece during which Letterman would call a number for a service and someone would answer and deliver a punch line. It was a premise similar to Carson's Carnac the Magnificent, exactly the kind of comedy that the *Lampoon* clique thought the show already leaned too hard on. "More dial-it services?" Meyer said to Breckman in the office after he had been named head writer. "We're doing that all the time!"

Breckman responded that Letterman wanted to do this thing. Gammill said, "We've got to reeducate Dave about what's funny." At that point, Dave walked in and said, "Reeducate me, huh?"

Breckman quickly perceived the difficulties of being head writer of this group, and managing a staff had never been his ambition. So the same day he was offered the job, he quit. The briefness of his tenure blunted the revolt from the *Lampoon* group, which now included Steve O'Donnell, who replaced Richard Morris, whose contract wasn't renewed.

With no head writer, Markoe had to try again. This time she picked up someone with more credentials, hiring James Downey, a *Lampoon* veteran who had been a major contributor to *Saturday Night Live*. Having him as the head writer consolidated the Harvard group in the writers' room. Max Pross marveled at the situation. "We went from being these two young idiots," he said, "to now we're stacking the show with our friends."

As soon as he started, at the end of 1982, Jim Downey brought the hipster spirit of *Saturday Night Live* to *Late Night*. He was handsome, laid-back, and smart but didn't sweat the small stuff. "He was the coolest guy I ever met," Hal Gurnee said. "He had a big dopey Cadillac and was very low-key."

He may not have lobbied Letterman as effectively as Markoe had, but he could be persuasive. "Jim Downey would say, 'Come on, you big baby,' and sometimes he could shame Dave into doing something," Meyer recalled.

Late Night had a very different aesthetic than *Saturday Night Live*. *SNL* was an elaborate production with costumes, sets, and celebrity hosts. It was built on punch lines and over-the-top characters. The early *Late Night* favored jokes that set a mood and reflected an attitude. *SNL* required hot-tempered commitment; *Late Night* was coolly disengaged. In comparing the shows, Lorne Michaels said, "You guys can play with the form. We have to take a full swing at the ball."

By that he meant that *Late Night with David Letterman* didn't have to commit, relying instead on its sarcastic attitude. That wasn't an entirely fair assessment, especially in the early days. *Late Night* was just committed to different things. "Words are very important on Letterman," Downey said. "And not only very important, but they're enough."

Saturday Night Live had premises that took a point of view on politics or social life. But Letterman could find the biggest laughs in something bizarre or silly. Steve Martin, who performed often for *SNL* and became one of the most prolific guests on *Late Night*, explained this distinctive sense of humor by saying that Letterman could be most tickled by the sound of a word. When Martin was asked to introduce Letterman to receive a Peabody Award in 2016, he went over a joke he was going to tell: "You're not just some A-hole who got some late-night talk show. You're *the* A-hole." Letterman laughed, but focused on one word. "He loved that I said 'A-hole,' as opposed to what the joke was," Martin said.

In its first two years, the scripted comedy of *Late Night* was dense, literate, and playful. "If you're ever in a discussion at *Saturday Night Live* and try to defend something, it would usually be to defend a dry, ironic piece," Downey said. "At Letterman, the kind of pieces that you had to defend were ones that were like too cheap or hacky or too easy."

As a manager, Downey employed a loose style like that of *Saturday Night Live*, where late nights were the norm. Another way to put it: Downey was a mess, badly disorganized, with an office littered with mail and laundry. Whereas Merrill Markoe was hands-on and high-energy, Downey could be remote. Markoe started work early and was finished by the early evening; Downey would often keep the production team waiting in the afternoon, without scripts to put on the cue cards. And he would stay up until 3 a.m. writing pieces.

The change caused some friction, particularly on the production side. "Downey had his own schedule," Barry Sand said. "Merrill you can count on. She would deliver and knew a deadline. With Downey, who knew? He was a loose cannon. He didn't have the discipline."

Downey was casual even when it came to his own salary. When he started at *Late Night*, he didn't sign a contract, relying on a verbal agreement with Jack Rollins. Downey saw his job as convincing Letterman to do things slightly outside his comfort zone, not running meetings and hitting deadlines. What mattered to him was that "the stuff be good, and that Dave be talked into doing the good stuff," Downey said. "That would make for a much smoother day than my being at the ten o'clock meeting."

Downey clearly had his favorites. He didn't like the stuff produced by Winer and Tiedemann, and they found it difficult to get jokes on the air. As the *Lampoon* alumni gained power, those two were marginalized, and in early 1983 their contracts were not renewed. "Downey would sometimes come into my office," Steve O'Donnell remembered, "and go, 'You can go home. Me and Max and Tom will think of something for tomorrow.'"

During the year that Downey led the writing staff, the *Lampoon* contingent imposed its will on *Late Night with David Letterman*. In part, this had nothing to do with Downey, but reflected a show that was moving further away from the morning show and developing its own identity. A major turning point was a sketch about the Museum of the Made-for-TV Movie, in which Letterman introduced fake exhibits devoted to TV movies. As he walked from one prop to another, he saw a doorknob the size of a watermelon sitting on a counter. He picked it up and asked a stagehand off-camera what it was doing there. His response was that the doorknob had gotten dropped off by the wrong truck, adding, "It's just plain big." Letterman looked delighted, even if the audience didn't roar with laughter.

A doorknob is not funny. A giant doorknob is really not funny. Which is funny. That's the thinking behind one of the most critical jokes in the first two years of *Late Night with David Letterman*.

The day after the Museum of the Made-for-TV Movie aired, Letterman brought the giant doorknob back, this time in a bit with a music teacher who could balance things (like the doorknob) on his nose. The next week, the giant doorknob had its own sketch. Sitting at his desk, Letterman said soberly that the doorknob had not been well received as a comic device. "Perhaps you don't realize how big it is," he said with the patience of a kindergarten teacher. Then he took out a board that illustrated the size of other things, and how they were smaller than the doorknob. The crowd roared. The doorknob had become a star.

Credit for the original bit goes to George Meyer, who found a giant doorknob in a catalog of joke props. He then sketched a pencil drawing of a man approaching a giant doorknob, with the phrase "It's just plain big," and handed it to Merrill Markoe, who showed it to Letterman. They both laughed about it for weeks.

In 1983, one of the most popular comedians in America was Gallagher, a frizzy-haired goofball who used oversized props to build a strangely popular stand-up act. The giant doorknob was poking fun at that kind of comedy, but Meyer was also creating something stranger and more streamlined than a mere parody. "What I was trying to do was reduce a joke to its essence," Meyer said. "What is the least tweak you can do to something and have it still be a comedy piece? I was influenced by Steve Martin, when he did giant stuff in his act."

In the late 1970s and early '80s, Martin was filling arenas with an act that, like Letterman's, skewered show business conventions. But his parodies not only didn't sting—they became so beloved that they lost any satirical punch at all, which was part of the reason Martin stopped doing stand-up. Whereas he had begun by sending up a specific kind of Las Vegas entertainer, his act became more mannered and sillier as he got more famous, turning scale itself into the joke. He asked his thousands of fans to repeat the "Nonconformist's Oath," mocking his own adulation, but also got laughs with a joke arrow through his head.

Like the arrow through the head, the doorknob was dumb. But it was also a joke *about* dumbness, just like Stupid Pet Tricks. After *Late Night* kept bringing it back again and again, it took on a third meaning: a meta-joke, a joke about the fact that they were running the joke into the ground. The giant doorknob lost any trace of satirical purpose and became something weirder, more surreal, and at the same time a familiar part of the landscape of the show. "It started as one thing," said Markoe, "and evolved into something else."

That something else helped define *Late Night*, distinguishing it in the public imagination and setting a standard for a new kind of inside-baseball comedy that would become an integral part of the show. Some of its best jokes undermined themselves, introducing a self-awareness that brought into question what the intent was. By bringing the giant doorknob back, show after show, *Late Night* pushed past hack comedy into something defined by its own self-consciousness, a piece of hack comedy that was so aware of its own cliché that it started to seem fresh. It also created a cult atmosphere, since, if you weren't a regular viewer of the show, the giant doorknob made even less sense—the crowd's loud response baffling, if not off-putting.

As with almost all recurring comedy bits on *Late Night with David Letterman*, the giant doorknob eventually did overstay its welcome, in a way that hinted at an aesthetic shift away from the freewheeling morning show.

On a later show, Letterman was interviewing strangers exiting the elevators down the hall from the studio. It was comedy that leaned on his making something funny out of spontaneous discussion, something he tried often in his first few years. (Another popular bit was called Mr. Curious, where Letterman would just approach people on the street and ask them personal questions.)

But on this night, once the elevator door opened, Letterman saw the giant doorknob sitting inside. He had not expected it. It was the kind of surprise that Merrill Markoe would have pulled on the morning show, and indeed she was the prankster this time. But Letterman's irritation about such surprises had hardened. "After the show, he was furious," Breckman said. "You could hear him and Merrill in his office. He was not happy. It was almost like your parents arguing."

Letterman did not want to be surprised on his show, and he was firmer about this point than he was on the morning show. He would know exactly what was going to happen on *Late Night*.

If Meyer made progress ushering in absurdist comedy, Gammill and Pross increasingly managed to incorporate elements of satirical sketch work. They wrote one recurring character called Little Susie, an angelic girl who would play Letterman's troubled daughter in various skits that interrupted the show. These exchanges satirized the benign relationships between parents and kids in sitcoms like *Father Knows Best* and *Leave It to Beaver*, where the kids are sweetly mischievous scamps and the parents are dependable moral beacons. Anticipating shows like *Married with Children* and *The Simpsons, Late Night* regularly ridiculed these sunny family portraits, first with a series of very funny scenes between Susie and an indifferent dad, played by Letterman.

In the first installment, Susie appeared as a baby. Later, she returned as a small blond girl named Susan. Letterman gently sent her on her way, off the stage and through the studio doors on a bike. After she pedaled offscreen, there was the sound of a loud car crash, then a wheel came rolling onstage toward Letterman. For a moment, it got awkward. Did *Late Night* just kill off a little girl for laughs?

Susan turned out to be fine, returning in that episode, but this sequence signaled that the *Lampoon* ruthlessness had entered the late-night show. Once Downey took over, the Susie character became even more fleshed out, returning frequently, expanding the narrative of this relationship. Susie shows up at age sixteen, wearing a bikini, and

Letterman tells her to cover up, which causes her to storm offstage. In a sign of the escalating absurdity, she returns a few months later, now twenty-one, after being caught shoplifting. "I've given you anything you wanted," Letterman tells her, then concedes, "Of course, I haven't given you any personal attention." In later episodes, she's a married woman.

Pross and Gammill wrote scenes that didn't call for Letterman to do much more than act with the same sense of authority that he otherwise would on the show. And while he was skeptical of straightforward satire, he did like comedy that showed disdain for television. Imitating and subverting the gee-whiz language of terrible, well-intentioned community theater and after-school specials was a hallmark of the arch comedy of Pross and Gammill.

George Meyer also wrote satire, though he favored nonsense, abstract jokes like the giant doorknob. In one sketch, he wrote a character who would interrupt Letterman, shout about Stupid Pet Tricks being fixed, and then get dragged off the stage. He became known as the Conspiracy Guy and was played by Chris Elliott, then a runner on staff. This sketch set the template for a series of characters played by Elliott in the same vein, including the Guy Under the Seats, the Panicky Guy, and the Fugitive Guy.

In a segment Meyer proposed, two stagehands participated in a contest between a humidifier and a dehumidifier. Letterman called this "the single most brilliant idea on the show ever."

Meyer could write dialogue that imitated genres with a pitch-perfect ear, but he then spun it in such a strange direction that his jokes veered away from parody. He used double meanings and metaphors to smuggle in ideas. For instance, Meyer found a way to write sketches with Larry "Bud" Melman that incorporated his dislike of the character. In one self-referential cameo, Calvert DeForest came on the show as Larry's brother Chuck to complain about how Larry was treated, chastising Letterman for "bringing him out here just to laugh at him." Dave explained that they were laughing *with* him.

The sketch ended with Chuck going backstage and having a conversation with his brother, whom we hear but cannot see. In a spoof of *Psycho*, he becomes a Norman Bates–like figure. "They're always laughing at you!" he shouts to himself, woodenly.

An even more critical take on Larry "Bud" Melman emerged in one of George Meyer's most influential ideas, a segment that first aired on April Fools' Day in 1983. It began with Letterman at his desk.

"In times like these, sure, it's easier to tear things down than build things up," Letterman said, pausing. "Much easier. Much, much easier. It's so much easier, in fact, that we went to the New Rochelle shopping mall, right here in New York, to see what you, the viewing public, would like to see flattened or completely destroyed by a steamroller."

What followed was a stunt so simple that its pleasures were almost primal. An object was placed in front of a steamroller, which rolled over and destroyed it. A shot would reveal the flattened remains. The suspense was in what these objects would look like afterward. Letterman liked the steamroller because it had a payoff. But also: What little boy doesn't enjoy watching things getting destroyed?

Meyer approached this juvenile stunt with meticulousness, particularly over which objects got crushed and in what order. A Smurf doll, for instance, earned a big cheer when crushed. Then the jokes got sillier, like crushing "a nutritious breakfast." And finally, inevitably, the giant doorknob. The steamroller moved toward it, but then Letterman begged for it to stop, saying he just couldn't do it. Instead he brought out Larry "Bud" Melman and asked him to lie down on the ground in front of the steamroller. Besides being the kind of cartoonish violence that the *Lampoon* crowd enjoyed, it was a knowing critique of how *Late Night* delighted in brutalizing Calvert DeForest.

"It was getting kind of dadaistic at that point," Meyer said of the steamroller's development. "That's what I liked about it. No one made you feel bad for suggesting strange stuff."

George Meyer favored conceptual jokes that dispensed with top-icality and risked leaving some audiences baffled. For Letterman, these jokes could be too indulgent. "Dave would say something that was in effect like 'Have something that's a little more accessible from time to time,'" Downey explained. "And those guys [Pross, Gammill, and Meyer] would be upset because 'Oh, God, no—we're way too accessible.'" But with the steamroller, Meyer had found something that fit with Letterman's sensibility.

It was a critical period artistically, and yet that was not reflected in the size of the audience. The show was doing fine but still not a hit, and morale was shaky. The *Lampoon* writers thought they weren't paid enough and were frustrated that Letterman wasn't accepting more ambitious ideas. Eventually, Jack Rollins gave Jim Downey a contract, which he said was less money than they'd agreed on. "So I just told him, 'I'm not comfortable signing that, because that's not what the deal was and you know it,'" Downey said.

Months went by, and eventually Downey asked Letterman to in-tervene. When Letterman talked to Rollins, Downey hurried to the door to listen in. "I hear Rollins saying, 'No, he's not getting fucking shit! Not a fucking dime! Not a fucking dime!' Then when Rollins comes out and sees me, it's 'Jim, I hope that you don't feel that I am in any way opposed to your getting . . .' Fucking scumbag!" Downey eventually got paid, ten months after he'd started working.

But this was a minor dustup compared with the soap opera that resulted when Downey slept with staff writer Steve O'Donnell's girl-friend. O'Donnell confronted him about it and they stopped talking to each other, creating an uncomfortable split on the small staff. Downey acknowledged that this alienated him from the rest of the writers.

"Every person on the staff took the view 'What a fucking asshole! How could you do that to Steve?!'" Downey said. "I said, 'Here's what I'll do: People who were friends, I will not make any effort to sell my case to them. I will voluntarily withdraw. I will plead guilty and my punishment will be self-exile.'"

It was the kind of office scandal that seemed more a part of the *Saturday Night Live* culture than of the repressed ethos of *Late Night*. The legacy of that show intruded on *Late Night* in a more concrete way in the fall of 1983, when its creator, Lorne Michaels, who had left *SNL* along with the original cast (though he would later return), announced that he was launching a sketch show on NBC called *The New Show*.

Many *Late Night* writers, including Downey, jockeyed for jobs, leaving the show for the opportunity to get on board with what looked to be the new *Saturday Night Live*. At the end of September, Pross and Gammill joined Downey. George Meyer left as well. Andy Breckman got an offer from *Saturday Night Live*, and since all the "cool kids," as he put it, were leaving, it seemed like a good time to take it. "Letterman was not what he would soon become," Breckman said, explaining his decision. "He was not a cultural phenomenon."

Pross and Gammill didn't see it as a difficult decision. Ratings had dipped from the first half of 1983. Rumors of a move to Los Angeles had spread. And the original *Saturday Night Live* remained the gold standard in comedy cool. They felt they had gone as far as they could with Letterman and now had an opportunity to join with the architect of the signal show of the era, to create something from scratch.

Gammill, Pross, and Meyer had helped shape the aesthetic of the show, and losing them was a major blow. Meyer recalled the awkwardness of telling Letterman he was leaving. "Dave was hurt," he said. "He was wondering why this mass exodus. I think he felt like 'What have I done wrong?' He just wondered what was so great about this new, untested show. I think it was just our great respect for Lorne."

To future writing staffs of *Late Night*, the work of these writers would become storied, a golden age that established the blueprint for the kind of work people aspired to do. But in the immediate aftermath, the *Lampoon* group felt a chill from the show. Downey had an unfriendly encounter with Markoe and Letterman at a New York restaurant in early 1984 that hinged on a dispute over *The New Show*'s hiring of writer Jack Handey. Letterman and Markoe felt that Downey had steered him away from working at *Late Night*. "So Dave gives me a kind of funny look, and Merrill comes over and says, 'Dave's really angry at you. That's a really shitty thing to do to Jack Handey.'" Downey claimed that he'd recruited Handey to be a writer for *Late Night*, but Markoe thought that Downey had steered him away from the job by telling him the story of Jack Rollins's taking ten months to pay him.

After *The New Show*'s run lasted only one season, Pross, Gammill, and Meyer would go on to venerable careers in television that had a titanic impact on modern comedy. Pross and Gammill brought their self-aware comic style to *It's Garry Shandling's Show*, which deconstructed the sitcom the same way that *Late Night* did the talk show. They wrote fourteen episodes of *Seinfeld*. Meyer started a short-lived humor magazine called *Army Man* that developed a cult following after only a couple of issues. Sam Simon, whom Merrill Markoe had introduced Meyer to in the *Late Night* office back when he was producing *Taxi*, loved it and asked if he would be interested in writing for a new show called *The Simpsons*, the seminal cartoon that would become a home for many *Late Night* writers, including Pross and Gammill.

"[*Late Night*] gave us the confidence to try the crazy style of comedy we did on the show," Meyer said. "Before Letterman, I don't know that *The Simpsons* would have had the swagger that it did. The confidence to try different forms of comedy, styles, jokes. If we hadn't had that success, it would have been difficult."

In Pross and Gammill's last month on the show, *Late Night* aired what may have been their greatest piece of comedy on the show, the culmination of what they had been pushing Letterman to do for years. It was a sketch Letterman had initially passed on, a send-up of after-school specials called "They Took My Show Away."

As with Little Susie, Letterman played a benign patriarch in a bizarre television family. But instead of warning kids about drugs or sex, the soft-focused short video let kids know that sometimes your favorite television shows are canceled. It began with Letterman at home with a young boy doing homework. "Jimmy, are you going to do homework all night?" he asked. "Don't you think you ought to watch a little TV?" The kid responded with pep: "I will, Mr. Letterman. I just want to finish in time for my favorite show, *Voyagers*." Then the show cut to a cover of the *New York Times* announcing that *Voyagers* has been canceled, followed by Letterman gently proposing that he and the boy take a walk.

The conversation between Letterman and the boy as they walked through the park echoed the prototypical talk parents have with kids when a loved one has died. Letterman broke it to the boy that *Voyagers* had been canceled, and Jimmy responded by running away. When Letterman caught up to Jimmy, he was ripping apart a *TV Guide*. "I don't think I'll ever watch television again," the boy said. Letterman responded gravely: "Jimmy, don't ever say that. Not even as a joke." The sketch ended with Letterman showing him the new NBC schedule and the boy finding hope in the new high-concept crime drama *Manimal*, about a man who can change into a snake or a bird.

After this short video first ran, it was replayed on two future episodes and became known as one of the show's greatest triumphs. Writers for the show most frequently cite it as *Late Night's* most important comedy bit. "It's kind of like how musicians talk about hearing "Like a Rolling Stone" for the first time," said Tim Long, who was the head writer in 1997. "I had never seen such pure contempt for television on television."

David Letterman and Merrill Markoe had always poked fun at television, and they slyly mocked the form on the morning show. Sarcastically skewering whatever it was he was participating in had been a part of his repertoire since college radio. But the original *Lampoon* writers gave him new tools with which to express himself, ones that he was previously hesitant about using. "They broke so much ground," said *Late Night* writer Matt Wickline of the influence of the *Lampoon* writers from the first two years. "They softened Dave up. It took a while for the door to open, and when it did, they had left."

PART III

THE ARCHANGEL OF IRONY

1984–1987

Dave, I've been meaning to ask you something: When
are you going to stop using sex as a weapon?

—Paul Shaffer, *Late Night with David Letterman*,
January 29, 1986

THE FOUNDING FATHERS OF LATE NIGHT

Steve Allen pioneered the modern late-night talk show, from the desk to the monologue to the man-on-the-street comedy. Yet as the host of *The Tonight Show* (originally called *Tonight Starring Steve Allen*), which premiered as a ninety-minute program on NBC in 1954, he was the face of late night for only three years. Once he left to focus on a prime-time weekly variety show, he struggled in the ratings opposite *The Ed Sullivan Show* and was canceled. He hosted another talk show on ABC that lasted thirteen weeks.

Jack Paar took over *The Tonight Show* from Steve Allen in 1957 and transformed the franchise to match his personality, adding an exhibitionistic and glamorous style. Paar commuted every day from Connecticut to an office in Manhattan's Algonquin Hotel, where he ate dinner at this fabled home of the Roundtable before each show, trading stories with friends like Noel Coward, Dorothy Parker, and George Kaufman (all of whom appeared as guests).

Adopting an intimate, chummy manner with guests, Paar made a nationally televised talk show seem like a living room in Beverly Hills. He talked to Richard Nixon like an old friend before inviting him to play the piano—almost three decades before Bill Clinton played the saxophone on *The Arsenio Hall Show*. Paar positioned the monologue as the centerpiece of *The Tonight Show*. It was a laundry list of jokes that made his own fevered personality the real spectacle. Paar may have looked elegant, but his temperament was mercurial. He was charming one minute and combustible the next, expanding the emotional palette of the talk-show host.

Paar's most famous outburst came when he walked off the set of his own show because, the day before, a relatively tame joke about a "water closet" had been cut by the network. "There must be a better way of making a living than this," he said melodramatically, before making his exit. He returned a month later, and on his first show back he began, "As I was saying before I was interrupted."

Paar turned his own tempestuous personality into riveting television. He constantly interrupted himself, got irritated on the air, and found comedy through discomfort as easily as he did banter with movie stars. Steve Allen never really told you much about himself (although his wife made cameos on his second show), while Paar's cool persona masked a need to divulge and confess. He talked about his daughter and his family and what was bugging him that day. Throughout his monologue, which he performed while sitting casually on a stool, he promised the audience that the stories he was telling were not fabrications. "This really happened," he would say, looking straight into the camera. "I promise you."

By the time he started creating his third talk show, Allen had begun to sound weary, if not cynical, about television. "It is not part of the world's true business, merely a distraction from that business," he had written two years before he started *The Steve Allen Show*, a syndicated show produced through Westinghouse Broadcasting that embraced triviality and turned it into spectacle. It was a talk show that often looked like an action movie.

In its premiere, Allen emerged in formalwear from a sewer on Vine Street in Hollywood. In later episodes, he swung on a wrecking ball into the building across the street and leaped through a ring of fire into a pool. He played the piano on top of a crane, and strapped himself to the hood of a car and drove through a wooden fence set on fire. He rode piggyback on a bear riding a motorcycle, and tied himself to a biplane and flew thousands of feet in the air.

In a particularly startling episode, Allen, a lean man in plastic glasses, walked onstage in an immaculately pressed suit, standing in front of an orchestra with musicians in skinny ties behind music stands. Then he coolly promised the biggest pie fight since the era of silent films. Minutes later, he walked into the audience, where the camera revealed hundreds of people wearing plastic parkas and hoods. Allen tossed the first pie, and in the following few minutes, a tornado of custard flew. A low hum of scampering feet and propulsive piano played while people dodged dessert. But what made this food fight exhilarating was not that it was such a silly idea, but the way the chaos was captured. The cinema verité–style camerawork shifted every few seconds to a bird's-eye view of this vast, striking, even beautiful mess. The shot transformed the ragged guerrilla warfare of pies whizzing past people's faces into an abstract image of a rectangle of dark chairs with a slowly expanding gooey white center.

David Letterman's family didn't own a television when *The Tonight Show* premiered, but they did when the pies and wrecking balls flew on Steve Allen's Westinghouse show. Letterman saw Steve Allen's show for the first time when he was a teenager, and he was immediately fascinated and delighted by its chaos, destruction, and silly charm.

Allen put on a joyful show that was a model train set spinning out of control. Paar aimed for more adult pleasures, hosting a salon lit up by his eccentric, dynamic personality. They were both innovators, of very different stripes, and set the paths for two distinct talk-show traditions. But it was the host who followed them whose name became synonymous with the late-night talk show.

Johnny Carson had by far the longest and most popular tenure of any of the hosts of *The Tonight Show*, extending over three decades. At his most successful, Paar rarely reached more than 7.5 million viewers. Carson more than doubled that, dominating the time slot with more than 17 million viewers every night in the late 1970s. To get a sense of how lucrative his show was for NBC, consider that a sixty-second commercial during this decade cost as much as $36,000. During his tenure, Carson was not only the biggest star in late night; he was arguably television's signature performer. His predecessors were adventurous artists, but it was Carson who turned the talk show into a blockbuster.

In his early years, Carson did some material in the spirit of Steve Allen (splitting a block of wood with his head, on instructions from a karate champion), but then he moved away from stunts to follow more in the tradition of Jack Paar, leaning on a long, topical monologue. But Carson was a stark contrast to Paar in temperament, with none of Paar's recklessness or self-revelation. In his monologue and with guests, Carson was quick, icy, and unflappable. In a definitive magazine profile in the *New Yorker*, Kenneth Tynan described Carson admiringly as an "immaculate machine."

Carson vigorously avoided reflecting the times. His producer Fred de Cordova boasted that Carson was the first comic to stop doing anti-Nixon jokes. With a big-band orchestra and a sidekick, Ed McMahon, whose baritone, yes-man laugh was straight out of a lodge meeting, his show aimed for the cool of Vegas rather than the coffeehouses of the Village. (He started shooting in New York but moved to Burbank in 1972.) His signature comedy bits, like Stump the Band

and Carnac the Magnificent, were retreads of concepts with the whiff of vaudeville.

His was a show that aimed to be for everyone and offend no one. During the heart of the Vietnam era, the generation gap didn't exist on Carson's *Tonight Show*. He didn't want to provoke or disrupt. Instead, he reliably gave his audience some light banter and pleasing laughs before going to bed with a clear head. There was a reason that when the unhinged lunatic played by Jack Nicholson in *The Shining* broke through the door with an ax, yelling "Here's Johnny," the nod to Carson was so incongruous.

There was a certain formality to the style of *The Tonight Show*, with its theatrical curtain and dress code of a tie and jacket for comedians. Steve Winer, the writer for *Late Night*, said that even in the 1960s, young people saw Carson as old-fashioned: "People my age, teenagers, whatever—we thought Johnny Carson was old hat."

When *The Dick Cavett Show* premiered in 1969, ABC offered viewers a sharp contrast to *The Tonight Show*: a loose, freewheeling interview show that aimed to capture the tumult of the time, culturally and politically. Cavett courted controversy by putting on late-night shows about censorship and draft dodging, as well as debates with intellectuals like Norman Mailer and Gore Vidal. Cavett gave a forum to enough activists to get the attention of Richard Nixon. "Is there any way we can screw him?" the president once asked his special counsel, Chuck Colson.

Johnny Carson, who soundly beat Cavett in the ratings, aimed for a larger demographic. His gift was in knowing just how far to push a joke to get a laugh without losing parts of the vast American public. In his jokes, he displayed a light touch, understanding that a glance could make a bigger impact than a punch line. He was also fiercely competitive. And he turned *The Tonight Show* into a formidable institution that could make careers and promote movies and television shows better than anything else on the air.

Carson's artistic legacy was marked by consistency and caution. "It's hard to criticize him personally on this, because he's been there for twenty years," Steve Allen said in a radio interview in the early 1980s. "Why should he bother to be inventive now?"

To many fans, *Late Night with David Letterman* was a rejoinder to, if not an outright rebuke of, *The Tonight Show*, reaching back to a more experimental era pioneered by the iconoclasm of Steve Allen and Jack Paar. It scorned the world of show business as much as Carson served it, mocking the kind of promotion at which *The Tonight Show* was best. Carson told jokes; Letterman deconstructed them. Carson was charming and even-keeled; Letterman was hostile and vexatious. Carson looked like he was born in a sport coat; Letterman wore sneakers with his suit.

While he was often portrayed as the hipper alternative to Johnny Carson, Letterman never saw himself in opposition to *The Tonight Show*. Throughout his career, he portrayed Carson as the model host, praising him not just in interviews but also at the office, to staff members. Letterman and Carson were friendly but not close. Markoe recalled one encounter in the green room of *The Tonight Show*, on a night when Letterman was a guest. Carson ducked his head in and said, "We should get together sometime." Letterman's response: "And do what? Interview each other?" Markoe described the response as "restrained chuckles all around."

Late Night with David Letterman might have looked like an insult to *The Tonight Show*, but Letterman revered Johnny Carson. What explains this discrepancy?

David Letterman owed his career to Johnny Carson, not just for putting him on *The Tonight Show* when he was an unknown comic but also for producing *Late Night*. Letterman had watched Carson since he was a kid, when he hosted the game show *Who Do You Trust?* (Ed McMahon was an announcer), and when Letterman gets specific about his admiration for Carson, it's telling what he singles out. His favorite episode of *The Tonight Show* was when Carson walked off the set and into the studio next door, where Don Rickles was shooting the comedy *C.P.O. Sharkey*. Angry that Rickles had broken his cigarette box when he guest-hosted, Carson confronted him on the set. "It broke that illusion," Letterman said admiringly. While that was a hallmark of *Late Night*, it was, however, an anomaly on Johnny Carson's *Tonight Show*.

Letterman also always admired how Carson transformed the failure of a joke into its own comedy bit, gently mocking himself by tugging on his collar, adjusting his tie. "He was at his best when something didn't work," Letterman said. Carson's influence on Letterman on this count is clear, even though they handled failed jokes very differently. Unlike Carson, Letterman made the most of luxuriating in the failure.

He might have aspired to Johnny Carson's onscreen persona, but he operated at a much higher temperature. His suffering appeared far more visceral and real, a peek at his true self, as opposed to a deft bit. Even when his jokes bombed, Carson never acted less than cool and in control. The older Carson became, the more his self-mocking seemed a reliable part of his shtick. As Letterman evolved, his temper turned volatile, and his much more disruptive personality led him to challenge convention.

Artistically, David Letterman had more in common with Carson's predecessors. He started fully embracing the irreverent silliness of Steve Allen in the mid-1980s, then he shifted into imitating the style of Jack Paar by the end of the decade.

He had both of them on his shows in his first few years at NBC. When Steve Allen came on as a guest on his morning show, Letterman praised him as a critical influence, which Allen appreciated, since Carson, he felt, took bits of his without giving credit. "You did the original *Tonight Show* for five years," Letterman said to Allen on his second-to-last episode of the morning show. Allen replied, "Three years. Seemed like five," before adding that Paar had done it for "five years—seemed like three."

When Letterman had him on again in the first month of *Late Night*, Allen explained his legacy to Dave's audience. "I would read letters. I would go into the studio audience," Allen told Letterman, before pivoting to look at the host in mock offense. "I am making an arrest."

Jack Paar was also an early champion of Letterman. "Of the newest personalities, David Letterman will unquestionably be a big star," he wrote in 1983. "He has an original style and a winning manner that is lasting. He will go the distance."

The artistic rapport did not lead to close friendship. When Paar invited Letterman to a party at his home (they both lived in Connecticut), Dave didn't want to go. Paar loved to entertain, but Letterman hated to socialize, particularly with people from show business. Hal Gurnee, who directed Paar decades before Letterman, convinced him by insisting that it would be low-key and relaxed.

As Letterman and Markoe entered Paar's mansion together that August day, they spotted a tennis game outside and a butler in a morning jacket with gloves, holding a silver tray. Letterman looked at Gurnee and said, "What the fuck have you gotten me into?"

Letterman recalls Paar regaling the party with stories about the Kennedys, Nixon, and Jonathan Winters. Andy Rooney was there, and when he approached Letterman and Markoe, displaying the same tact he had on *60 Minutes*, he asked, "It's a shame—why don't you two get married?" Letterman's face tightened. Rooney pressed forward, asking Letterman if he had been married before. Dave said he had, but that it hadn't worked out. "Andy said, 'You have to make things work out,'" Letterman recalled.

"Dave just wanted to slip under the table and slug him. That was a bad moment," Gurnee said. "Somehow it became my fault."

Then, around 8 p.m., something happened that changed the mood. "Jack gets pissed off at something at his side of his table, leaves, and goes to bed," Letterman remembered, smiling at the thought of the talk-show host living up to his reputation as a guy willing to prematurely exit. "So we're sitting there. Where's Jack telling stories about Ethel Kennedy? Hal said, 'Maybe we should go home.'"

By late 1983, *Late Night with David Letterman* had reached a crossroads. About half the writing staff had left the show. At one point, there were only six writers. "I do remember there being a small element of desperation and fear," said Steve O'Donnell, who replaced Downey as head writer. Letterman was concerned. When another *Lampoon* writer, Jeff Martin, interviewed, Letterman asked when he could start. Martin said he could quit his job tomorrow. "That's just the kind of loyalty we're looking for," Letterman said sarcastically.

But Martin would become part of a new team of writers who stayed together for around six years, through the first explosion in popularity for the show. This new group was composed entirely of white men. This blanket homogeneity was in part a reflection of the comedy scene, marked by institutional sexism and racism, but it was also specific to the show. Its only female writer was its first, Merrill Markoe, who had a major role in hiring the first group of writers. One of the lessons she took from the morning show was that the disparate voices on the staff didn't mesh well. She aimed to get people who could do one thing: write for the sensibility of the host. Having people who were similar seemed like an asset. "That seemed good to me back then, because it was harmony," she said, "people who all thought the same."

As a comic coming up in the 1970s, Markoe understood the sexism in show business, and she was wary of tokenism. "In those days, women were just starting to get jobs, and they used to hire one or two women on the staff," Markoe said. "That was absurd to me, not realizing, of course, that they would later get rid of the tokens."

Letterman periodically worried that there were too many Harvard graduates on staff (it was why they later passed on Conan O'Brien, according to Steve O'Donnell), but there was almost no serious discussion of racial or gender makeup on the staff in the 1980s. "The joke among the writers was that the interview was just to make sure you weren't black or a woman," said Randy Cohen, another new writer. "The show was not actively hostile to either. It didn't go out of its way to recruit them, either."

Since the pools of talent where talk shows looked to hire writers were dominated by men (*Harvard Lampoon*, comedy clubs, writers' rooms for other shows), not prioritizing the hiring of women or African American writers ensured that *Late Night* would suffer from a lack of diversity. The paucity of female writers narrowed the comedy but also meant that the show had blind spots to certain gender stereotypes. This was evident from the start, but it would become a more overt issue later in Letterman's career.

There was a certain prankish fraternity house strain to Letterman's humor that attracted young men. "I would sometimes hear criticisms in the eighties and nineties about 'Oh, Letterman. That's like a frat-house-type show,'" Steve O'Donnell said. "And I'd go, 'Have you ever been to a frat house?'" The level of comments and the verbal quality of what was going on in the office and on the air was not like a frat house."

For the next six years, Steve O'Donnell steered the comedy of the show as the head writer. It was a difficult, even punishing, job. Merrill Markoe survived for less than a year. Jim Downey lasted for around the same duration. Andy Breckman was around less than a day. Gerard Mulligan also did it for a short stint in 1984, when O'Donnell took a hiatus, long enough to realize he never wanted to do it again. "Merrill said it once: It's like chasing a truck down a hill," Mulligan said, adding, "You bring stuff to Dave, and that can be scary. If it starts out badly, there's a real sinking feeling."

O'Donnell had the perfect background to prepare him for the job of running interference between the host and his writing staff; he'd gotten his training in diplomacy growing up one of ten children. Like the host, he came from a working-class midwestern background. The son of a welder and a homemaker in Cleveland, he had worked as a furniture mover and a teacher's assistant, but he had the Harvard pedigree of many of the writers. Most important, O'Donnell had a first-class temperament, patient to a fault. He would need it, because the job required him to soothe egos, deliver bad news, and endure constant rejection. It also meant understanding what comedy worked best for Letterman and reading his mood, which could shift quickly from glum to doomsday. In an interview in the fall of 1983, Letterman conceded that the show was getting complacent.

> To our discredit—maybe that's too harsh a word—you get less and less experimental. You reach a plateau and you tend to get a little complacent. Recently we've had a big changeover in the writing staff, so that's good because it forces us into a little bit more experimenting.

With new writers, *Late Night* started to change, adding oddball stunts and conceptual gimmicks, moving toward the legacy of Steve Allen. If you were to tune into *Late Night* in the middle of the decade, you might see bowling balls dropped from the roof or Letterman heckling people with a bullhorn from the window of his Rockefeller Center office. There was a show where the camera slowly spun 360 degrees and an entire show that took place inside a jet plane. At the center was David Letterman, smirking. Barry Sand described the show this way: "a man in a suit and a tie surrounded by madness."

Letterman became looser, louder, and more demonstrative. He began to realize that in order to really distinguish himself, he needed to be bigger onscreen, a more heightened version of himself. One turning point was a bad review in *New York* magazine in which James Wolcott wrote that Letterman seemed happier doing stunts than talking to people: "He's suavely repressed, as if anything ragged and wild would be mortifyingly uncool." The line in the review that really stung was Wolcott's description of *Late Night* as "a creaking, facetious contrivance—a choochoo forever wobbling off the tracks."

This review bothered Letterman, and it stuck with him more than three decades later. "It affected me," he acknowledged, and he started to increase the energy of his performance. "I can't be the head of a show and it be creaking. No one wants to watch the real me. I had to come up a little."

I n 1984, one idea changed the course of *Late Night with David Letterman*, helping to usher in a new, broader brand of comedy. It was a suit made of Velcro. Letterman wore it, then hopped on a mini-trampoline and stuck to a wall. It was an instant hit. The press loved it. And unlike most of the previous scripted comic highlights of the show, this was not satirical or rooted in language or a skewed perspective. It was much sillier than smart. And more than on the rest of the show, Letterman abandoned his outsider's perspective. To jump on a wall, you needed to participate. There was no way around it.

"Part of the point was not just to make people laugh. It was to engage them," said Joe Toplyn, one of the new writers, who—along with Sandy Frank—came up with the idea in a brainstorming session to find something "Steve Allen–like" for their host to do.

The Velcro suit spawned many sequels. Letterman put on a suit of Alka-Seltzer tablets and jumped into a giant glass of water to make himself fizz. He wore a suit of chips and was lowered into a giant vat of dip. He wore a suit of Rice Krispies and lay in a bath of milk. At the start of the show, Letterman refused to wear costumes or funny hats or work with props, but once these stunts started to get attention, he became more accommodating. To expand his show and reach for a larger audience, Letterman showed a sillier side. But to devoted comedy fans, it was more than that. Letterman was working off the playbook of Steve Allen.

Allen brought a herd of cows into his studio; Letterman ushered in sheep. Allen once covered himself with dog food; Letterman put on a suit of food and went into a cage before having chickens enter to peck at him. The chickens were indifferent, and the bit fell apart, which allowed Letterman to wallow in the failure. He embraced stunts, and *Late Night* became known for them. "The stunts and informality and the fun of today's talk shows—the stuff on Fallon—is the offspring of Letterman and Merrill," said Carol Leifer, one of the first stand-up comics regularly booked on *Late Night*. "Carson was really an interview show."

The only idea that might have been as popular as the Velcro suit was heading to the top of a building and throwing things off the roof to see them go splat. Sandy Frank and Joe Toplyn proposed the idea of tossing watermelons, which, when they hit the ground, exploded like fireworks in a vivid red mess. Then they showed it again in slow motion. This led to tossing turkeys and bowling balls (the turkeys were frozen ones, and they landed on small trampolines).

David Letterman had a deep appreciation for silly humor that tapped into childish pleasures. He respected it enough to know that it was more than just pandering to the crowd. "The problem with 'silly' is that it sounds low-class," said Steve Martin, who was delighted to see *Late Night* update the aesthetic of Steve Allen for a new era. "But

Steve Allen and David Letterman elevated the meaning of 'silly' and gave you the right to enjoy silliness in an adult package."

There was also something about these bits that seemed radical, a touch of juvenile pointlessness in the middle of late night. It tapped into the pleasure of making a mess, the kind of thing kids understood far better than adults. "Dave was this punky kid throwing watermelons off a roof," Martin Short said, explaining how he connected with young people. "Our parents wanted to see Steve and Eydie."

Letterman brought to these stunts something different than Allen did: misery. Steve Allen played the role of a game, if occasionally reluctant, guinea pig delighted to be part of his experiments. He followed jokes with a big, booming cackle. By contrast, Letterman didn't appear to be having a good time. He looked uncomfortable, like a man forced into this situation.

When Letterman would promote these stunts, his voice signaled that it was absurd to be making such a big deal about something so stupid. As usual, he participated while also being in opposition to the thing he was doing. Even when sitting in a giant bowl of cereal, Letterman found a way to distance himself from the spectacle with a glance, a sigh, the posture of a man who looked like he wanted to be doing something else.

In 1984, in part due to the stunts, *Late Night with David Letterman* turned into a hit. Its ratings steadily rose, especially in the prized baby-boom demographic. By the fall, 60 percent of the audience was people born after World War II. Hollywood noticed. When Eddie Murphy, the biggest *Saturday Night Live* star of the decade, made a guest appearance, he told Letterman that *Late Night* was the "hippest show on television." *Playboy* magazine announced that "an heir apparent to America's talk show throne has finally emerged."

This was not lost on the king himself. Johnny Carson appeared on *Late Night with David Letterman* for the first time in 1985, when the show made its first trip outside of New York to tape inside the Burbank studios of *The Tonight Show.* The crowd was much louder than the ones in Rockefeller Center. There were huge lines for tickets. Carson surprised Letterman by bringing a large piece of cardboard, opening it up into a desk, then placing it next to Letterman's. Setting up shop next to him, Carson was doing the kind of stunt that Letterman was known for. For the staff at *Late Night*, this was validation, but it also represented how much David Letterman had pushed the culture in his direction.

Letterman had dreamed of succeeding Carson on *The Tonight Show*, although in interviews he was circumspect about the prospect, in part out of deference to Carson. But there was also a sense that what made his show great was distinct from what the Carson show did. In an interview on *The Phil Donahue Show*, Letterman waved away the suggestion. "I don't think the kind of show we're doing is the kind of show NBC would move to a reasonable time slot," he said.

Saturday Night Live was no longer the coolest show on television, and the praise it had once received as the most adventurous, zeitgeist-capturing comic showcase now went to David Letterman. Jim Downey, who returned to *Saturday Night Live* after *The New Show* was canceled, recalled when he first noticed the shift. "There was a review in *People* where they go, 'How bad is the new *Saturday Night Live?*' Meanwhile, the geniuses at David Letterman continue to come up with incredibly inventive things like dropping things off a tower?" he said, exasperated. "I thought, 'Really?' That was just George Meyer's steamroller."

THE WRITER UNDER THE STAIRS

n the middle of 1983, Chris Elliott, then a production assistant, sat down at his cubicle on the sixth floor of Rockefeller Center and slowly, meticulously cleared out his desk. He put his things in moving boxes, placed a cup of coffee on his empty desk, and waited. People started whispering, wondering if he was changing jobs. His prank had worked.

The point of this performance was to make clear that Elliott was frustrated with his job getting coffee and making copies and was restless to join the writing staff. It didn't produce any immediate results, however, so at the end of the year, when there was an opening, he decided to try a more direct tactic, charging into David Letterman's office to lobby for his case. Elliott found the host in his underwear, in the middle of changing his clothes. Then it got awkward.

After some quick greetings, Elliott asked if there was a job for him on the writing staff. Letterman was standing below his ceiling filled with the upside-down pencils that he regularly tossed like darts, which he had been doing since his days in local television in Indiana. He looked annoyed. He did not enjoy getting into the weeds on staffing, contracts, or anything managerial.

"What if there isn't?" Letterman said caustically. "Are you going to quit?" Confronting the boss was beginning to look like a miscalculation. Elliott shifted course and said he wasn't planning on quitting, but that he needed money to get his teeth fixed, then made a quick exit.

It's impossible to imagine any other writer on staff being this aggressive toward the host—let alone being rewarded for it by getting the job, as Elliott eventually did. But Elliott had an unusual connection with Letterman. They shared a wiseass comic sensibility, a love for sarcastic gibes and smart mockery. The *Lampoon* writers were as cutting as Letterman, but they were snobbish about comedy in a way that he was not. Elliott had a deeper appreciation for all manner of pop culture. He found pleasures in terrible art. "I remember George [Meyer] being sour about the crap we were doing," Elliott said. "To me, the crappier the stuff was, the funnier it was."

Elliott not only hadn't gone to Harvard; he hadn't gone to college at all. Nor did he have any credits with a national television show. He had done a little acting, but he didn't pursue a career in theater or the movies. At *Late Night*, his pitches were riddled with spelling errors. (The staff joked that he couldn't read due to his expensive progressive education.) But anyone who worked on the show could tell that none of this stopped Elliott from having more brazen confidence than any other writer on staff. He was always imitating staffers, needling them in the way a little brother does to get attention.

Elliott recalled being on a remote with Letterman one day on the streets of New York when a delivery guy walked by them at the same moment that Letterman laughed at something Elliott had done.

Thinking he was the butt of a joke, the delivery guy stopped, shot a dirty look, and asked, "Did I do something funny?" He was angry, and the moment was charged with the threat of violence. Letterman assured him that he wasn't mocking him, and the guy walked away. Then Letterman turned to Elliott and said, "That shit's been happening to me my whole life."

Elliott could say the same thing. But his feelings of alienation came from a different source. He had gotten a comedy education earlier than college and had an elite credential that no university could give. Elliott's father was Bob Elliott, one half of the radio team of Bob and Ray, whom Letterman and his father had listened to when Dave was a kid. Bob Elliott appeared on the show several times in the first two years. In his second week, Letterman had both Bob and Ray on the show, and said in the monologue, "If you want to tell if someone has a good sense of humor, ask them if they like Bob and Ray. If they like Bob and Ray, they're okay."

Chris Elliott grew up on the Upper East Side ("I never went to the West Side," he joked) and attended the Rudolf Steiner school, an elite school founded by an eccentric Austrian. "I was the kind of guy who laughed at the kid who got the answer wrong, then looked the other way," he said. He made prank calls to the local church and then turned those into a play produced at school. He briefly attended the Eugene O'Neill Theater Center but didn't find a home there. He didn't have the patience for the theater.

"I never had the chops," he said, explaining how this led him to make fun of such artists. "It's a safety net. I don't have to be good. I can make fun of someone else and get laughs without having to do things myself. I'm a coward."

His father encouraged him to get a job at NBC, so once he graduated, he went to work at Rockefeller Center's observation booth, which was where he first met David Letterman, who was taking his mother on a tour. Elliott introduced himself as the son of Bob Elliott.

Letterman, then hosting the morning show, said he would love to have his father on the show. Elliott responded, "My dad only does Carson," then charged him the kids' price for the tour.

Letterman found such disrespect amusing and remembered it when Elliott applied for the job on the show. Elliott went into the interview wearing a thin tie, a vest, and bright Zodiac shoes, which were very popular in the 1980s. "Are you going bowling?" Letterman said by way of greeting.

Elliott got the job and moved into an office with Barbara Gaines and Jude Brennan, both veterans from the morning show. They encouraged his mischievous humor. This was a tremendous asset, because Gaines and Brennan had developed a trust with Letterman that would continue for decades. "They were amused by me, and Dave loved them, and I think that helped Dave love me," Elliott said.

With the exception of Markoe, no writer in the history of *Late Night* had a greater influence on the show, though Elliott is not often even thought of as a writer at all.

The talk show had traditionally been a collection of loose parts: monologue, interview, desk piece, music. Its structure owed a debt to the variety show, but in the middle of the decade, *Late Night* maintained a much more unified aesthetic, to some degree because of its embrace of conceptual theme shows that integrated all their disparate parts under one concept.

Letterman initially was skeptical about concepts that took over an entire show, particularly after an ill-advised episode in which they hosted a bar mitzvah, featuring a family much too enthusiastic about being on television. They seemed so in on the joke that the religious ceremony hijacked the show. "There was a kind of Munich syndrome," O'Donnell said. "Any kind of theme like that would be pitched to Letterman. Like "Oh, no. I don't want another bar mitzvah."

Elliott, along with his writing partner, Matt Wickline, changed that by proposing the Custom-Made Show, the first of many hour-long experiments they worked on. "It was the turning point," Elliott said, referring not just to a move to theme shows but also toward a *Late Night* where he became a star. "It gave me the bona fides."

The two-page pitch for the Custom-Made Show (originally called the Tailor-Made Show) was succinct: "Dave allows the studio audience to design tonight's show exactly the way they would like it to be." Wickline and Elliott imagined a series of questions such as "Would you like the band to play the theme to *Hawaii Five-0* or *The Brady Bunch* during the opening credits?" or "Would you like to see the writers play all the band's instruments?"

It was a very savvy pitch that didn't ask for Letterman to do anything too ambitious. He didn't have to act or leave the studio. And it had him interacting with the audience, asking them questions in a way that he was skilled at. "Chris had an awareness of Dave and his comfort zone," Wickline said. "Dave had done a lot of game shows. There were lots of structured things on the show, so the Custom-Made Show seemed to make sense."

The show opened with its host sitting in the aisle in the audience. "Most of you watching at home are probably watching on television," Letterman said, before asking pointedly, "Do you really think you're watching a show that you want to watch?"

Then Letterman emitted a condescending guffaw. "No, you're not watching a show you want to watch. You are watching a show that some high-powered network executive wants you to watch. All that is going to change tonight."

Letterman announced that he was going to let the audience decide on every element, from his own suit to the guests, in the style of a game show, with the host offering the audience choice after choice, settled by audience applause, as measured by the "applause-o-meter." "We thought there was something campy about it," said Steve O'Donnell. They had done a narrower version of this joke in the first year, but for only one segment, providing one member in the crowd a choice of what they wanted to have happen next: (1) an interview with the star of *Annie*, (2) a better seat, or (3) "say hello to my grandmother." But this was more extensive, stretching through the entire show. Just as they had done since the morning show, this celebrated the amateur, demystifying television by showing that anyone could do it. The Custom-Made Show was also a parody of pandering to the audience, with Letterman playing a host who would do anything for applause. You want a new theme song? Sure. Would you like me to do the interview after inhaling helium? You got it. Decades later, Jimmy Fallon would have guests speak after inhaling helium, for a reliable cheap laugh, but Letterman had a satirical aim as well. He was skewering what would become two of his favorite targets: the hype of show business and pointless innovation.

The Custom-Made Show set a precedent for theme shows and served as creative validation and one of the central calling cards of *Late Night*, celebrated in the entertainment press and becoming modest broadcasting events. It won *Late Night with David Letterman* its first Emmy Award. The Custom-Made Show was followed by the Reverse-Image Show, in which, after much sarcastic promotion and talk of the miracle of special effects, Letterman switched the picture so that the two sides were flipped, with Letterman on the left and his band on the right. *Late Night* also produced four different International Shows that featured guests from other countries. It did a dynamite hour-length parody of a cheesy morning show, complete with aerobics and Carol Channing, and a seventies variety show, both of which Letterman had done for real, with little success, earlier in his career. They were elaborate parodies that felt like exorcisms.

In one of the most original theme shows, the Too Tired to Do a Show Show, Letterman told the audience they could go home and shot the episode entirely in his office, wearing a baseball jersey and jeans. It doubled as a parody of a behind-the-scenes documentary, showing the office and the host talking to his producer about preparation for the show. Letterman played a jerk of a talk-show host. After telling Robert Morton, who wrote the questions for the guests, that he hadn't seen the movie his guest, Teri Garr, had been in, he introduced her, calling the movie "wildly entertaining." Garr played the shallow, fame-obsessed star to Letterman's indifferent phony. As soon as she came on, she told an anecdote about being on a plane with Diane Sawyer and Sally Field and wondering: if the plane crashed, who would get top billing?

Since it took place in the office, this show had no studio audience, and while it looked like a television show, it had the unusually quiet sound and intimate feel of an off-Broadway play. No jokes got big laughs, which changed the entire atmosphere. In early 1986, the highwater mark for these kinds of experimental theme shows, Letterman did another show inside the office. This time, the theme was Parents Night and it unfolded like a typical show, except in the cramped office, with every staff member, musician, and even guest alongside their mother and father. David Letterman had his mother pick up a bullhorn and yell out the window that she was Jane Pauley and she was trapped with Willard Scott, who "had no pants."

For the fourth anniversary, the same year, *Late Night* was shot in an even smaller venue, inside a 747 airplane heading to Miami. Hal Gurnee set up a control room on the plane. The news anchor Connie Chung was painted on the side of the plane. The band brought portable instruments, and Letterman sat at a desk. The show didn't entirely work. Letterman looked like he was working on a set even when he was in flight, and he couldn't entirely hide his disappointment when promoting the show. The night before it aired, he teased it on air, telling his viewers to watch: "It turned out," pausing, "ehhhh." Still, it won another Emmy.

Even if the execution was lackluster, it didn't matter. *Late Night* had become the rare talk show willing to truly experiment with form, and a consistent aesthetic thread was emerging that connected many of the conceptual shows. "You move the show into a different setting and it plays out in every single detail," said writer Randy Cohen. "What the opening montage looks like, even what the typeface in the closing credits is like. What you see out the window behind Dave. It was extremely self-conscious about every element in the show. And we would do millions of variations on putting the show in different settings."

During this period, Chris Elliott distinguished himself from the rest of the staff, becoming a star through a series of regular guest characters who appeared every week. Like Paul Shaffer and Larry "Bud" Melman, Elliott's bizarre characters gave Letterman someone else to react to. But Elliott had a bolder approach, injecting a new kind of overt hostility and darkness into the comedy. While in the past Letterman's anger was implied, now it came roaring to the fore. Elliott was critical in transforming not just *Late Night* but the way it revealed the host.

First Elliott played a disgruntled intern, then the Conspiracy Guy, who would shout accusations at Letterman and then get dragged off the stage. That was fairly one-note compared with his next character, the Panicky Guy, who returned at various stages of his life, including his wedding and finally his death. Both of these were high-energy characters playing in scenes with a barely trying Letterman. It made for an entertaining comedy duo. Elliott barreled onto the set, clashed with the host, and then dramatically exited.

What Elliott's characters shared with Letterman was a half-baked commitment. Like Letterman, Elliott didn't really pretend to be someone else when he did characters. He essentially played Chris Elliott doing the character. He wasn't really doing parody so much as a parody of parody. There was always the sense that Elliott could break character and speak directly to the audience at any time. Emphasizing the artifice of these characterizations, Letterman would introduce him as "the Panicky Guy played by Chris Elliott." The sketches were as much about the actor Chris Elliott and his relationship with Letterman as they were about the characters.

In one scene, Letterman visited the Panicky Guy in the hospital, as if they were shooting a made-for-TV movie about his life. "Dave, I have been, and always shall be, your friend," Elliott said from the hospital bed. The scene ended on a downbeat note as the credits rolled and images of clouds emerged on the screen. Elliott was poking fun at certain kinds of maudlin drama, but more pointedly drawing attention to the ridiculousness of him and Letterman being in an emotional scene. If there was a joke, it was that a jerk like Chris Elliott would commit emotionally.

"The narrative of these characters is the same," Elliott explained. "I am this guy who wants to be a performer who is stuck doing this on the show." He paused to underline how he saw these performances but what was lost to the audience: "It was about the relationship Dave and I had in the office."

One day, Elliott came to work determined to speak only in rhymed couplets—at his desk, in meetings, at rehearsal. What started as a funny diversion became so annoying to those in the office that Letterman eventually shot back: "Roses are red, violets are blue, fuck you." On another summer day, Elliott spent the entire day without a shirt on. After an argument about a sketch, he charged into Steve O'Donnell's office and wrote YOU'RE INSANE in big letters on his desk.

"It's the stuff I used to do in high school at recess," Elliott said. "I thought of it as 'I'm making people laugh in the office.' The show was the show, and the office was the office. But for [Letterman], it blended together. I felt doing that showed Dave an attitude I have toward my work he welcomed on the set. He knew I would do anything."

Letterman was delighted by Elliott's obnoxiousness. Elliott did not defer to him at all. In fact, he made a big joke of insulting him in the office, looking up from making coffee when Letterman walked in the room to say, "Oh, look at Mister Big Shit, funny man." Sometimes Elliott would even get genuinely angry. When Elliott's girlfriend, who worked on staff, bought a Christmas tree for the office, Letterman made fun of its size, sending her out of the room in tears. Elliott went into Letterman's office and started arguing with him. Eventually, he shouted, "Fuck you," and left.

Not everyone enjoyed his playful gibes. The writer Fred Graver had worked on the show for less than a week when Elliott walked up behind him on a Friday afternoon and whispered, gravely, "Dave can't stand you. I'm telling you. You're out the first option."

Graver froze, rattled. "It ripped me up," he said. This fed on all of his insecurities as a young writer wanting to do a good job in a high-pressure job. He stewed, running over questions in his head: What had he done to mess up? How could he have wasted his big break? He went home and cried for an hour. On Monday, he came in to work and walked into Merrill Markoe's office to see what he could do to save his job. She told him not to worry; it was just Elliott's needling. Then she gave him some advice: "The name of this show is Dave's Attitude Problem," she said. "Every night people tune in to see what's bugging Dave."

Clearly, Elliott's pride of place rubbed some writers the wrong way. He moved from being an assistant to a writer to an on-camera star who worked less with the other writers and more on his cameos. Frustration with Elliott's behavior and special status on the show exploded in early 1986. One day, the writers were calling one another women's names. The next morning, continuing the joke past its expiration date, Elliott approached writer Kevin Curran and called him "Nancy." Curran turned around and punched him in the face.

"I was stunned. I had a good welt, fat lip," Elliott said. "I said,

'Kevin, I just called you Nancy. What's going on?' He was shaking and said, 'Well, you shouldn't have.'" Then he went into his office and talked to Fred Graver, who came out and told Elliott that Curran was having personal problems. But there was more going on here. "Because Chris has this golden child position, there was probably resentment," Graver said.

Elliott's characters argued with Letterman on the show, but they were also a vehicle for the host to express his own contempt and self-deprecation. That became explicit in Chris Elliott's most famous character, the Guy Under the Seats, which found him emerging out of a trap door to talk to Letterman at various points during the show. The conceit was that he was a kind of Phantom of the Opera figure tormenting the host. Elliott would interrupt Letterman, who would stop what he was doing and introduce him to the audience as the Guy Under the Seats. This invariably annoyed Elliott, and the two pretended to be in hostile conflict.

Letterman would pay him a condescending compliment on his acting. This annoyed Elliott, who would respond sarcastically, then shoot back something like, "Not up to your usual standard of excellence." Then Elliott would deliver the same warning while opening the trapdoor and descending beneath the stairs: "I'm going to be right here," he would sneer like a Grand Guignol villain, "making your life a living hell!"

Almost every scene between Letterman and Elliott tracked this way: Elliott breaking into the show interrupted the host, followed by a patronizing remark from Letterman that led to intense hostility and a creepy warning. All of the other regular players on the show, like Larry "Bud" Melman and Paul Shaffer, provided targets to be mocked by the host, whereas Elliott was always the first to attack. And in the Guy Under the Seats, you started to see something other than an eccentric to ridicule. You saw a layer being peeled back on Letterman, an acerbic critic who poked fun at the show. Elliott was the start of the show's becoming a vehicle for Letterman to reveal more about himself.

"Merrill saw that at the start—that you could push him to be more self-revelatory," said Graver. "The Guy Under the Seats was a character who essentially voiced Dave's id."

When Andy Kaufman died, in 1984, *Late Night* lost one of its most inspired guests, a guy who had license to rattle the host and unsettle the audience. Chris Elliott filled this role, but his sabotage was scripted and more sensitive to the audience. Whereas Kaufman walked the line between real and fake, Elliott was more domesticated. Not only did we know he was playing a part, but he performed so halfheartedly that he let us know he was playing a part. His acting style was a direct match for Letterman's joke-telling—a comedy that mocked itself.

Elliott became so successful playing these characters that when Lorne Michaels returned to *Saturday Night Live* after *The New Show* was canceled, he attempted to recruit Chris Elliott to join the cast, even visiting Letterman to try and finesse this transition. Letterman recalls that Michaels compared Elliott's leaving to when he lost a star, Chevy Chase, in the early years of *Saturday Night Live*. But while Michaels had little trouble convincing writers from *Late Night* to come to *SNL* only two years earlier, he now found a different landscape. Elliott decided to stay with *Late Night*, although a decade later he would briefly join the *SNL* cast.

About a year after he suggested the Custom-Made Show, Elliott came into the green room to directly pitch Letterman a spoof of Bing Crosby holiday specials. Letterman laughed. What emerged was less a series of comic ideas than an elaborate comic play. There was precedent in the Little Susie sketch and "They Took My Show Away," but this was even more elaborate, an entire special called "Christmas with the Lettermans." It would win *Late Night* its second Emmy.

At the start of the show, Letterman introduced his (fictional) family, which included two smiling blond boys in suits, a mouthy daughter, a composed wife with a frozen smile, and his bitter brother, Darryl. When Darryl brought out the boy playing Letterman's younger son, Kyle, he said with a sneer, "I thought Kyle could use some adult supervision . . . for a change." Letterman chuckled.

Something was clearly wrong with this family. Letterman then sent Kyle out to find a Christmas tree, in exchange for a gold coin. Late in the show, we saw the kid being chased by a gang of teenagers in a nightmare scene out of *Taxi Driver.* More chuckles.

In this dark sketch, Letterman wasn't just a terrible father. He was also a bad husband, making snide remarks about his wife, who sat silently through the whole show. At the end, he apologized for not having time to let her sing a song. In other words, he bumped his own wife. And besides being a rotten father and husband, his relationship with his brother was marked by steady, simmering tension. Darryl mentioned that he had to change his insulation business because his brother had sued him.

This scene played like a dysfunctional family drama, with Letterman once again the soulless patriarch, just as he had been in the segments with Little Susie and the video "They Took My Show Away." When his daughter said she wanted to be a ballerina, her brother interrupted sarcastically, "Yeah, by then maybe they'll be tired of the tall, skinny ballerinas." Letterman laughed at the startling, mean insult and said, "Good one, Hank."

The first guest was Pat Boone, promoting precisely the kind of Christmas show that Letterman was mocking. After shaking hands with Audrey, Boone gamely said they were all such a wonderful, emotional "real family," before saying that it reminded him of the special on which "John Davidson and Andy Williams brought their families together with their lawyers." Boone was completely clued in to the joke, even though he was the butt of it, as was evident when Letterman showed a clip from "Pat Boone's Old Fashioned Christmas," airing on the Christian Broadcasting Network, which included a corny song-and-dance number just like the one that started this show. Letterman treated Boone respectfully to his face, but the entire enterprise did not. Boone played along like a good sport.

"Was he inside the joke or was he the butt of the joke?" Randy Cohen asked about the role of Pat Boone. "It was a very ambiguous relationship." But for Chris Elliott, it wasn't complicated. "We thought Pat Boone was cheesy. And we thought it would be funny to make fun of him."

In its first year, the Christmas special was marked by the low-rent amateurishness of the morning show. This new Christmas special wasn't such a lark, representing a new ambition that would mark the second great era of the show. It stung its target with a refined script and a tricky point of view. Letterman became not so much a host as a comedian who may or may not be playing a character.

Part of the reason Pat Boone seemed corny was that his specials suggested that you could get to know him. They had a contrived intimacy that, at its heart, was phony. Letterman told you nothing about himself, and he mocked anyone who did. This would change by the end of the decade, but for now *Late Night* was a show of stunts and smirks. When Letterman got serious, his message came across as simply this: Do not trust me.

THE LETTERMAN GENERATION

n May 1985, *Esquire* magazine published an essay by a twenty-three-year-old Yale graduate named David Leavitt, who set out to do nothing less than explain his generation. It belonged to a long, dubious journalistic tradition in which a major media outlet sums up young people for its readers, using an envoy from their tribe. These stories follow a certain script: Mix some reported anecdotes with a few references to politics and pop culture trends, add a tone of alarm, and then draw a sweeping conclusion about wildly different groups of young people. The piece's title: "The New Lost Generation."

Leavitt argued that those coming of age in the Reagan era saw the idealism of the 1960s vanish and substituted a cynical and steely veneer. They sighed at political activism and rolled their eyes at passion and engagement. Unlike the hopeful kids from past decades, they were not marked by a particular cause to fight for. They were more likely to find all of politics contemptuous. What united them was a jaded outlook about not just politics but even the nature of honesty itself. "We are determined to make sure everyone knows that what we say might not be what we mean," Leavitt wrote, building to a crescendo: "The voice of my generation is the voice of David Letterman."

By the next year, David Letterman not only had won Emmy Awards for the third year in a row but he was also the co-host of the awards show, with Shelley Long. He appeared on the cover of *Rolling Stone, Newsweek,* and *Esquire.* Doing a guest spot on his show became as much a status symbol for performers as making Johnny Carson laugh. "You wanted to impress him," Martin Short said of the reputation of the show among guests. "You did certain shows where you couldn't give a shit if you impressed the host. But this was the hip show. Tom Hanks would say the same thing. Steve Martin would phone me up three months before appearing on *Late Night* with a potential bit and say, 'Tell me if this is funny.'"

Late Night had not become as popular as *The Tonight Show,* an impossibility, considering their respective time slots, but its cultural impact had surpassed it. By the middle of the decade, Letterman was the rare host who stood for something bigger than a television show. He was increasingly mentioned as the talk-show avatar of postmodernism, a movement marked by self-awareness and challenges to dominant narratives that was then shifting from academia to the mainstream press. He became the host who didn't believe in hosting, a truth-teller whose sarcasm rendered everything he said suspect, a mocking challenge to anyone who pretended to take the ridiculous world seriously. Letterman became the face of an ironic sensibility that permeated comedy, television, and popular culture.

Letterman's early years satirized the show business world, but as his aesthetic strains hardened into conventions, he began to create his own, with distinctive rituals, codes, and in-jokes.

Late Night's humor transformed from being mostly reactive to establishing its own eccentric voice. The evolution of Paul Shaffer was part of this shift. He began the show playing a caricature of a Las Vegas entertainer, a spoof who parroted cheesy lines designed to be smirked at. But after a year, he started to fill out his character, improvise more, and become his own kind of oddball sidekick. "Dave got through to me: Let's just have a conversation," Shaffer said. "I also ran out of clichés."

Shaffer, who increasingly acted in sketches, doing the kind of physical comedy and character work that Letterman shied away from, built up his role as part of an absurdist double act with the host. In one episode, Letterman and Shaffer had an extended argument about whether or not the show they were appearing in was a rerun.

On the eve of his fourth-anniversary special, Letterman mused about what would happen next. "Then the exposé comes out," Shaffer said. "'The David Letterman Show: What Really Happened Backstage.'" Letterman laughed, then tensed up. Even though this was an obvious fiction, the prospect made him visibly nervous. A deft reader of his host's moods, Shaffer added: "I'm not going to talk to the people."

Letterman responded, "I appreciate that. Don't talk to them," and then grimaced, balled up a piece of paper, and tossed it behind him at a fake window, triggering what had become a familiar sound effect: a canned window crash.

In exchanges with Letterman, Shaffer often played the ham or the beleaguered fool. On one show, Letterman's insults on the air stung a little too hard even for Shaffer, and he called Dave the next day to say he'd gone too far. "David said, 'You can come back at me,'" Shaffer recalled. "'We're just trying to fill the hour by creating some dialogue.' That changed things for me a lot."

Shaffer's relationship to show business became more complex, moving from being a parody of Las Vegas insincerity to something that blurred the line between satire and his real voice, which displayed genuine affection and enthusiasm for show business. Randy Cohen, a *Late Night* writer who saw the show as directly in opposition to traditional show business, thought Shaffer diluted the point of view of the show. "I had a hard time with Paul and his relationship to Vegas entertainment," he said. "If you laughed because you enjoyed the thing at face value, he'll accept that. But if you laughed because you thought he was offering this sort of sly dig, he'll accept that, too. I think he was obfuscating his own position."

Implicit in Cohen's argument is that *Late Night* was a rejection of the values of commercial entertainment, which is how many of the show's fans saw it as well. But a hit network talk show could exist in opposition to show business for only so long before it also became a part of it. Letterman spent years making fun of the conventions of the talk show, but now *he* was the host of a popular talk show, and his job was to talk to celebrities. He was a distinct part of the world he was famous for disdaining. Even when he was dismissive of stars to their face, they joined in the joke. You could say that Letterman was co-opted by his own success, but that would imply that he began with more of an intent to disrupt the establishment than he did. It was Merrill Markoe who cared more about challenging the conventions of show business.

What David Letterman was truly committed to was a lack of commitment. His defining feature was not scorn for actors or revulsion toward the theater of the media, but how he surrounded himself with layers of ironic distance, creating an elusive and detached style that had become the quintessential Letterman pose.

Other comics deployed smirking detachment in movies and television. But they weren't in people's living rooms every night, talking directly into the camera to millions of viewers, establishing an intimate relationship that is unique in entertainment. David Letterman didn't invent comedic irony, but more than any other performer of his era, he brought it into the mass culture.

As his reputation became more pronounced, he embraced comedy that turned in on itself and made more shows about the process of making a talk show. He regularly left his desk to go backstage to his dressing room or his office, and often to the neighboring studio. His opening remarks operated on two levels: the jokes and his running commentary on his jokes. The latter often became far funnier and baroque, commenting upon his comments about a joke that commented on something else. Letterman criticized himself way before anyone else did. As a self-loathing perfectionist, it was a task he was suited for. Even with an ordinary joke, he would constantly signal that he found it lacking, pausing extravagantly, repeating the punch line, then sighing, casting side-eye. "If a joke wouldn't work," Letterman said, explaining his strategy, "I wanted to be able to excuse myself from it."

Many comics, of course, ridiculed their own jokes. But no one fought his own material as consistently and with as much creativity as Letterman. He didn't just sigh. Letterman looked hurt, off-kilter, at odds with his own material. Sometimes he would stop mid-joke to let the audience know the punch line was coming, or veer off into tangents that made a mockery of his own performance. If one diagrammed the structure of Letterman's jokes, they would look like a series of concentric circles increasingly putting distance between him and what he was saying. Years before the term "Generation X" moved into circulation, David Letterman made ironic detachment seem like the most sensible way to approach the world.

More than any other comedy figure, Letterman redefined countercultural cool as knowing, square, and disengaged. Authenticity, the currency of cool for ages, was out; only a fool still believed it existed. What mattered was signaling that you knew it. You saw this clash of old and new styles play out when the pop star Billy Idol appeared as a guest on *Late Night*.

Idol adopted a glossy version of Sex Pistols style with all the usual signifiers of a punk rock aesthetic: black leather jacket, shock of white spiky hair, a scowl. Idol told Letterman that his songs were so popular that drug dealers were naming their products after them. Instead of chuckling merrily or changing the subject, Letterman injected some antagonism into the exchange and sneered, "You must be a very proud young man."

A different host might have made this sound toothless, a self-deprecating remark that drew attention to how uncool he was. Letterman, wearing a suit, tie, and a short, neat haircut, looked like the anxious conservative figure in this exchange. His clothes did not telegraph counterculture rebellion the way Idol's did. Yet his stern old man's locution came off as more shocking than anything the musician was peddling. His sarcasm was laced with an attack, striking skeptical notes that refused to take Idol's provocation seriously. His attitude was clear: Idol was just more show biz. Letterman flipped the script of the rebellious rock 'n' roller shocking the conformist. He made Idol look like a poseur, a guy trying too hard. They were both fakes, but at least he was willing to admit it.

David Leavitt's *Esquire* essay didn't just trumpet the influence of David Letterman. It also hinted at an intellectual critique of him that would become more common toward the end of the decade. Letterman, the argument goes, was a reflection of the political moment, a figure who, if not in tune with the Reagan revolution, had a disengaged style that provided no opposition. In the 1960s and '70s, young people embraced antiwar folk singers and polemical comedians who took aim at the status quo. If Letterman was a hero for young people in the 1980s, what did he stand for? It was hard to tell, perhaps nothing. Characteristically, Letterman drew attention to this criticism while making fun of it, wryly saying on three different episodes from the middle of the decade that *Late Night* was "all form and no substance." Letterman made engagement itself seem a little ridiculous, particularly any earnest kind. In his history of transgressive humor, *Going Too Far*, Tony Hendra argued that Letterman made it "bohemian to be anti-bohemian."

Every night, Letterman invited the audience to join him in mocking something foreign, strange, or other. Jokes can be a cudgel against the powerful, but just as often they create a norm that excludes or stigmatizes difference. As he became more successful, Letterman risked moving from throwing the spitballs from the back of the room to being the one hurling them from the front.

Letterman was no conservative, but he did have a certain aversion to lefty self-seriousness. ("He used to make fun of my Berkeley roots by saying, 'You were probably off burning goats or whatever you hip people all did,'" Merrill Markoe said.) And in the 1980s, he frequently employed flag-waving images in sketches that riffed on Cold War populism.

Just as he did with show business, Letterman poked fun at gung-ho patriotic fervor in a way that could be seen as indulging in it as well. In one Viewer Mail sketch, Paul Shaffer responded to a letter from the Department of the Army with a rant against warmongers, saying we should cut funding for the military and use the money to plant flowers and support modern dance. In the middle of this parody of liberal do-gooder protest, Russian soldiers entered and grabbed the bandleader, who converted suddenly, pleading, "Nooo. Army, help me!"

Letterman ended the sketch by explaining that it had been a dramatization to illustrate the need for a strong military, then the screen faded to a clip of a waving flag as the host said, "God Bless America." The sketch was not right-wing. It made fun of a certain simplistic patriotic view, but it also made an ironic joke rooted in a conservative view of the weakness of liberals. In later decades, Letterman would become overtly liberal on the air. But in the 1980s, his politics, like his comedy, was elusive.

Context informs the meaning of comedy, and *Late Night* had developed into a popular show among young men in the heart of the Reagan era. (In 1986, 68 percent of its audience was in the eighteen-to-forty-nine age group.) Steve O'Donnell said the point of the flag-waving bits might not always have aligned with how they were received. "The joke was on television and entertainment and how cynically they will trundle out something to get a rise from a crowd," he said. "Sometimes the crowd will respond sincerely."

The author David Foster Wallace saw something insidious in the triumph of the ironic comedy of David Letterman. He disliked Letterman the way only someone who also loved him could. He wrote about him with the passion of a convert. Early in his storied literary career, Wallace became known for a certain self-referential, hyper-clever literary style, before becoming a sharp critic of these same tendencies in art and literature. He bemoaned the rise of the dominant ironic voice as good for cheap ridicule, but not much else. He worried that it closed off emotional responses, earnest declarations, and other actual expression—irony was good for debunking and exposing illusions, but it was a dead end. To Wallace, Letterman was "the ironic '80s' true Angel of Death."

Few artists dare to try to talk about ways of working toward redeeming what's wrong, because they'll look sentimental and naive to all the weary ironists. Irony's gone from liberating to enslaving. There's some great essay somewhere that has a line about irony being the song of the prisoner who's come to love his cage.

Wallace dramatized this condition in a short story, his first published in a major magazine. "Late Night," which ran in *Playboy* in

1988 (and was later retitled "My Appearance"), captured what an unusual figure David Letterman had become in the middle of the 1980s.

The plot focuses on an actress preparing to appear as a guest on *Late Night with David Letterman*. That this show business slice of life plays like paranoid horror is a testament in part to the reputation that Letterman established for treating his guests harshly, which became a concern for him. During commercial breaks, he would ask staffers if he had been too rough on a guest. "The great thing about Dave is, if he wasn't interested [in his guest], he could turn it into entertainment," Steve Martin said. "He survived the sitcom actresses."

He did that by being cutting or dramatizing his own irritation with the interview. He seemed to particularly relish poking fun at female guests. At various times in the history of his show, he made a female celebrity into a running joke that he would bring up repeatedly. He did this to Joan Collins, Oprah, Cher, Shirley MacLaine, Madonna, and others. Cher famously told him on the air that she hadn't come on his show for years because she thought he was an "asshole." She was not the only one. The first actress to receive his persistent needling was Pia Zadora, a show-biz lifer. In the first year of *Late Night*, her name became a kind of shorthand for "callow star." Letterman clearly enjoyed the sound of her name and would say it playfully, over and over, night after night. He delighted in oddball sounds. When she eventually came on the show, Letterman seemed at first uncomfortable, then rather blunt, then nasty. "There are women your age still waiting in that long, lonely line of show business who feel, you know, envious of you," he said. She responded, "You're picking on me because I have a wealthy husband. Look, I can work as hard as the next guy."

It was an unusually contentious exchange, a departure from the playful softballs that talk-show interviewers typically offered up to actors. It also got laughs. But it was positively collegial compared with the most painfully tense interview of his early years. When the actress

Julie Hagerty came on the show to promote a sequel, *Airplane II*, the result was a cringe-inducing exchange between two socially awkward celebrities. Hagerty was nervous to the point of paralysis, answering questions abruptly, though not rudely. She was polite, but clearly shy. Letterman did nothing to put her at ease. In fact, her inability to perform seemed to anger him, his temper rising.

After a few questions, he didn't become flustered so much as antagonistic. But the way he communicated his fury was by pointedly matching her in small talk, being boring to comment on her boringness, mocking her through imitation. It was brutal. First he asked mundane questions: Was it fun to work with Woody Allen on *A Midsummer Night's Sex Comedy*? Had she gone back home for the holidays? When she responded with short, colorless answers, he started talking about himself, in a passive-aggressive attack. "I went to L.A. over the holidays," he said, "and the weather was nice." It was a classic indirect Letterman insult. "I remember watching that on the monitor in agony," said Jon Maas, an NBC executive.

Even though he had no connection to Hollywood when he wrote it, David Foster Wallace, in his story, captured the chilling impact that Letterman's interviews could have on movie stars like Zadora and Hagerty. The main character was nervous, even terrified, about appearing on *Late Night*. Explaining his story's provenance, Wallace said that he was inspired by the interview with Billy Idol, but he clearly also borrowed from an appearance by Susan Saint James, the star of the sitcom *Kate & Allie*, who was married to the NBC executive Dick Ebersol.

The guest in the original story was named after her, but his editors made Wallace change it to avoid any possible litigation. Saint James was actually a savvy guest who never seemed to get too flustered by Letterman's slights, in part because she was so familiar with his style. (She had been a guest on the first *Tonight Show* that Letterman guest-hosted.) They had playful, bickering chemistry on her many appearances on *Late Night*. He would invariably open interviews with her by asking if she played Kate or Allie. She pushed back, needling him for not attending one of her parties, and even once brought a clip from her show of a character blissfully ignorant about Letterman. In one interview, she talked about doing an Oreo commercial for fun, and this is re-created in the Wallace story.

But whereas a show business veteran like Susan Saint James was slyly clued in to Letterman's sensibility and played along, Wallace's version of her character, named Edilyn, was at first naive about show business, which suited Wallace's purpose of portraying Letterman as a bullying dark force. The story hinged on the question of how a guest should act to perform well on *Late Night*. Her husband cautioned that the most important thing was to avoid being sincere. "That's the cardinal sin on *Late Night*," he said. "That's the Adidas heel of every guest that he mangles."

After some hand-wringing, she took his advice and performed oily, ironic glibness, presenting herself as a hack and a sellout for his amusement. After being coached by her husband to mock herself before the host does, she announced on the air that she had no talent. By telling the story from the perspective of an actress appearing on his show, Wallace presented a more ominous version of this pop culture transaction than viewers saw. *Late Night* was portrayed as a gauntlet of ridicule and humiliation you could overcome only by sacrificing a vital part of yourself.

In joking self-deprecatingly, Edilyn won laughs from the audience and from Letterman himself, but at a price. By the end of the story, her performance had created a rift in the relationship with her husband. There was a sadness between them, a connection broken between this couple who now saw each other without illusions. Letterman had shaken their ability to trust their own perceptions of each other. It was a cautionary tale about the danger of ironic distance.

Wallace was not the only literary figure to worry about the cultural impact of David Letterman. Toward the end of the decade, *Spy* magazine ran a cover story called "The Irony Epidemic," a manifesto by Kurt Andersen and Paul Rudnick. Andersen was one of the first prominent journalists to recognize Letterman's talent, but his cover story took a more anxious tone, warning of a pervasive cultural style described as "Camp Lite." As in Leavitt's essay about the new lost generation, Letterman was cited as the poster child.

"Camp Lite uses irony as an aesthetic, an escape route. It is a breed of timidity," they wrote. "Camp Lite can redeem itself, by cultivating some danger, some bracing recklessness, some of the alienating weirdness that spawned it. Otherwise, Camp Lite will remain a smug reflex, a painless roost for guys 'n' gals without imagination or real spunk."

That these brainy critiques of Letterman's style exist at all is evidence of his ascendant stardom and unusual influence. He was being held to the standards of a public intellectual or an artist leading the culture, not just another talk-show host who helped actors publicize a movie. Wallace, Rudnick, and Andersen also located a real pitfall in the style of David Letterman: if he could redeem terrible acting, hack jokes, and stupid pet tricks with the help of a raised eyebrow and a knowing gibe, how could you tell when his standards fell? But perhaps more seriously, they warned that ironic distance limited an artist's scope of expression.

Alex Ross wrote a perceptive analysis in the *New Republic* about Letterman that suggested a counterargument. Called "The Politics of Irony," it made the unlikely comparison between the performance style of David Letterman and that of Rush Limbaugh. Even though they differed politically, Letterman regularly listened to Limbaugh in the mid-1980s and found him compelling. As a former radio host, Letterman was impressed at how the right-wing pundit filled hours of time with meaty monologues of talk. "I thought he was very enter-taining and also full of shit," Letterman said.

Limbaugh had also clearly watched Letterman, and borrowed many of his tics when he had his own television show for a few years in the 1990s, including tossing cards behind his head. Ross regarded both as supremely gifted verbal performers, arguing that Letterman created his own mode of speech out of clichés, strings of banal phrases that, through repetition and attitude, he breathed life into. A guarded midwesterner whose natural inclination was to hold in his emotions, Letterman was by nature shy, repressed, and not inclined to hit any-one over the head with a message.

For an artist of this personality, an ironic pose helps him find a way to express himself, even if not everyone could detect what he was saying. Letterman often proved himself most articulate in what he re-fused to say or what he seemed to imply. It was clear when he thought a guest was peddling nonsense or when his jokes were failing.

Ross didn't see Letterman's ironic attitude as a dead end for ex-pression, as Wallace did. In fact, it enabled Letterman to use a coded language to say things that he couldn't say directly. He had become "a sly virtuoso of layered meanings, a contrapuntist of revealed and concealed messages," Ross wrote.

Letterman smuggled in messages of disapproval or irritation through tone of voice, a glance. But as he built an audience tuned to his frequency, alert to his tells, he was developing more ambitions as a communicator. Ross described an essential attribute of the Letterman style. What he shared with Rush Limbaugh was an ironic mode that reveals itself in reaction to something else. In the case of Limbaugh, the foil was liberal elites, but with Letterman, Ross argued, it was television. These performers were animated by their resistance to and scorn for a dominant language, by rejection rather than creation. This captures something essential about the limitations of David Letter-man, which is supported by those who worked most closely with him.

"He's not a comic, exactly," Steve O'Donnell said, trying to describe the essence of the host. "But he's not a broadcaster, purely, either. He's a personality and a commentator, a responder to things." When asked about his strengths and weaknesses, Rob Burnett, who would become his head writer in the early 1990s, said his strength was in reaction.

A performer like that needs the right target. In the first years of the show, Letterman found several, none better than television and show business itself. His greatest antagonist was his own network. He had mocked its programming choices as far back as the morning show, but a major event would help him turn this foil into something richer. It was several days before Christmas 1985 when Letterman found a new focus for his sarcasm and, despite being a star, turned himself, onscreen at least, into an underdog doing battle with the powerful.

Letterman began his show reporting some news. General Electric, he announced, had bought NBC. "They're calling it a merger," he said, before leaning toward the camera, almost as if he was about to tell the audience a secret. He made an "okay" signal with one hand, indicating that this was clearly a lie. Just in case you didn't get the point, he added, "It was one of those gun-to-the-head mergers."

Letterman then imagined the conversation between the network execs and their new owner. "'How much do you want?' 'Six billion dollars,'" he said, setting up his punch line. "'Okay,'" he responded, voicing the part of the GE negotiator. "'How much without *Punky Brewster?*'"

He used GE as a punching bag for the entire monologue. In between scripted jokes, he enumerated the things it had invented, like push buttons, before sarcastically praising how revolutionary they all were. "You know, in the old days, we used a switch," he said, pantomiming turning a switch on and off, his eyes wide in mock amazement. When Letterman moved to his desk, he didn't let up, asking

Paul Shaffer what he thought of the deal. Shaffer expressed enthusiasm that may or may not have been genuine. Letterman would not have it.

"No, you don't," he told Paul. "We don't want to be taken over by GE. What are we going to do when these knuckleheads come in here?" he said, glaring at his bandleader. Letterman looked strangely angry. "Well," Paul muttered. "They're . . ." Letterman cut him off again: "Listen, they're wimps."

Letterman had long mocked or caused trouble for his employers. He did it when he was doing college radio; he did it on his morning show; he did it right from the start on *Late Night*. Earlier in the year, he had tormented Bryant Gumbel and Jane Pauley from the seventh-floor window, shouting at them from a bullhorn while they were shooting the *Today* show. But there was something else going on here. When General Electric took over, Letterman found something he badly needed: a good villain.

His anger at General Electric was not an act. It was real. Much more than a stand-up comic, Letterman identified as a broadcaster, and he resented businesspeople who thought they understood better than those in front of microphones. Decades later, explaining his feelings after learning about his new bosses, he sounded just as heated:

> I had a degree in broadcasting when RCA was the Radio Corporation of America. General Electric made oscillating fans or something. I didn't know what the fuck they did. This was genuine. I was up in arms.

GE was a target that resonated, and not just for the reasons that Letterman intended. For the host, GE was primarily an electronics company, but it actually did have a long history in media, which he knew about as well. When Letterman was ten years old, the third-highest-rated show on television (behind *I Love Lucy* and *The Ed*

Sullivan Show) was *General Electric Theater*. Produced by the public relations arm of the company, the show featured many of the biggest stars of the day putting on crime stories, dramas, and other genres between promotions for GE products.

Its host was the faded movie star Ronald Reagan, who joined General Electric in the 1950s. Working for the behemoth company, one of the original twelve listed on the Dow Jones Industrial Average, Reagan spent two years touring the country, giving speeches at its facilities, and this was when he developed his stump speech about the perils of government overreach and the value of free markets, which sparked his political career.

On *General Electric Theater*, Reagan played the part of the forward-thinking patriarch showing the home audience the marvelous General Electric products in his own home. He used his real family in the show. And he would preach the gospel of GE technology, telling his viewers that "when you live better electrically, you lead a richer, fuller, more satisfying life."

This show represented two of the main sources of mockery on *Late Night with David Letterman*: the hollow promise of new technology and the benevolent television authority figures of 1950s sitcoms. Letterman had already ridiculed such television families with "They Took Our Show Away" and the Christmas special, and his Custom-Made Show was the start of what would become a sustained attack at hucksters of technological progress. When Letterman talked about the new cameras or Japanese technology, he could have been satirizing *General Electric Theater*.

When Ronald Reagan was running for president, clips of *General Electric Theater* were often shown on television and used as jokes about the absurdity of having an actor as commander in chief. It became a comedy cliché of the 1980s. "The writers and clip guys were always mentioning the old *GE Theater* as some kind of potential wraparound," Steve O'Donnell said, referring to a premise for a comedy bit on the show. He added that it seemed too politically on the nose and hack for *Late Night*. Still, Letterman jumped at the chance to skewer General Electric.

David Letterman was not a comic who believed in only punching up. He mocked eccentrics and outsiders, whether it was immigrants or people from small towns (this was part of the premise of Small Town News) or the overweight (he had a weakness for fat jokes). His tense interviews could come off as mean, and once he became a star, his aggressive brand of comedy risked looking petty.

Building General Electric up as the enemy enabled Letterman, at the height of his cultural influence, to reclaim the role of the little guy. It also put him in the tradition of comedians saying the things to their bosses that you always wished you could say to yours. Letterman, who still wanted to be seen as an underdog, turned *Late Night* into a drama for playful complaints about the corporate giant. He staked out his most aggressive stance toward his bosses in April 1986, when he ventured out to the headquarters of General Electric to give them a welcoming gift, with a camera crew in tow. With his arm around a large fruit basket, he entered the revolving door, only to be stopped by security. "We received your letter," a woman told him, adding that he had not gotten authorization. "We need authorization to drop off a fruit basket?" Letterman asked.

Randy Cohen had the idea to do a remote piece on getting to know GE. And they spent the day visiting GE appliance dealers, washing machine repair shops, and other stores. None of that footage was used. The short video became Letterman going to the headquarters to deliver a fruit basket.

It was the kind of gonzo stunt that Michael Moore would turn into a trademark only a few years later in the documentary *Roger & Me*, which he started making around the same time that Letterman showed up unannounced at General Electric. Moore also played the ordinary working-class guy walking into corporate headquarters—this time at General Motors—looking for answers or at least some semblance of humanity, after massive layoffs. His clever editing also echoed the stark juxtapositions in Markoe's remotes.

In the video, a GE security guard approached Letterman aggressively, and later walked up to Hal Gurnee, who had been filming the scene. Both Letterman and Gurnee extended their hands for a handshake, and the security guard started to do the same before having second thoughts, pulling his hand back abruptly. In the editing, Hal Gurnee saw this moment and knew it would make for the key part of the comedy. On the air, after showing the remote piece, Letterman gave this aborted greeting a name: the General Electric Handshake. He smiled when he said it.

Letterman may have become a star celebrated on college campuses and on the covers of magazines, but he still found a way to position himself as an outsider. In turning the network into the unseen antagonist of the show, he found the perfect thing to react against, artistically, at least. As for a career move, mocking your boss has a way of backfiring.

THE TWO DAVES

S teve O'Donnell was sitting in his office in Rockefeller Center when he saw a magazine advertising a top-ten list of eligible bachelors on the cover. It seemed arbitrary, as these lists often do, which gave him an idea. And thus was the Top Ten List born.

Randy Cohen recalled its origin differently. He saw a list in *Cosmopolitan* of the ten sexiest men over sixty and thought it absurd, but inspiration struck and he brought the idea of a top-ten spoof to the rest of the writing staff, who kicked around ideas, and out emerged the Top Ten List.

After polling the *Late Night* writers, O'Donnell's theory had more supporters, but Cohen's had a rather important one. In a television interview, David Letterman said that the Top Ten was Cohen's idea, although that does not end the discussion. "Dave gives credit to Randy, but he doesn't always know," said Barbara Gaines, Letterman's longest-tenured employee.

There is also a third theory. Jim Downey, the head writer whom O'Donnell replaced, says he was its real creator, even though he left the show years before the Top Ten List premiered, in 1985. So how could a writer who wasn't even working on *Late Night* at the time come up with the idea? Downey said that after he left and moved to *The New Show*, he wrote a list of jokes called "The Top Five Causes of Death of College Students in Fort Lauderdale," which appeared on the show.

It was not a top-ten list, but the concept was the same. Downey said that Jeff Martin, one of the *Late Night* writers as of 1985, called him to compliment this idea, which Martin then brought to *Late Night*. And so the Top Ten List lurched to life. It sounded far-fetched, but when I approached O'Donnell with this alternative history, he, remarkably, withdrew his own story and threw his support behind Downey.

So that would seem to settle it, except that when you ask Jeff Martin, he denies calling Downey at all. He gives credit to O'Donnell, who, as it happens, won't take it. Are you lost yet?

That you can fill up a third of a top-ten list with the varying origin stories of the Top Ten List illustrates the importance of this comedic conceit. No one, for instance, argues over authorship of Small Town News. But the Top Ten became a staple of David Letterman's talk shows for three decades. Two books of Top Ten lists made the bestseller list. Letterman read Top Ten Lists during his hosting of the Emmys and the Oscars. It became his signature.

What matters more to the history of the show than who came up with the idea is how it evolved. The first lists were absurdist satires of these lists that even at that time were a media standby. On *Late Night*, the first list was "Top Ten Words That Almost Rhyme with 'Peas.'" The top three were: (3) Nurse, (2) Leaks, and (1) Meats. Another was "Top Ten Keebler Elf Euphemisms for Death."

The original Top Ten List started with a bizarre sensibility, but it evolved into a structure for topical punch lines. "It started as conceptual," O'Donnell said. "But it became a place for John Sununu jokes."

This reflected an aesthetic tension that had always been on the show, and one its writers needed to navigate. "There are two Daves," explained writer Matt Wickline, describing the challenge of coming up with jokes on *Late Night*. "First there's the one who likes the meat-and-potato stand-up jokes. Then there is the weird Dave."

The Top Ten was at its heart a conventional series of very short jokes. It became almost like a second monologue, with less room for setups. But reducing the Top Ten List to middle-of-the-road jokes doesn't give it enough credit. What made the list such a quintessential part of the show was how it incorporated the host's peculiar sensitivity to language. Letterman was always delighted by the humor of words, not just punch lines. And the conciseness of the Top Ten List forced the writers to make every word count.

Brevity allowed the Top Ten to be a showcase for the quiet humor of funny sounds. And if there is one artistic constant throughout David Letterman's career, dating back to his days in Indiana, it's his intuitive belief in the power of language itself to be funny. Mixing formality with folksiness, his sentences are filled with florid transitions ("heretofore"), obscure words ("comptroller"), and dopey phrases ("Them bats is smart").

In scripted comedy, Letterman could be as stubborn and exacting as an old-fashioned English teacher about grammar and word choice. In preparation for the show, his notes on the comedy often focused on the way something was phrased. He could get exercised about the distinction between "further" and "farther." Of course, what was technically right was not the same as what sounded better or funnier. Letterman loved snatches of clichés, repeating them over and over until they took on the tone of an incantation. But he also liked jargon and official-sounding words, the obscure juxtaposed with the blunt.

The Top Ten filtered the Letterman sensibility through the standards of head writer Steve O'Donnell, who created and oversaw the first few years of the list. He had an ear for the sound of Letterman's humor and grasped the comedic poetry of these jokes.

The Top Ten Lists favored certain words ("squeegee," "Spam"), some of which were whimsical, but others had a kind of blue-collar simplicity ("taking a leak," "what's the deal"). The list also developed its own loose formulas. Typically, it opened with a strong, short joke. The second was usually weak, and the fifth was the start of a new screen, so it needed to be dependably funny. "Three is the funniest," writer Fred Graver said. "During the laughs, Dave can throw those last two away, and you're out of there."

The Top Ten didn't just take up time that would have gone to prop pieces or a man-on-the-street video. It became such a signal element that it ate up much of the time in the process by which *Late Night with David Letterman* was put together. The office day now started with the staff poring over newspapers to come up with three or four ideas that O'Donnell could bring to Letterman. By lunch they had settled on a topic and then began sifting through ideas to show to the host. Each writer came up with twenty or thirty Top Ten jokes, then read them at a table. O'Donnell compiled the best ones, brought them in. Letterman rejected the vast majority. Then O'Donnell would go back again, asking, "One more please, just one more." Then the writers went back to work.

"It felt like those Top Ten Lists were dangling meat over a shark tank, with all the writers desperately trying to get a line onto the list," Merrill Markoe said, describing its popularity as a turning point. "I just avoided that whole thing. I just thought, 'This is not what I meant when I envisioned being a writer.'"

While the Top Ten was hardening into a staple of *Late Night*, Markoe was editing a book that was designed to show off the more lit-

erary accomplishments of the show. It was a collection of short comedy pieces from *Late Night* translated to the page, along with some
new comic essays by the writers. A photo-by-photo version of "They
Took My Show Away" was one of the many comedy bits from the
show that were used. It was an unusual challenge to convert comedy
written for television to a book, but the early *Late Night* was the rare
talk show that could be as funny on the page as it was on the screen.

There were some errors in the production of the book, which bothered some people on staff, but when Letterman promoted the book
on the air, his irritation was strangely out of proportion. After his
opening remarks, he couldn't bring himself to say anything positive
about the book. "The book is kind of like the owner's manual if you
buy a Pinto," he said, adding that the publishing house had printed it
without captions. Then he advised the audience that if they bought
one and there were no captions, "Hang around the store and be really
impolite for a couple of days." Then he flashed a grumpy look and
tossed the book behind his head like trash.

Letterman's perfunctory and hostile mention of *Late Night with
David Letterman: The Book* was a metaphor for his show's artistic direction. The center of power was moving away from the writing staff.
So was his troubled relationship with Markoe. They tried couples
therapy once, but to little avail. "He got angry and never came back,"
Markoe said. "I had a tendency to get in and solve his problems. It was
very Zelda Fitzgerald."

Markoe started working more outside the show, including writing
an episode of a sitcom called *Buffalo Bill*, about a depressed, lonely
talk-show host played by Dabney Coleman. She and Letterman were
still dating, but they were often on different coasts, with Markoe
spending more time in Los Angeles. When Garry Shandling appeared
on *Late Night* for the first time, he joked about relationships before
turning to Letterman to ask, "You're sort of leasing with an option to
buy?" Letterman didn't respond.

It was more awkward when Markoe appeared on the show in a segment called Get to Know Your Staff, during which Letterman would interview people who worked with him. Markoe planned a bit where she would answer the question of what Letterman was like in bed. The joke was that she talked about their sex life in the sober, technical language of a scientist. She had a chart that mapped his pulse rate and sleep patterns. Letterman thought it would sound weird to do this bit as an unmarried couple, so he told Markoe they should say at the top that they were engaged.

When Markoe announced it, the audience cheered, throwing the entire piece off-balance, striking a tone that was sentimental instead of dry. "It was meant to be this cynical thing," she said. "But it became this announcement of getting married."

By the end of the decade, *Late Night* looked inward. The best way to get a job was no longer to come from *The Harvard Lampoon* but to take an internship at *Late Night*, bide your time, and keep an eye out for openings. Matt Wickline, Chris Elliott's writing partner, had been the first intern to get hired as a writer, followed by numerous others, including Rob Burnett, who went on to produce the show in the next decade. *Late Night* was not terribly intrepid in searching out new talent.

"An early nugget of insight that Merrill gave me is 'Dave would prefer to go with someone he knows,'" Steve O'Donnell said about hiring writers. "That proved to be true more and more as time went on. Sometimes people who weren't the most spectacularly gifted in their task were better because of familiarity with Dave. That doesn't mean it's bad for the show, because if Dave is comfortable, that's better for the show."

Late Night's artistic center was also moving away from the writers' room, and its most dynamic comedy became as much about the visual image as the written word. Much of the credit for this goes to Hal Gurnee, the rare auteur director in late-night talk. By the mid-1980s, Gurnee, a shambling, avuncular man with a calm, bemused voice, had established a trusting working relationship with Letterman. In a *Rolling Stone* interview, Letterman even went so far as to call Gurnee one of his best friends, but what that may have revealed the most about was how few friends Letterman had. Off-camera, Letterman and Gurnee rarely discussed the show, nor anything personal. But in the office and on television, they had an easy rapport. Gurnee's understated calm proved soothing for Letterman.

"I don't think he had any idea where I came from, who I was," said Gurnee. "The only reason I know about him is because he invited me out to Indianapolis a couple times and I met his mother out there. If you've been to Indianapolis, they are different. They're politer, superficially politer. And a lot of awkwardness."

On the air, Letterman and Gurnee shared a towel-snapping camaraderie. When he appeared, usually as an off-camera voice talking to the host, Gurnee could be sternly paternal, while Letterman played the misbehaving kid, repeatedly mispronouncing his director's name as "Hal Gurtner." Their exchanges were improvised, but followed a consistent pattern, with Letterman grumbling to Gurnee, who acted as if he didn't think anything was worth getting too worked up about.

Gurnee expanded the aesthetic of the show, becoming not just an on-camera character, but one of its most important writers, albeit one who crafted visual jokes. Until the mid-1980s, talk shows were shot like filmed plays. *The Tonight Show* kept the camera on the action and retained a static image. But television camerawork was starting to change, due especially to the influence of slickly shot NFL games. Sports had become the most overproduced genre on television, with a dizzying number of camera angles for every NFL play. *Monday Night Football* pioneered this style, placing cameras not only on the field but above it, and also in the stands. Football games leaned on instant replay and slow motion, which transformed the way viewers digested events on television. These technological breakthroughs improved the viewing experience. On the other hand, they were often pointless exercises trumpeted by networks as more exciting than they really were.

The rise of MTV, whose young audience also watched Letterman, similarly ushered in a flashy style that approached its subjects from many angles, shifting cameras for no reason other than to hold your attention. It was a cheaper version of what networks were doing with sports.

Adding technological bells and whistles to broadcasting became a major theme of *Late Night with David Letterman*, one that its host returned to throughout his career. Letterman's television career overlapped with the computer revolution and the Internet era, and he regularly mocked fetishizing technology in a way that was refreshing and sharp, but also risked looking behind the times. (When Bill Gates explained the Internet to Letterman in 1995, he mocked the idea that you could follow a baseball game on the computer. "Does radio ring a bell?" he joked.) In the same month that the Top Ten began, Letterman introduced his own Sky-Cam, which floated above the ceiling, giving the audience the view of a bird racing through the studio. Gurnee had used something similar on the episode of the morning show in which Letterman informed the audience the show was being canceled.

The next week, Letterman showed the Sky-Cam again, accompanied by a showman's bluster. "This is the only television show in America using the Sky-Cam," he said. "We were the first. One day, all talk shows will be like this." Several weeks later, he invited three Japanese men in suits to observe. Just like the Top Ten, the Sky-Cam began as a parody but evolved into something more particular to the aesthetic of the show. Letterman seemed to move from poking fun to genuinely enjoying it.

Hal Gurnee had experimented with these high camera angles on the morning show, but this rushing, chaotic camera made the talk show look like a horror movie. It was silly, but also so different that it got your attention. *Late Night* took advantage of its success by offering variations on the theme. Tom Hanks wore a camera, and the Guest-Cam was born. Paul Shaffer did the Band-Cam. There was the Thrill-Cam, which shook and added horror movie sounds. These cams were part of a tradition of showing new perspectives that was part of the start of the show, but they weren't one-off gimmicks. They became hallmarks.

In another idea cooked up by Gurnee, *Late Night* satirized the sporting world's indulgence of constantly shifting angles by doing a show with thirteen cameras that kept changing perspectives on Letterman for no reason other than that they could. It was a vivid parody of the pointlessness of technological innovation and the courting of attention-deficit-disordered audiences.

The most memorable of these camera stunts might have been the Monkey-Cam, in which a camera was strapped to the back of a trained chimpanzee that hopped around the studio while Letterman tried to talk to the radio host and sex therapist Dr. Ruth Westheimer. As his attention wandered to the chimp, she angrily told Letterman to stop paying attention to the animal and talk to her. These cameras were poking fun at technology, but they were also mocking television itself in the way that Letterman had since the beginning of *Late Night*.

But instead of using sarcasm or insincere hyperbole, he was now getting his point across visually, through form as much as content. Just as David Letterman mocked show business while also engaging with it and poked fun at patriotic displays while waving the flag, he made fun of technology while pioneering it. The camerawork made the look of the show unpredictable, but it also called attention to its artifice. As *Late Night* featured more of these cameras, Letterman became more playful in how he interacted with them, taking a second to look inside it from close up, blowing air on it, and rubbing the screen to clean it up. These maneuvers highlighted the fakery of his show and broke up the traditional way the talk show looked, tactics that became standard.

In a joke on the show, Gurnee shrank the screen down to a tiny fraction of the set, with the rest of the screen black. It made the host look like he was shrinking. In a bolder experiment, *Late Night* slowly rotated the camera over the course of the hour, so that the screen was upside down halfway through. It was a great opportunity for self-deprecation. "If you think it's annoying now?" Letterman said. "Just wait ten minutes."

It was a perfect satire of our obsession with high tech, executed with a certain delightful old-school panache. But it was also exploited for a deliriously inspired and silly joke. At the midway point, when the image was inverted, Letterman introduced Larry "Bud" Melman, dressed in a jacket and tails and dancing, to make it look as though he was dancing on the ceiling. If the whole show was jerry-rigged to create this one surreal image, it was worth it.

Many viewers called in to the network to complain about the 360-degree show, but the ratings, which were tracked every fifteen minutes, didn't go down. "If the show has an interesting central idea, it's about how people watch TV," said Randy Cohen, who wrote the 360-degree show and many of the more conceptual theme shows of the second era of *Late Night*. "No matter how unpleasant you make it for them, they'll whine and complain, but they won't stop watching."

Most television comedy is loath to confuse the audience, and goes to great pains to explain the joke, with its host repeating its premise repeatedly. Letterman himself satirized this tendency, but by the middle of the decade his loyal audience had come to expect oddness and eccentricity. Being confused made sense in the context of this show. And Letterman understood that, which changed his relationship with the audience. He could get away with different kinds of jokes than he could when *Late Night* premiered.

Hal Gurnee's signature comedic innovation, the one that created an entirely new genre of late-night jokes, was the cutaway shot. It was a simple maneuver where, in the middle of a remote piece or an interview, Gurnee shifted the camera away from the people talking to an angle that showed you an onlooker's response. Sometimes this was entirely random. Other times, Gurnee used the tactic to save an interview, juicing it up with some new point of view. He said he did it to liven up a boring moment, but its roots went back to when he worked for Jack Paar on *The Tonight Show*.

> Before that, when you did interviews, it was a shot of the person asking the question. Jack asked the person a question, then you cut to the person answering the question. Then you cut back to the guy asking the question before. And I figured it was more interesting to watch the person's face as he's being asked the question than to see the guy who was reading the question. And that worked.

Gurnee found the silent shot of a person listening just as compelling as a person talking. And the juxtaposition could result in a good joke. He would cut away from Letterman's opening remarks every night to someone in the audience watching, which would get a laugh. Maybe it was because the person looked bored, or had a strange look on their face. Or it was the way this shot changed the timing of the jokes, since Letterman would become confused or add a joke about this person.

A classic example of this technique was in a remote film that turned out to be one of the best pieces ever aired on *Late Night*, in which Letterman responded to a letter from a woman asking about his shoes by visiting her at her job at Sears. He first went to her house, where he met her brother and mowed her lawn. At the end, Letterman and the woman shared a meal with the crew, but then, for seemingly no reason, the camera shifted to a man taking a bite out of an ear of corn. It was an absurdly unnecessary shot, but it also allowed for a pause before Letterman delivered the last line of the piece. The camerawork changed the rhythm of the joke.

These cutaways could seem indulgent, but only rarely, since Gurnee had such a resourceful improvisational mind and knew exactly when to sit still and when to go for laughs. For Letterman's interview with the performance artist Brother Theodore, Gurnee delivered the biggest laugh. When Theodore announced apocalyptically, in a booming voice, "Don't ask me for whom the grave is dug. It's dug for you!" Gurnee shifted to a shot of Billy Joel standing with Paul Shaffer, both looking unimpressed. The hilarious contrast between the existential rant and the relaxed pose of the pop star was achieved in one cut and no words. Letterman didn't have to do a thing.

The most famous example of Hal Gurnee's cutaway might have been the time, a decade later, when Madonna cursed more than a dozen times during an interview that quickly turned awkward. Gurnee, recognizing Letterman's discomfort, took control of the segment by shifting the point of view to an elderly couple in the audience. As Madonna cursed and Letterman groused, Gurnee simply kept returning to shots of members of the audience, which gave the host something else to talk about.

What other television director would take the focus away from the biggest pop star and television comedian of the era with a simple camera switch? Who even had the leeway and courage to do it? Gurnee did, and it worked, getting a big laugh.

Late Night with David Letterman created something that few talk shows had: its own distinctive visual aesthetic. *The Tonight Show* gave a familiar vignette every night, but *Late Night* had a constantly shifting, unpredictable palette. It was the most interesting-looking talk show on television, by far.

By the late 1980s, Letterman had become more distant to his staff. He kept to himself, often remarking to his head writer that people on staff didn't like him. In the style of the old-fashioned comedy legends, Letterman smoked cigars. He talked about celebrities with occasional fondness. "He became statelier in a way," O'Donnell said. "He seemed to not be a big Barbara Walters fan for years. And then, when she was going to do an interview, he would start talking about her around the office in a way that was much more admiring or something. And I remember going, 'What happened, Dave?' And he'd go, 'These are like my peers now.'"

David Letterman had become more famous than almost all of his guests. Offers started arriving from Hollywood. Disney signed him to a multimillion-dollar deal to make movies. Unsure whether there was a project that would suit him, Letterman asked some of his writers for help. Steve O'Donnell suggested he should play a cranky H. L. Mencken type. Letterman called his old writer George Meyer and asked him to write something for him. Flattered to be asked, Meyer came up with a project that reflected the self-awareness of *Late Night* and the blazing cultural cachet of its host. He explained the premise of the movie, which never settled on a title, this way:

> It was a movie within a movie. And it was partly about the challenge of doing that. It turned into a James Bond parody, which was like Austin Powers in some ways. That was the closest thing to what I was going for. He was playing himself for the first part of the film. In the second, it was the movie within a movie, where he was playing James Bond essentially.

Letterman told Meyer he liked the script, but he never made the movie and decided to give the money back to Disney.

Letterman stopped putting on Velcro suits and being dipped into tanks. He stopped doing segments like Mr. Curious, in part because he couldn't go outside without being swarmed by people. Letterman would tell head writer Steve O'Donnell, "Steve, my van-riding days are over." He would still shoot segments, but they were more scripted, with less room for spontaneity or even surprise. He improvised less.

The show also started screening remote pieces in front of a live audience to see if they worked before running them on the air. This eliminated some of the stranger segments that may not have gotten a laugh in a theater.

Letterman started turning down more and more of the theme shows and told more jokes in the opening remarks. He didn't want to leave the studio. He had always made interactions with strangers on the street a part of his show, but now he preferred to have these exchanges from his desk, mediated by a phone or a camera. He could stay behind his desk and call pay phones outside to find people they could invite up to the studio rather than approach people on the street.

When they realized that the technology existed to allow them to talk through a camera (*Late Night* staffers called it the Hurlycamera, after the bar in which they shot their first remote with it), they started leaning on it as a way for Letterman to interact with people without leaving his desk. "A lot of what we were doing then was because Dave wanted to insulate himself from the public," said Rob Burnett.

Letterman had begun loosening up his onscreen persona, becoming quirkier, more ornately self-referential. He set up the premises repeatedly, mocking the way comics simplify and underline their jokes, then, right before setting up the twist, he would look off-camera and smirk, bailing on his own joke before delivering the punch line, then mocking it repeatedly. Letterman constantly promised that his show would be magical and his guests were talented and beautiful. His hyperbole became more and more extreme in its gushing.

Chris Elliott's characters had always been a reflection of the show, and his on-camera role only increased through the decade. Elliott had a falling-out with his partner, Matt Wickline. "We were very good friends, but he was also someone who wanted to be a star," Wickline said. "It just got frustrating. He wanted me to be part of that thing. It was just a little too much of the crazy train, so I took a step back."

Taking his place was a talented NYU graduate, Adam Resnick, who collaborated with Elliott in creating the characters he played on the show. (They would eventually make the movie *Cabin Boy*, which featured Letterman in a rare cameo as an old fisherman.) Elliott shifted from playing frustrated, angry ranters like the Guy Under the Seats to bloviating celebrities like Marv Albert and Jay Leno. Working with Resnick, Elliott created a series of cartoonish buffoons not dissimilar to the kinds of parts that Will Ferrell would become famous for.

In a parody of show business rituals, Elliott would often greet Letterman with a two-handed embrace, then turn to the crowd and raise his arms in triumph or put his hands up to his chin in a prayer gesture. Elliott mastered the body language of a certain kind of phony. He was playing a show-biz type just as divorced from reality as Paul Shaffer. But he was more arrogant. What remained constant from his earlier group of characters was the ironic distance built into the performance. Elliott didn't break character as often, though he wasn't entirely committed, either. But his performances had a new swagger.

His most famous recurring character was Marlon Brando, an actor who had been satirized so much that it had become cliché. But whereas most impressions (like the one by John Belushi on *Saturday Night Live*) did the mumbling, intense Brando from *The Godfather* or *On the Waterfront*, Elliott played the later Brando: bloated, pretentious, a guy on his own island. He was a man whom show biz had driven mad, but also oddly likable in his absurdity.

When he barreled onstage and sat down next to Letterman, Elliott's Brando said, "From time to time I'm going to be stopping by, giving you a feeling of awkwardness, a feeling of uneasiness." Then he made a threat that could have doubled as a misguided mission statement for *Late Night*: "I'm giving your audience a choice: Either they can laugh or they can sit there and be baffled."

Elliott also did a character that poked more direct fun at Letterman: the host of a late-night talk show called "Night Life with Chris Elliott." In its first incarnations, he played a flashy entertainer who seemed nothing like Letterman. But when he brought the character back the following week, he had a smirk and a demeanor that echoed his boss. With a wry, self-mocking smile, Elliott introduced the "Chair-Cam," then was interrupted by a character called Panicky Boy, played by Adam Resnick.

Chris Elliott was clearly putting on a mini-version of *Late Night with David Letterman*, including a mini-version of Elliott, several feet away from the real thing. *Late Night*'s self-obsession had reached another level, satirizing itself. This segment was built on so many inside jokes that it collapsed in on itself. "Dave nixed it after I tried to crush something," he told me, referring to a bit that Letterman had become famous for. "I always thought it hit too close to home."

Toward the end of the decade, Letterman started relying more on extemporaneous talk. His confidence as a talker able to keep an audience's attention had grown. His stories regularly dramatized his own thought process. Letterman became more of a storyteller, not just in his monologues but at the desk, where he would describe a mundane thing that had happened to him with great wit and suspense.

So much of his persona during his first years on the show was about being a guy who did not reveal himself. Now Letterman started talking more and more about real life, turning personal anecdotes into comedy at his desk. His life became grist for the show. When a mentally ill female stalker named Margaret Mary Ray repeatedly broke into his house, Letterman started adding the story to jokes and desk bits. In one, he picked up the phone, called, and let it ring. When no one picked up, he said, "Good. It's my house." Such jokes needed little explanation. "It was a watershed moment," O'Donnell said. "That surprised us on staff."

Letterman was putting on a show more in the vein of Jack Paar, who moved *The Tonight Show* away from the giddily juvenile stunts and flamboyant showmanship of Steve Allen. Letterman often said that Paar told him it was okay to show anger on television, which he seemed to take to heart. Letterman never went as far as Paar by walking off the set on the air, although he did unexpectedly walk offscreen a few times. In 1987, the actor Crispin Glover had clearly planned to do his spot in character, rambling madly and challenging Letterman to a fight. It was the kind of idiocy that Letterman could destroy with a one-liner. But when the host saw Glover act up, he looked upset, ignoring his guest and talking to Shaffer.

"Paul, is this the first time you've seen another guy drown? Is this the first time you've watched a guy die?" Shaffer looked confused: "Him?" he asked. Letterman said, "No. Me." Letterman wasn't in the mood to play along, not even with an insult. He saw this as another disaster, another way that he was messing up. Glover responded by standing up and kicking his foot up into the air. He wasn't close to hitting Letterman, but it didn't matter. Dave said he was going to check on the Top Ten List and walked away from his desk before they cut to commercial.

Most late-night talk-show hosts would find this great television. But Letterman wasn't interested. He hated that this stunt was unplanned, and by walking away he took control. Letterman's onscreen presence also shifted. The show could take dark turns. In one running bit, Letterman would blow up in a fury at the writer Gerard Mulligan for some small infraction and fire him on the air. Mulligan would walk away pitifully, before Letterman flashed a guilty look and told him it was just a joke. One version of this cruel prank ended with Mulligan hanging himself. In a remote piece two months later, Letterman responded to feeling down by taking a walk in the park and beating up some old people.

He brought back his fictional family for another Christmas special, but this sketch, which they had first done in 1984, was now bleaker. He called one of his sons "a sissy," and it became clear that his brother's wife had married him only so she could get closer to the talk-show host.

After Shaffer chirped, "You can't spell 'Season's Greetings' without GE," Letterman said, "We want to do something with all the love, warmth, and sentiment that I am capable of faking for a stretch."

Letterman's physicality also became more eccentric. He wrestled with his clothes, yanking his tie, fidgeting with his hair, and adjusting his suits. He cleared his throat before jokes, stretched out his neck, and cracked his knuckles. Letterman's body language was restless, charging toward the camera and even rubbing it with his sleeve, pantomime cleaning it during the show. And when he made a joke he didn't think was that strong, he emitted a loud, flamboyantly insincere guffaw.

Letterman would often tell a joke, find himself tickled by a particular phrase, then repeat it incessantly throughout the show—between jokes, in asides, in response to frustration—for reasons that were entirely unclear. The phrase operated like an incantation for Letterman, a theme that had no meaning outside of being something that he repeated, connective tissue that tied together a bit. Its meaning may have been elusive to most, but fans of Letterman came to recognize this as one of his distinctive verbal tropes.

Some of his comedy became so inside that it became barely even comedy at all. Letterman set up a fountain with rainbow lights in front of his desk that he called Dancing Waters, and he would turn it on at various times during the show. The audience loved it, but why was this funny? In the spirit of giant props, Letterman brought out a huge Swiss Army Knife, which wasn't even a new joke but was in the tradition of a joke they had done in the past. Letterman added a smirk and it killed.

This was the height of the weird comedy era at *Late Night*, the kind that would blossom in the following decade with the explosion of the alternative comedy scene where comics like Maria Bamford and David Cross experimented with longer storytelling and oddball jokes at venues like the Uncabaret in Los Angeles or the Luna Lounge in New York. Letterman no longer seemed comfortable if a joke didn't get a laugh, and at times he could seem utterly disinterested in jokes. His show had such a firmly established reputation for absurdity that his wry sensibility could turn most anything into a laugh.

At times, this could become insular, if not indulgent. "I remember thinking, 'We're doing a lot of stuff that you'd be hard-pressed to say what the joke is,'" said Jeff Martin, one of the writers. "'Because the world has decided that we're cool and cutting-edge, the stuff we're doing is cool. What's cool about it? It's cool because we're doing it.'"

Late Night had become as much about the star power and personality of its host as about whatever comedy he was performing. If the audience was entertained by dancing waters, do you even need scripted material? In 1988, when his writers went on strike, David Letterman would put this to the test.

PART IV

WRITER'S BLOCK

1988–1993

Charles Grodin: Ten years ago, when you were on in the daytime, you were nothing. Have you changed?

David Letterman: Oh, yeah, I've gotten quite peculiar.

—*Late Night with David Letterman*, May 11, 1990

COMEDY IS NOT PRETTY!

Every weekday at 1 p.m., David Letterman went to rehearsal in his studio in Rockefeller Center, where he would run through the comedy he would perform that night. In the downtime between bits, he tossed around a football with staffers and played the drums. Then he retreated to his office, got in makeup, changed into a suit, splashed cologne on his face and on the ground. Before every show, he snacked on pineapples and Hershey bars, carefully broken into small squares.

At one point, he said the chocolate tasted waxy, so a new plan was hatched, wherein boxes of chocolate were shipped directly from Hershey's headquarters in Pennsylvania. Letterman drank cup after cup of coffee—in the morning, before the show, and during commercials. He tried caffeinated soda for a while but returned to the stronger stuff. Of all his habits, the one Letterman was dedicated to the most was worrying about his health. He was a spectacularly committed hypochondriac, and close watchers of *Late Night* could tell. "I have the worst cold in the history of television, and you know what keeps me going?" he said to the audience at the opening of one show. "Your love."

He would begin shows looking into the camera, flashing a severe look. "I feel really sick. I am deathly ill," he said one time. Then he would pause dramatically. "But I'm going to do a great show for you tonight." It came off as a melodramatic joke.

Off-camera, his health anxieties were even more pronounced. In the office, he would often study a well-worn copy of *The Merck Manual*, searching out symptoms in an effort to speculate about what disease was going to threaten his life next. He was very careful about his diet, eating a small bowl of pasta for lunch every day. He fixated on certain illnesses but also invented others. His former agent Deborah Miller recalled getting a call from him at an airport, panicked that he had overdosed on aspirin.

For weeks, he would be obsessed with mercury in teeth fillings and bring in doctors to talk to him about it. On one vacation, Letterman decided he had what he called "heart tumors" after analyzing *The Merck Manual*. Merrill Markoe tried to reassure him that it was probably nothing, but he insisted on going to the doctor. Later in the day, she returned home to find him smoking a cigar in the hot tub. When she asked about what the doctor had said, Letterman replied, "The doctor told me he never heard of heart tumors."

His back was a constant source of pain and tightness, which dated back to a car accident. A masseuse was in and out of his office. The complaints about the back were nothing compared with the neck. "You could do a chapter on Dave's neck," Steve O'Donnell said. "It had an effect on lots of things. It is partly responsible for Dave's imperious reputation. Guests would hear, 'Don't touch Dave.' His neck was fragile. He would occasionally have a brace."

Everyone on staff knew never to touch his neck. Letterman had a habit of moving his head to the side and cracking it onscreen, a tic he had leaned on since his stand-up days. The reason he threw the football at rehearsal, Robert Morton explained, was to loosen his neck up. Letterman would tell people that he believed he had a broken neck. He also suffered from dizziness that he diagnosed as disequilibrium, and he became so darkly concerned about it that he traveled the world to find a cure, once visiting a Munich doctor for two days of examinations. "He called me into his office and said, 'You know, there's nothing wrong with you,'" Letterman explained. "'You're still holding on to this idea that you're injured. The house is not on fire. Stop it.' And then it went away."

Late Night was the rare show with a staff doctor who gave every employee a flu shot. Hillary Rollins, the daughter of Jack Rollins, recalled her father talking about the star's various crises: "'He thinks he's dying. He thinks he has a brain tumor.' My poor dad had to manage a lot of crazy comedians, and Letterman did not disappoint," she said.

To those who worked with him, the most striking change with David Letterman was how isolated he was becoming inside his own office. Once he'd become the host of a hit show for a few years, he hardly ever talked to the people who came up with his jokes, with the exception of his head writer. "The running joke was: 'You might get to meet him when you leave,'" writer Steve Young said. "Howard Hughes–like, I always say. He had a few trusted lieutenants but didn't want to interact with those outside. He had various OCD traits."

The office of *Late Night with David Letterman* reflected the boss: tense, anxiety-ridden, and increasingly shut off from the world. Letterman was an intimidating figure to many of the younger staffers, one who could flash a cutting wit that stung even more because he was less accessible than he had been in the early days of the show.

Hal Gurnee recalled one harsh joke he made at the expense of an intern along for a remote shoot. She asked something about the weather. "Then Dave very carefully explained how weather works—how toward the end of the summer it starts getting colder and colder, and then pretty soon the leaves will come off the tree, and then it really gets cold sometimes," Hal Gurnee explained. "And this girl's going, 'Uh-huh . . .' Some people would think it was cruel. To me it was just very funny."

The writer Dave Hanson recalled Letterman sitting down next to him at a Christmas party at the skating rink in Central Park. "So you're going skating," Hanson said, to which Letterman responded, "Masterful powers of observation," got up, and took off. Hanson remembered another time when he wished him a belated happy birthday that got curiously tense. "What do you mean by that?"

Interactions between the writers on the show and the host became increasingly rare. By the end of the decade, even head writer Steve O'Donnell had difficulty pitching material in person, often having to wait to talk to Letterman by phone at night, during his car ride home. In 1986, Letterman met with O'Donnell twice a day to go over ideas; two years later, there were days when O'Donnell could get an audience for pitches only after midnight.

Barry Sand, who had been his producer since the morning show, started having similar trouble getting time with Letterman. He had the distinct impression that he was being phased out, and became the first of many longtime Letterman collaborators who left *Late Night*.

Sand was critical in putting together the show, and for years he did the dirty work, like securing last-second bookings or dealing with rising costs, salary complaints, and firing employees. But he had become a polarizing figure. To the writers, he was a yeller who meddled in their work unnecessarily. He and Letterman were never close. "He wasn't a hearty-laugh kind of guy," Sand said. "He thought he wasn't show business. He was a weatherman, a guy's guy. What host wears white socks?"

Sand shifted from confidant to outsider, falling out of favor with the boss but not being fired. Part of his problem was that the talk-show field was starting to get more crowded, and Robert Morton, a longtime segment producer at *Late Night* who had aspirations to be the executive producer, had already taken a leave to produce *Max Headroom*, which the *New York Times'* critic compared to *Late Night with David Letterman*. Morton was getting offers from HBO and Fox to work on new talk shows, including one hosted by Joan Rivers. Morton let people at *Late Night* know that there was a risk that the show could lose him.

Morton, whom Letterman called Morty, a nickname that stuck, had no ambitions as a writer and got along with staff members better than Sand did. And as talk of Letterman possibly succeeding Johnny Carson heightened, Morton seemed better suited to help the host transition to a larger platform in an earlier time slot. He was as gregarious and accessible as Letterman was introverted and prickly. Sand was strong-willed and organized. Morton had a lighter touch, both with the press and with the network executives. A regular at events around town as well as at the Catch a Rising Star comedy club, Morton had good connections in the media and at NBC. He was already the face of the show in certain New York circles. Most of all, Morton got along with Letterman. They were closer in age and ribbed each other around the office.

Sand's relationship with Letterman had become icy, and the producer could no longer accurately anticipate what his host wanted. One time, a guest dropped out for the following night's show, at 11 p.m., causing an all-hands-on-deck crisis. Sand worked the phones and somehow secured Mel Gibson, who was at the height of his *Mad Max* fame. When he entered Letterman's office triumphantly to deliver the news, the host's response was, "'Who the hell wants Mel Gibson?' Letterman said, 'I don't want him.' I said, 'We don't have anyone.' He said, 'I don't care.' So we wound up with Kamarr the Discount Magician."

Letterman was loyal to his longtime employees, and he knew that Sand had played a critical role in streamlining his morning show, turning it into something that would resemble *Late Night*. But by 1987, Sand felt pressure to quit. He was often not clued in to major developments in the show. Staffers noticed that in some meetings Sand didn't know what was going to be on the show.

The final break occurred when *Late Night* spent a week in Las Vegas in the summer of 1987. Seeing a great opportunity for Letterman to use Las Vegas as a foil, Sand lined up a bunch of Vegas entertainers whom Letterman could play off, but the host nixed them. Part of the problem was that the Las Vegas that Paul Shaffer sent up barely existed anymore. "It was misguided from the beginning," Shaffer said. "It was unclear why we were there."

It was in Las Vegas that Letterman asked Sand to become an executive producer, in what Sand viewed as an obvious attempt to get rid of him through a promotion, leaving room for Robert Morton to fill his place. Sand refused. "I didn't want to be a figurehead," he said. "What followed was not contention, but silence." Sand said this made his job effectively impossible. "My job is confidence and communication, and it wasn't there," he recalled. "I was uncomfortable."

This was consistent with Letterman's passive-aggressive management style. "It became something that I saw year after year, decade after decade—Dave not being able to personally fire his friend," recalled Dency Nelson, a stage manager. "There would be some other mechanism of removing the guy. Whether it was a blessing or a fault, he didn't have the guts to look the guy in the eye and say, 'This ain't working. I'm so sorry.'"

Letterman claimed that he did fire people face-to-face and presented Sand's leaving as a function of his no longer getting along with the writing staff, which was true. "It got to the point where it seemed it was causing an impasse," Letterman said. "If the writers were doing what they wanted to do, Barry was upset. It was my choosing the writers over Barry."

In an episode in August 1987, Letterman sat at his desk and awkwardly explained that Sand, his longtime producer, was leaving. He looked down at his desk. "We will certainly all miss him," he said. "So best of luck to you, Barry." Then he paused before adding coldly, "So we wanted to take care of that now."

Sand left as *Late Night* was changing. Carson's exit from *The Tonight Show* was a source of constant speculation. Letterman was looking for more people to play off of, but also someone who could shift the show in the public consciousness to set him up for a move to an earlier time slot.

When Robert Morton took the job, Letterman approached his new producer and asked him if he minded being on camera, saying he wanted to talk to someone else during the show. Morton said that would be fine. "He said, 'When I'm out there, it's really lonely,'" Morton remembered.

It would become more during an industry-wide strike in early 1988, over residuals and money for foreign markets and VHS rights. There had been several strikes in the history of the show, but no labor dispute had been as long or as meaningful as this one. *Late Night* was off the air for half the year. Letterman held out longer than the rest of the late-night talk-show hosts but he paid the staff during the break. He stayed in Los Angeles with Merrill Markoe and was restless, eager to return to the show. During this period, Margaret Mary Ray, his stalker, broke into his Connecticut home again, moved furniture around, and tried on some of Markoe's clothes. Letterman had made jokes about Ray on the show, but he would come to regret them. She committed suicide a decade later.

Markoe recalls Letterman using Johnny Carson as a gauge for when to go back. "We had an answering machine where we had two friends who did dead-on Carson impressions who would call,"

Markoe said. "So we'd get a call. And we'd hear Carson. And then we'd do a version of 'Oh my God! Pick it up! It's Carson! No, no, it's not. It's Jeff Altman. It's Harry [Shearer].'"

Letterman had been involved in a contentious, high-profile strike before, as a comic for the Comedy Store in the late 1970s, in a dispute over the right to get paid for doing a stand-up set. Letterman had walked the picket line, which had strongly helped the strikers' cause and led to a change in policy at the Store. He understood the stakes.

But when other hosts started returning to the air, including Carson, he decided to return on one condition: He would not hire or use any new writers. There would be no scabs, and he wouldn't keep quiet about the situation on the air. It was a tricky position, because Letterman himself was also a writer for the show, so he was arguably crossing the picket line. But he did not want to be the only talk show not on the air. "I felt personally betrayed by Dave going back," writer Randy Cohen said. "No matter what he said after that, all that hairsplitting about 'We won't use writers, yeah, fuck you'—that was just self-serving. That was dishonesty that he's not usually guilty of." Letterman said he now wishes he'd stayed out longer.

What followed when he returned to the show was a fascinating test case for a show in transition. *Late Night with David Letterman* had begun as a talk show whose comedy was defined to a large degree by its writers. Its signal bits, from Viewer Mail to the remote pieces to scripted sketches like "They Took My Show Away," were created by them and filtered through Letterman's ironic attitude. There was always a tension between Letterman and the jokes he was telling, but they were both essential.

As he became a bigger star, and segments like the Top Ten List became more regimented, the balance shifted. Letterman's sarcasm became so well known that he would get laughs regardless of the joke, and he leaned less on his writing staff. But this process reached a culmination during the strike, when, for the first time, Letterman got a chance to see what *Late Night* would look like without writers.

D avid Letterman walked toward the cameras in his dark studio, looking unhappy. After one joke fell flat, he punched the air as if he had just hit a game-winning shot, looked to his right, and asked bandleader Paul Shaffer if he noticed how quiet the audience had become. Then Letterman sighed before hyping himself up again. His performance was frenetic, a hustling anxiety fueling his jokes.

"Are you like me?" he began a joke, in a parody of the kind of opening gambit that broadcasters and stand-up comics employed to seem relatable. "Do you like following the global financial scene?" Then he imitated the crowd's knee-jerk response. "Yeesss, Dave," he said, suggesting by the tone of his voice that his crowd would agree to anything. With manic comic aggression, Letterman mocked his own audience, highlighting how easily they were manipulated.

After sitting down at his desk, he introduced two acrobats from Cirque du Soleil, a French Canadian circus that had recently become a cult hit in the United States. You wouldn't know it from Letterman's condescending introduction, which referred to their work as "that pointless hopping around."

The strike shows revealed more starkly than ever Letterman's slow-boiling hostility, a suppressed rage papered over by a thin tissue of sarcasm, until it wasn't. Without writers, Letterman delivered a more nakedly emotional performance, one closer to how he was backstage but at a much higher energy level. "I was very angry," he said bluntly at the desk. "These guys at NBC . . . What's his name, Robert Wright—what's he, the CEO of NBC?" One running joke was Letterman's inability to remember the names of the most powerful executives at the network.

He then told a story of NBC throwing him a party in honor of his one thousandth episode, revealing that he'd received a present from NBC: a toaster. By this point, Letterman had been consistently mocking GE for nearly three years, describing this mighty corporation as merely a maker of cheap electronics.

Sitting at his desk next to the toaster, he said, "Since the writers are on strike, because the producers are . . . By the way, what are they, Paul?" Letterman shot a look at Shaffer, almost as if he was forcing him to say something he didn't want to. "Money-grubbing scum," Shaffer said woodenly, and Letterman nodded his head, repeating the insult. In the absence of his writers, Letterman said, he was going to entertain America by making toast on the air. "Let's just sit here and wait for the toast."

And so he did. Letterman made toast on television. It had to be the first time that making toast had become a defiant protest, one perfectly in keeping with the mock-apathetic aesthetic of David Letterman. He didn't stay on strike, but in the heart of the dispute, he thumbed his nose at the network by using their show to do essentially nothing on the airwaves. If you take away my writers, he seemed to suggest, I will turn your show into waiting around for breakfast.

The strike shows marked a turning point, a shift into a new era. *Late Night* was no longer a man in a suit surrounded by madness; he had gradually turned into a fascinatingly disgruntled eccentric trapped inside a more traditional talk show. The mercurial personality of its host was now the show's center, and its most unpredictable element. Letterman had accordingly become much more unguarded about his emotions. "He's the only guy in the history of television whose mood has been chronicled on television," said Bill Scheft, a comic who would join the writing staff in 1991.

The strike shows were a logical extension of the direction the show was already going in, away from the writing staff. Among the movies that David Letterman watched around the office, one of his favorites was the fist-shaking TV drama *The Comedian*, which juxtaposed the smiles of television hosts with their backstage sneers, decades before the cynical HBO masterpiece *The Larry Sanders Show*. The movie also had kitsch value, because Mickey Rooney, the quintessential child star of the golden age of Hollywood, played an angry television comic with a morose and monstrous alter ego. In one scene, Rooney barked at his head writer, "You write the comedy. I'll breathe the action into it." Letterman was tickled by this self-serious portrait of the behind-the-scenes entertainer.

That overheated boast captured a typical power dynamic between television hosts and their writers. David Letterman's writers had come up with many concepts for their host to breathe action into. They constantly tinkered with the form, and Letterman narrated these experiments, using them for jokes. *The Tonight Show* had the same basic elements every night; *Late Night* did not.

The high concepts and stunts had started to slow down by the end of the 1980s. *Late Night* had fewer theme shows and more major stars as guests. Letterman's jokes increasingly became about the failure of those jokes and his reactions to them. "That was a common complaint among writers—that he would sell out the material," said writer Kevin Curran.

The strike took the writers out of the show entirely and forced *Late Night* to radically reshape its process. Instead of a team feeding jokes to Steve O'Donnell, people in production filled the breach. The day started with producer Robert Morton, director Hal Gurnee, production coordinator Barbara Gaines, and associate producer Jude Brennan sitting in a room with Letterman, brainstorming ideas. They had been working with Letterman for nearly a decade and understood his style, his preferences, and the things that irritated him. "Before, the head writer was the gatekeeper," Brennan said. "Now it was a coffee klatch."

The result was a scrappier, if coherent, process that pushed *Late*

Night to return to the looser, more unscripted style of the morning show—except now the host was a major star and far more seasoned, confident, and open about his own feelings. During these shows, his monologue had three jokes, maximum. Around the punch lines, Letterman kept reminding audiences he had no writers, mocking the weakness of the gag he was telling, and sighing and chatting with people offscreen. His mannerisms became more ornamental and, considering that his audience was constantly being reminded that he was working with a handicap, were even more knowing than usual.

Instead of scripted comedy pieces to perform at the desk, Letterman filled the airtime with whatever his production people could find. The cabaret performer Michael Feinstein played the piano in the control room. Most memorable was Hal Gurnee's Network Time Killers, a segment in which Letterman would check in with his director in the control room, who would introduce time-wasting events like having the audience watch him button his shirt or proving that Abe Vigoda was still alive by having him breathe on a mirror. Letterman would introduce this with much fanfare, including drum rolls, then he would milk the anticlimax at the end.

Many of these bits had no punch lines, and they were only tangentially related to show business. There was some absurdity, but it wasn't heightened so much as the product of seeing these low-rent activities through the prism of David Letterman's sarcastic voice. In a way, all of *Late Night with David Letterman* had turned into a Stupid Human Trick. The subtext was the same as when Larry "Bud" Melman introduced the first show: Can you believe this is on television?

One of Gurnee's ideas was to have a tailor measure Letterman on the air and then make him a suit, which he would bring him later in the week. The whole thing played like a documentary about an incredibly boring subject that took place entirely in a television studio. Letterman spent more time talking directly to the camera about his life. He'd chat with Robert Morton, with Hal Gurnee in the control room, and then turn to Paul Shaffer for feedback. *Late Night* had the feel of a conversation dominated by one person.

The strike forced Letterman to experiment. He had always been a deft storyteller who could turn a small irritation into an operatic lament. Now he took this further. In the past, he would only hint at his offstage persona: shy, self-critical, obsessed with his own health. It would emerge through a sensibility that viewers had been conditioned to not entirely trust. He didn't abandon that attitude, but now he brought his angst and hypochondria to the forefront. Letterman was quite open about his anger toward NBC. And he didn't always try to be funny. He just told stories of getting through the day, with all the attendant irritations, and that was enough to get laughs. In one video remote in 1989, when he helped a woman pick out a wedding dress, he even talked about his quickie first wedding to Michelle Cook. "I was married once by a justice of the peace in his garage," he said, adding, "And I was really drunk." Leaning on his broadcasting skills, he turned extemporaneous stories into compelling television.

His interviews accordingly became more revealing. Letterman was quicker to get annoyed at a guest, and less game to tangle. Only a few days after he returned from the strike, Sandra Bernhard came on the show and brought along her friend Madonna, in her first appearance on *Late Night*. When Bernhard talked over Madonna, saying, "Isn't she delightful and charming?" Letterman retorted: "Well, if you'd shut up we'd find out." Bernhard was surprised by her treatment. "That show bothered me," she said. "I brought this big star to the show, and he didn't appreciate it. It upset me. Could you not be a little nice to me?"

How was *Letterman* without writers? To the dismay of some on staff, just fine, and in some ways he was better. It was riveting to see Letterman talk himself through this ordeal. He dramatized the misery of his situation in a way that put you on his side. Letterman made a point of calling himself a broadcaster, as opposed to a comedian, putting himself in a tradition of radio disc jockeys and news anchors. But in these shows, Letterman proved that the television talk show could be bluntly personal comedy. They provided a template for what the show was about to become.

In a *New York Times* story titled "Seriously Now, Can Writerless Comics Cope?" Glenn Collins argued that the strike shows underlined the strength of *Late Night*, which was not jokes but the host's attitude and instinct for self-parody. "The show invited the audience to share the adventures of a talk-show host beset by a writers' strike," he wrote. "It has always been difficult to discern the presence of writers in his nightly 'lame swipe at a monologue,' as Mr. Letterman has called it. In a sense, the Letterman monologue has always seemed to be a wry comment on Mr. Carson's; the typical Letterman joke isn't dependent on his writers' rim-shots as much as his self-referential delivery."

The story ended with a question: "Will 'Late Night with David Letterman' ultimately be transformed by the strike experience?"

The answer was yes. The strike shows proved that David Letterman could do a completely different kind of comedy show, one that was not packed with bits but could instead float along on blunt conversations and irritated stories from the host's personal life. Bits developed during the strike remained after the writers returned. Hal Gurnee kept doing Network Time Killers.

But as successful as these shows were, they also set a precedent that would forever change *Late Night*, and not always for the better. It became more dependent on the performance chops and prickly personality of its star. It also empowered the production team, which wasn't even unionized. They organized the following year.

"All the writers were in first class, while the producers [and the] talent department didn't get residuals. We didn't get health insurance," said Madeleine Smithberg, who worked on the production side. "I circulated a petition saying it was unfair that a show that generated so much money could not provide basic benefits. That's why everyone has health care and benefits to this day."

Once the strike ended, the show was moving in a different direction. Letterman's mood remained dark, and he indulged it, at times even seeming to cultivate hostility in his performance. Letterman lost his cool when Harvey Pekar visited him just a few weeks after the strike was over. A cult Cleveland cartoonist (Steve O'Donnell, a Cleveland native, had suggested him as a guest), Pekar had become famous for his cranky, grousing appearances on *Late Night* in which he would angrily announce his own authenticity in a world full of nonsense. "I'm no show-business phony," he boasted to Letterman, a host who had built a reputation on not being one, either.

Pekar came on the show and challenged Letterman about crossing the picket line. Letterman became visibly upset, telling him he would not be back on the show and referring dismissively to "his little comic book." Pekar smiled, delighting in having provoked the late-night host. Letterman later regretted saying this about Pekar.

Two weeks later, Letterman appeared not angry but wounded during an interview with Teri Garr. "Please make fun of me," he told Garr, to which she said, "You feel you deserve it." Letterman: "I do. I really feel that way. I'm full of self-loathing these days." When Garr pressed him on what he was worried about, he said he couldn't because they were out of time. Letterman hinted at such feelings on the air, but he became overt about it here. His misery could be made funny.

His obsession with health and his fear of sickness began to take center stage on the air. In one episode, Letterman brought on a nurse to give him a physical, making the show seem like nothing more than a trip to the doctor. It was a bizarre ten-minute segment in which Letterman gave blood and talked at length about his health, with few jokes. Later, Shirley MacLaine sat down to chat as a guest. When

Letterman poked fun at her for believing in past lives, she said, "Maybe Cher was right. Maybe you *are* an asshole." Letterman's comeback: "Would you like to give some blood? Give it the hard way?"

In one high-concept show, he just watched a rerun, his face popping up in the corner to comment on the show. In one of the rerun's bits, the writer of a Viewer Mail letter asked about writers' dreams and aspirations. Merrill Markoe appeared on camera inside the shape of a heart, saying she dreamed of finding a man who was "in touch with the little boy he once was, but senses the threadbare pile of hopeless human wreckage he'll become." Gerard Mulligan appeared, saying that he was "looking for a cheap, meaningless backstreet affair that fills me with self-loathing so that at least I'll feel something for a change." At the end, Letterman's face appeared in the corner of the screen with a cigar and said that Gerry was the only writer who'd had his dream fulfilled. "He really is filled with self-loathing," he added, with an intentionally hollow laugh.

Some writers noticed a dip in morale, while others felt Letterman was becoming less receptive to bold new ideas and more focused on good bookings and solid jokes. Before the strike, Matt Wickline and Randy Cohen had proposed one of the most ambitious theme shows ever: the first talk show filmed underwater.

It was exactly the kind of idea that flourished in the middle of the decade. It sent up pointless technology while also showing a perspective that had never been seen before. The pitch imagined Letterman and the band wearing round, transparent helmets, like in a science fiction movie. Wickline found a French company that made a self-pressurized bubble helmet and said they would do it for free. All the same, it was an expensive show (about $70,000), but when it was pitched, in February 1988, Letterman was interested and participated in a run-through in a pool in New Jersey, assisted by a scuba instructor. It looked like a talk show dreamed up by Jules Verne. After the strike was over, Wickline found out that the underwater show had been canceled. "I heard years later that he had a really sore neck from doing it and was in excruciating pain," Wickline said. Letterman was also moving away from that style of show.

In a 1989 interview, Letterman balked at being called avant-garde. "I think it's true that in the early days we felt like we had to establish ourselves as being different, so maybe it was easier for us to do odd things and take more chances," he said. "But I think what has come over the years is a more consistent spirit."

At the same time Letterman proved that he could put on a funny show without writers, his relationship with the writer who had helped create *Late Night with David Letterman* ended. By 1988, Merrill Markoe was spending most of her time in Los Angeles and had little to do with *Late Night*. She was delivering weekly video reports (called "Merrill's L.A.") for a local station, in the style of her old remotes, and she did several pilots and wrote and directed a special for Showtime called *Merrill Markoe's Guide to Glamorous Living.*

She still talked regularly with Letterman by phone but could tell something was awry. Their conversations were dominated by Letterman's pessimism about his health, with dark talk of death and dying. They spent less time together. In her diary, she wrote, "He says he really misses me. I guess if only he weren't so burdened by having this darned vacation we would be together."

Once the strike was over, an already distant relationship fell apart entirely when she learned that she wasn't the only woman in his life. "I (ahem) intercepted some letters that came to the house and became aware of a lot of other stuff as well," Markoe explained circumspectly. In one of their final fights, she told him, "Look, you are either dying or you are dating. But you can't be both. Don't tell me you were dying and then it turns out you are dating. Pick one."

In the fall of 1988, Markoe changed her phone number and drew a cartoon of a talk-show host at a desk with a big slash through him. She put it on the front door of her home. It was over.

Rumors circulated around the office that Letterman had begun dating Regina Lasko, the unit manager on the show. And indeed, there is dispute over when the relationship with Markoe ended. Letterman would later say on the air that he and Lasko had started dating two years before he and Markoe broke up.

In a *Rolling Stone* interview reflecting on the end of this relationship that lasted about a decade, Letterman confessed that he "did not behave well at the end of that relationship." Soon after, Lasko left *Late Night* to work as a unit manager for *Saturday Night Live.*

"When Merrill left the show, the show in my view really suffered," said Cohen. "She brought him along in a certain way where he saw, even if they weren't his favorite pieces, he saw the value of doing them. No one else could be as unrelenting. One of her many fine qualities: if it were a piece she enjoyed, she would fight for it."

When asked about her impact on the show, Letterman said simply, "Without her, you and I wouldn't be sitting here."

That Letterman moved from a relationship with a writer to someone in production paralleled the power shift on the show. *Late Night* began as a show led by a dynamic writing staff, and much of their creativity and influence was due to Merrill Markoe, who embraced the cerebral silliness and ambition of her remote pieces, which were comic masterpieces. She also advocated for the show to be loose and improvisational.

The offices of *Late Night with David Letterman* were not a place where high-minded debates about comedy dictated the direction of the show. Everyone was too busy scrambling to fill the hour, but, as with any successful show, the people working on it were engaging in an implicit artistic debate: What exactly is this show's primary strength? The strike clarified a change: *Late Night* had become about the host and his eccentric personality. The audience didn't want to see him as a delivery system for jokes. They wanted to see his take on the world, which was neurotic, angry, and decidedly odd. "The show became more and more like what it is now," Jeff Martin said during Letterman's final year on the air. "A pure conveyance of Dave."

Merrill Markoe and David Letterman. Their creative partnership created the foundation of *Late Night*, and its legacy long outlived their romance. (COURTESY OF MERRILL MARKOE)

In the summer of 1980, David Letterman started hosting his first NBC show in the morning. It was canceled after four months but proved to be a critical test run for his late-night career. (COURTESY OF DENCY NELSON)

Merrill Markoe *(center)* helped find several writers who proved essential in establishing the comic voice of David Letterman, including Max Pross *(left)* and Tom Gammill *(right)* who created some of the finest satire of the first two years of *Late Night*. (COURTESY OF MERRILL MARKOE)

In the mid-1980s, *Late Night* embraced Steve Allen–inspired stunts. In this rehearsal from 1985, head writer Steve O'Donnell is wearing a suit of sponges before being dunked in the water.

At the end of 1983, most of the writing staff left, providing an opportunity for a new group that would define *Late Night* in its greatest era. *From left to right*: Sandy Frank, Randy Cohen, Matt Wickline, Chris Elliott, Eddie Gorodetsky, Joe Toplyn, and Jeff Martin.

Besides being the rare talk-show director with a singularly funny and innovative visual aesthetic, Hal Gurnee *(left)* made a considerable mark on late-night television because of his close bond and comedic chemistry with David Letterman. (COURTESY OF MERRILL MARKOE)

When Jack Rollins's powerhouse management company signed David Letterman in the 1970s, it gave the comic credibility. Rollins *(right)*, who also managed Woody Allen, would later become an executive producer of *Late Night* for a decade.

The *Late Night with David Letterman* staff playing softball in Central Park. Letterman has his arm around Barbara Gaines *(far left)*, who had worked with him since the morning show, ending her run as a producer at *The Late Show*.

From left to right: Maria Pope, who worked as everything from writer to producer for Letterman; head writer Steve O'Donnell; David Letterman and his assistant, Laurie Diamond.

Late Night with David Letterman won the Emmy Award for Outstanding Writing in a Variety, Comedy, or Music Program three years in a row, ending with this 1986 victory for its fourth-anniversary special, which took place on a plane in flight.

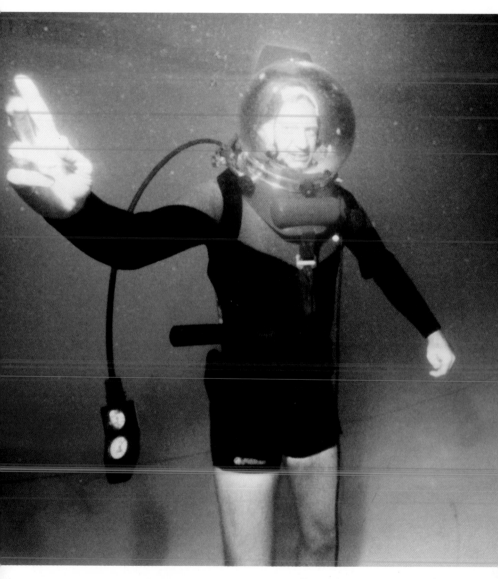

In 1988, *Late Night with David Letterman* attempted one of its most ambitious ideas, an episode underwater. This is a shot from a run-through, filmed in a pool in New Jersey. The idea was scrapped, as *Late Night*'s era of theme shows was coming to an end.

David Letterman's mother, Dorothy *(second from the left)*, became a regular fixture on *Late Night* toward the end of its run on NBC. Larry "Bud" Melman, another popular figure from the show is next to her, laughing.

Regina Lasko *(left)*, who worked for *Late Night* for several years in the late 1980s, and David Letterman. In 2009, they married.

David Letterman attending a 2011 staff holiday party and photo gallery exhibition given by his staff writer Steve Young *(on the right, in the distance). To the left*: Eric Stangel, one of the head writers, holding a glass.

(ROBERT CAPLIN)

MEG AND MOM

On February 11, 1991, the first shot in the late-night war was fired, a story in the *New York Post* titled "There Goes Johnny: NBC Looking to Dump Carson for Jay Leno."

As Bill Carter detailed in *The Late Shift*, the essential chronicle of the battle to succeed Johnny Carson, Leno's manager, Helen Kushnick (who had represented David Letterman in the 1970s), was the source for this story, which reported that Leno would replace Johnny Carson within a year. (It turned out to be a year and three months.) In the article, NBC spokesman Curt Block denied the claim but conceded that Leno "probably will replace Carson." David Letterman was not mentioned at all.

Letterman had been a leading candidate to succeed Carson since the late 1970s. Henry Bushkin and Dave Tebet, both of whom worked for Carson, had met with Letterman twice and told him they wanted him to eventually take over. Letterman assumed one day he would get a call from Carson or the head of NBC to offer him the job. It never happened.

By the early 1990s, Letterman had fallen out of favor among some at NBC, and many executives preferred Jay Leno, who was then the permanent guest host of *The Tonight Show*. Rick Ludwin, head of late-night programming at NBC, respected Letterman as a great entertainer but was skeptical that he could draw the broad swath of viewers that made up the *Tonight Show* audience. He also saw Letterman as difficult to deal with. Whereas Leno was friendly and approachable, Letterman was distant, even hostile. NBC's president, Warren Littlefield, had no personal relationship with him. Brandon Tartikoff, his predecessor, had told him, "You can't have a meal with Letterman." When he asked why not, Tartikoff said he was not "comfortable having food with people."

In an attempt to make a connection with the star, Littlefield had once sent Letterman a crystal decanter as a present. Letterman took the gift, put it on his desk during one show, and explained what it was to his audience, then proceeded to smash it with a hammer on the air. It didn't endear him to his bosses. "It was a little shocking to me," Littlefield said decades later, the memory still fresh in his mind. "He intimidated me."

When told this years later, Letterman emitted a hollow laugh: "Oh, that's delightful," he said sardonically, before describing himself as having been consumed with unearned righteous anger at the network at the time. Now he found his response ridiculous.

But it wasn't only his lack of a diplomatic touch that hurt his chances of getting *The Tonight Show*. Letterman's on-air shift to a crankier, more confessional persona concerned some at NBC. Ludwin saw his comedy as distinct from that of *The Tonight Show*, and didn't even see him in the tradition of Jack Paar. "Jack Paar would turn revelations into a joke," Ludwin said, explaining the difference.

"Dave didn't always do that. Sometimes it would end in bitterness and something nasty."

Since the strike, Letterman's ratings had slightly faded, particularly among younger viewers. It was nothing dramatic or even surprising. His audience was aging with him. "From the numbers, we knew his appeal was getting narrower and narrower in the demographic," said Sari DeCesare, who tracks ratings for NBC. "From 1988 to 1991, his audience got five years older. He wasn't picking up new viewers. The cranky Dave was not getting ratings in the demo."

Late-night talk shows had become a huge business for NBC, with *The Tonight Show* earning $75 million in revenue and *Late Night*, which charged about half as much for every thirty-second ad, making around $55 million. For NBC, this decision really mattered. What made it more complicated was that by the 1990s, the field was getting more crowded. Fox was looking for a new show after Joan Rivers hadn't panned out. ABC was trying to figure out how to introduce late-night talk while holding on to its news franchise with *Nightline*.

The Comedy Channel, an early incarnation of Comedy Central, had premiered *Night After Night with Allan Havey,* a show influenced by *Late Night* (it had viewer mail). The comic Dennis Miller, who had experience telling jokes behind a desk on Weekend Update at *Saturday Night Live,* was launching his own syndicated talk show. Letterman kept an eye on the competition. "I remember when Rick Dees got a talk show," said Madeleine Smithberg. "Suddenly it was: 'We've got to up our bookings.' I was like, 'Really?'"

Letterman was no longer the only cool alternative to *The Tonight Show.* The comic Arsenio Hall's syndicated late-night show captured younger audiences with a style that provided a sharp contrast. Letterman mocked show business; Hall wallowed in it. Letterman welcomed guests with halfhearted enthusiasm, while Hall turned these introductions into their own event, pumping up the crowd with his fevered patter. Letterman made fun of catchphrases; Hall called his band "my posse" and every night shook his fist to pump up the crowd, shouting phrases like "Let's . . . get . . . busy!"

In a *GQ* story with the cover line "Is He Still the King of Hip?" Letterman offered Hall faint praise: "You get the sense that fun is taking place," he said. In the monologue of one show, Paul Shaffer nodded to the competition by turning to Letterman and asking, "Are we your posse?" Letterman shook his head, at a loss for words.

The feature presented a portrait of a lonely man who had lost his longtime partner and girlfriend and even his dog. Bob, the dog who had stuck by the host since his first marriage and through several remote pieces directed by Merrill Markoe, had died. His photo was taken down from the set. "I've had this job longer than any other I've ever had," Letterman said. "When you do that, you become more focused and introverted than maybe is a good idea. So I think that's caused me to change a bit."

Letterman became increasingly gloomy. On the air, when a joke bombed, he could become existential, sometimes acting as if he was past his prime. "I'm feeling more and more like Bob Hope," he said to Paul Shaffer during the monologue of a March 1990 show. That the show was coasting became one of his running jokes, such as this entry Letterman read in a list of the top ten reasons *Cheers* was going off the air: "Unlike this show, they decided to quit when they ran out of ideas."

The day after the *New York Post* story, David Letterman had a conversation on the air with a book publicist named Meg Parsont. She had made her first appearance when he called the building across the street to see who was still at work at 5:20 p.m. She answered, and this prank call led to a peculiar on-air friendship spanning three years. On *Late Night*, Letterman called her about once a month to chat and make small talk in front of an audience of millions.

On this episode, Letterman was particularly cranky, ribbing Parsont about attending the show's anniversary party without saying hello, then asking her if she noticed all the "weasels there." Parsont seemed unimpressed by Letterman's celebrity. She didn't watch *Late Night* or know that he regularly called people from NBC weasels and pinheads. She was unaware of any stories about Jay Leno getting the job at *The Tonight Show.* She didn't know what he was going on about. Letterman wasn't interested in explaining, either. He vented.

"That's what sickened me at that party," he said sourly. "The staff and the crew, they're fine. But then there's the planeloads of weasels."

Letterman had talked to strangers on the street since the start of his show, but his conversations with Meg Parsont were something different. She became part of the cast of characters, but she wasn't an inept actor like Larry "Bud" Melman or a member of the staff. With her, Letterman became a boyish flirt, and the comedy of their segments didn't come from jokes so much as the tension of their chemistry. The relationship felt as real as the memories of a first date.

Letterman saw his conversations with Meg Parsont as one of the signal bits of his entire television career. "If you want something to represent the show, it's that," he said, with unusual pride. "You're not going to see that anywhere else. The chances of that working are minuscule. It didn't have the life of Stupid Pet Tricks, but in terms of an idea that, 'By God, we're going to show you how to do TV,' that was pretty good."

Letterman began talking to Meg Parsont right before reality television exploded in popularity. Ordinary people had been on television in game shows, documentaries like *An American Family*, prank shows like *Candid Camera*, and occasionally talk shows. While there were antecedents like *Real People*, the breakthrough for reality television was when *The Real World* premiered on MTV in 1992. This was when the mundane dramas of everyday people became weekly soap opera fodder for mass consumption.

Focusing on the anxieties of romance and the banal details of strangers living in a house, *The Real World* slickly edited the most meaningless spats among a diverse collection of young strangers to build narratives that for many people proved far more gripping than prime-time drama. Its characters (who became a new breed of television stars, the forerunners of the contestants on *The Bachelor* and even the Kardashians) still seemed more real than the characters on fictional shows.

Since the writers' strike, *Late Night* appealed to the same voyeuristic pleasures that would soon be exploited by the reality show genre. It had its own contrived narrative that its fans followed closely, and after a decade of peeling back the artifice of his show, Letterman invited you to see him as the protagonist of his own drama. He played the role of the ornery, aggrieved employee, furious at his bosses, an eccentric you could identify with, in part because he was surrounded by overly intense employees (Chris Elliott), phonies (Paul Shaffer), and doddering fools (think Larry "Bud" Melman). Then there was the love interest he fawned over (Meg Parsont) and the maternal figure he rolled his eyes at (his mom, Dorothy). You might say that *Late Night with David Letterman* became what happened when one talk-show host stopped being polite and started getting real.

D orothy Letterman made her first appearance on *Late Night with David Letterman* in the mid-1980s, on a "Take Your Parents to Work" theme show in which the band, staff, and guests all performed next to their mothers and fathers. Letterman occasionally mentioned his mother in jokes, where she was portrayed as vaguely disinterested in her son and his career. Letterman called her "the least demonstrative person in the world" and has told the story on his show of her coming backstage when he did one of his first big stand-up shows at Butler College, near his hometown in Indiana. Waiting anxiously for her response, he saw her enter his dressing room. She didn't compliment the performance or even mention it. In his telling, she said nothing but "We'll be going now."

After her husband died, Mrs. Letterman remarried a German man whom Letterman occasionally joked about around the office. "[Dave] called him 'the white angel of death,' which seems unfair, since he fought for us in World War II and got a Purple Heart," Steve O'Donnell said. Dorothy Letterman didn't become a regular character on the show, however, until June 1990, when her son called her on the air for help with a Top Ten List. She read the top ten things found in her refrigerator. Letterman got the idea of putting his mom on the show from Howard Stern, who used to call his mother on his radio show. Letterman was a regular listener to Stern's show and, as with Rush Limbaugh, respected his ability to create compelling conflict and stories over hours of broadcasting.

Later that month, Letterman called her again, asking her to review Driving Miss Daisy and Dick Tracy. They also talked about her Thanksgiving plans. In these exchanges, Letterman came off as the exasperated son, and Dorothy Letterman as polite and soft-spoken. One time, he played a prank, telling the audience his goal was to get his mother to mention a particular flower, so he called her and asked questions designed to get her to mention it. When she did, the audience cheered and Letterman threw the phone in the air. The joke was about how predictable Mom could be.

Unlike her first husband, Dorothy Letterman was not outgoing. Letterman had a more distant relationship with his mother. At times, he had trouble talking to her. "He loves his mother, but I think the relationship he has with her on the show is as close as they come," said Madeleine Smithberg.

As late as 1989, Letterman said his mother didn't watch his show, and years later he claimed she was embarrassed he was in show business.

Late Night writer Steve Young said Letterman once told him, "The only time my mother called me to say she enjoyed the show was after Ventriloquist Week. The only time ever."

Merrill Markoe could see things from his mother's side. "I remember one time we showed up in town and she didn't know we were coming," she said about a trip to Indiana. "And we showed up, and she was alarmed we were there. And he took that as a sign that she wasn't very happy to see him. He didn't give her an hour's notice; he just showed up. Who wouldn't be?"

In Dorothy Letterman's conversations on the show, she came off as sweet and sunny, if reserved, while her son acted flustered. The conflict of these exchanges was in seeing him gently prod her into expressing something outside of midwestern nice. When she would gently approve of a movie, Letterman pushed her on it. He would demand tougher treatment. She said, "It was just for fun."

M eg Parsont started appearing on the air at the same time that Dorothy Letterman did—in early 1990—and they both played critical roles in the first few years of the decade, the last of his show on NBC. By this point, Letterman ventured onto the street rarely, preferring to stay at his desk, talking to these women who had become regular characters: a potential love interest and a parent.

But the most riveting drama starring David Letterman was taking place offscreen, and now it was slowly inching its way onto the show. The tumultuous battle to succeed Johnny Carson was being covered exhaustively in the press and becoming its own soap opera. Its narrative was a kind of patriarchal struggle between two comics, David Letterman and Jay Leno, with intertwined histories. Leno had been an early influence on Letterman when they were both at the Comedy Store and yet owed much of his fame to regular appearances as a guest on *Late Night* throughout the 1980s. They both wanted the approval of Carson, and, of course, his job.

The late-night war changed *Late Night with David Letterman*. Before he finished his run at *Late Night*, his crankiness and natural irreverence toward his superiors started to take on a more urgent meaning. If you thought Letterman deserved the *Tonight Show* job, his complaints about General Electric as a soulless company with no idea about broadcasting now seemed confirmed. His grievances had a resonant context, filled out in the culture and business news regularly.

Parsont may not have known what Letterman was complaining about, but much of his devoted fan base did. Letterman had been making cracks about NBC for years, but they had grown increasingly personal and severe. In a guest spot on *The Tonight Show* in late 1990, Letterman complained about NBC for several minutes, before telling Carson that he had to go and "drop the audition tape off at CBS."

When the media started reporting that Leno would be the next host of *The Tonight Show*, Letterman's gripes began to carry a new frisson, his anger more purposeful. At times, Letterman seemed as if he was broadcasting behind enemy lines, sneaking in subversive messages when not actively trying his hand at sabotage.

On July 30, 1991, Jay Leno was guest-hosting *The Tonight Show*, and at a commercial break, the nightly promo that teased *Late Night with David Letterman* featured the usual shots of guests (Robert Klein!), followed by Letterman at his desk. "Hi, we're on NBC," he said, smiling through a pause, "for the time being."

Letterman had long played the hero who hated his boss; that was a role he'd inhabited since college. But with so much speculation over who would succeed Johnny Carson, he ramped up the hostility. Letterman had been a student of the genre. He knew how Arthur Godfrey had hurt his reputation by firing a colleague so publicly, and he understood the power of Jack Paar getting upset at NBC and angrily walking off the air. And he saw how Johnny Carson and the stars of *Saturday Night Live* poked fun at the network.

Letterman had become known for his dyspeptic personality, so he was suited to play the oppositional role. Why walk off your show like Jack Paar did, when you can *look* like you are about to walk off the air but stay, adding suspense and danger to your performance? Letterman and Leno were hardly the first stars to jockey for the same job on television. But David Letterman was the first to integrate this kind of backstage drama into the comedy of his show while building himself up into a cause. Dave Chappelle and Conan O'Brien turned their troubles with their respective networks into grist for comedy in the following decade, similarly becoming heroes to their fans.

L*ate Night* started taking on traits of a reality show right after its writing staff had its second major turnover. The staff had remained fairly consistent for six years. Some of the writers were frustrated by an inability to get bits on the show, but many also realized that they could make more money in Hollywood. With the expansion of cable television and the comedic ambitions of the Fox network, the entertainment universe was growing, and more jobs were opening up for comedy writers. Being a writer on the most influential show in late night made you in demand. Creative Artists Agency agents started calling them, talking up new shows and moving to the West Coast.

Kevin Curran was one of the first to move to a sitcom when he took a job at *Married with Children* in 1989. The next year, *Late Night*'s eighth-anniversary show was shot in Los Angeles, and Jeff Martin recalled an eye-opening visit with Curran. "He had us over to his house, and he had a good-sized house in Hollywood Hills. And we were like 'Wow!'" Martin said. "And you start thinking, 'I know I'm as good as this guy.'" Martin later went to work at *The Simpsons*.

Joe Toplyn and Matt Wickline went to work for the sketch show *In Living Color*. Toplyn then moved to *The Tonight Show*. Fred Graver went to work for Norman Lear. Chris Elliott and Adam Resnick started their own sitcom, *Get a Life*, on Fox. Letterman tried to keep Elliott, but he had yet to get his own production company, Worldwide Pants, off the ground. "He had the rights to Howdy Doody," Elliott said. "He brought it up to me after I brought up *Get a Life*. He said, 'Is there anything we could do with the Howdy Doody idea?'"

A new staff of young talent was hired, including Paul Sims, Steve Young, Spike Feresten, Joe Furey, Bill Scheft, and Nell Scovell. Young was a devoted fan, but now that he was on staff, he had trouble figuring out what the host wanted. The writers typically sat in a windowless conference room for four hours after the show, trying to come up with jokes for the next day, the vast majority of which Letterman either rejected or agreed reluctantly to try. There was an air of desperation in the room.

"The old-timers, like Randy Cohen, were saying we would never stay late after the show," Young said. "There was a feeling I arrived too late and missed all the fun."

Letterman had long distanced himself from his material with sarcasm or a self-mocking gibe. But he became more blunt in his disdain for a failing joke. In one show, he walked onstage, took a look at the cue cards, and clearly didn't like what he saw. A frozen smile was plastered on his face. He shook his head and told the unseen stagehand to skip it and move to the next joke. The audience chuckled. Letterman didn't like that one, either. So he gave up on the opening entirely and walked to his desk without telling a single joke. Letterman had the look of a guy who was sick of the grind and decided to just not show up for work. This wasn't an anomaly.

Letterman's grumpy mood was in tune with the style of the late-night-war era, one in which the host's unease became the main subject.

Instead of making fun of the jokes that his writers had worked on, now he just ignored them entirely.

He didn't want to do remotes with strangers and ceased making phone calls for audience members. (The last straw may have been when he called a widow who said the person they were looking for was dead.) That left fewer options for the staff as they looked for ways to put him in situations where he could improvise and ad-lib. What he would do was talk from his desk, with familiar people, mediated by technology. He called pay phones on the street or random people in the telephone book in other cities to ask about the weather. He sent cameras into the street and asked strangers in photo stores, "Can we see your photos, please?"

More of *Late Night* became about Meg Parsont. Her segments all began the same way: Letterman asking Paul Shaffer for "a little dialing music," then shifting to a shot of her window across the street. "We provide this service for snipers," Letterman said in one setup. While the first episodes with Parsont shifted right to a shot of the back of her head, this eventually became prefaced with a view of closed blinds from inside the office of *Late Night*. Then you saw a hand open them, revealing Parsont's building across the street. Then the long shot zoomed in to a woman in one of the cubicles.

It echoed the famous image out of Alfred Hitchcock's *Rear Window*: an attractive blond woman inside the square window. The camera lingered there as Letterman dialed the phone, putting the viewer in the position of voyeur. We saw her, but she didn't know anyone was watching her—or at least it appeared that way. (She later came to expect calls on certain days and would be given a heads-up.) Then her phone rang. She picked it up. The whole setup appealed to the natural curiosity of anyone who had ever looked up at a skyscraper and wondered about the lives that it holds.

The conversations between Letterman and Parsont were filled

with chat about her weekend, holiday plans, and other small talk. If Letterman pried too much, she balked. Their early conversations had an odd formality, like that of a date at the soda fountain. "I am very fond of you," Letterman would say. "Thank you," she responded.

After talking to Parsont every month for a year, Letterman became increasingly forward, asking her pointed questions about her boyfriend, deliberately misremembering his name. He sounded like an eager member in a long-distance relationship, charmingly giddy to see his lost love. "Have you missed me? Have you thought about me?" Letterman would ask Parsont, sounding like a man with a broken heart. When she said she did, he paused, then became more aggressive: "In what sense, exactly?"

The audience picked up this charged dynamic and started hooting and whistling when she came on the screen. Her boyfriend, incidentally, did not like her segments. (They later broke up.) It's no surprise, considering that Letterman often extravagantly flattered her, his attention veering from the sweet to the inappropriate, with a leering innuendo or a mumbled hint to disrobe.

Their early discussions occasionally enlisted her in stunts, like dropping a paper airplane or a roll of toilet paper out the window. These tasks aimed for a visual effect, but they eventually took on the feel of the tropes of a romantic comedy. For an early birthday gift, Letterman sent over thirty floral arrangements. The next year, on her birthday, he had the Jamestown High School marching band perform on the street below her window in a formation that spelled out "Meg." Another time, he sent over clams and even a live turkey. One day, he sent over a horse to ride down a Midtown street.

The relationship was, of course, one-sided. We found out about Parsont, but she didn't ask anything of Letterman. We saw her, but she couldn't see him. Letterman always kept her at a distance, which was how he was most comfortable. Off the air, Letterman and Parsont almost never talked. But on the air, they bantered like old friends, which in a strange way they had become. She was one of the few people on the show who could make David Letterman look happy and calm. Often he would go for minutes without any jokes. But their conversations were far more unpredictable than the comedy bits on the show, and they made Parsont an unusual celebrity.

People magazine profiled Parsont, and she was invited to appear on radio shows. Before the Internet made every person one viral video away from celebrity, a random stranger becoming a television star was unusual, even bizarre. Parsont still seems a bit baffled about why her exchanges with Letterman were popular. She now lives on the Upper West Side of Manhattan and remains in publishing as a freelance publicist. "There was a slightly voyeuristic quality, and I was aware of that," she said recently, offering up a theory. "They were gazing into my office."

The way Letterman talked about sex on the show changed. In his first few years on *Late Night*, he cringed at the subject, playing the prude for laughs. When Dr. Ruth Westheimer suggested that women could use cucumbers to pleasure themselves, Letterman walked away from his guest, leaving his desk empty. George Miller, one of Letterman's best friends from the Comedy Store days, who had regularly appeared on *Late Night* since the beginning, did an imitation of Letterman engaging in foreplay, saying, in a stilted television anchor voice, "Let's get on with it, shall we?"

By the end of the decade, Letterman was working in a brand of comedy that tapped into the smirking humor of blunt innuendo and leering that would only expand in later decades. When interviewing a female talk-show host from China, she asked him about exotic foods, saying, "Have you ever had the hump of a camel?" Letterman's face lit up. "No," he said, then added, "But when I was young, I was pretty good."

It's hard to imagine Letterman making this overtly sexual joke in his early years on television. But it became a regular part of his comedic repertoire. "In the beginning, I was doing Johnny," Letterman explained, about how he imitated Johnny Carson's self-conscious awkwardness toward anything sexual. By the 1990s Letterman had become a star, and he shifted his approach to getting an easy laugh from a sex joke. "I think it comes from being on the air too long, being tired, lazy."

Models became regular guests, and it often seemed that their purpose was nothing more than to be the subject of boorish advances. When interviewing Jerry Hall in a cleavage-baring dress, Letterman said, "Sitting next to you, I get the awful feeling I may have overinflated my tires."

Letterman turned his infatuation with the news anchor Connie Chung into a running gag, inviting her on the show and mercilessly poking fun at her husband, Maury Povich. When he had Dolly Parton on, he asked if she exercised, and she said she did. "Yeah, I'd like to see you sweaty," he said.

Was Letterman satirizing or just indulging male fantasies? By the end of the decade, having become a star cheered on by his crowds, it was more of the latter. Letterman lavished attention on actresses' appearances, introducing many on the show as "leggy." He had always poked fun at such clichés, but if you repeat something often enough, the satire can fade away.

"That's super-complicated," Steve O'Donnell said, explaining Letterman's relationship to women. "We liked using a phrase like "leggy supermodel" because it seemed jarring, but you couldn't disentangle the pleasure Letterman got from it. At first it was a joke, another show-biz cliché, but then you couldn't tell how much Dave was enjoying the Brazilian supermodel."

The show started booking more models, not just as guests but also in remote videos. One began with Letterman shopping in a hardware store, setting up a scene in which he might find comedy from interactions with customers or salesmen. But that was how the early version of *Late Night* would have handled a remote. In the middle of this bit, Letterman said to the camera, "Let's hang out with models." Then he jumped in a car with a team of beautiful women and they played on the beach. At one point, he saw Paul Shaffer, with actors playing his kids and an overweight wife looking miserable.

The joke emphasized that it was good to be rich, famous, and hanging out with beautiful women. It was pure fantasy, with no ironic distance. "At the time, it was supposed to be bizarre, not leering," O'Donnell said. "But nevertheless, the leggy supermodels started appearing more and more."

Letterman had long been a host who refused to show any emotion. But he was becoming someone else, at least on his show. His strength as a talk-show host was his willingness to explore his own personality, but he also increasingly riffed on his image, inhabiting different roles. He was a nervous son needling his mother and an immature suitor trying to make a girl like him and an obnoxious jerk objectifying a model. Letterman was showing us more, filling out his television character, and not necessarily in an appealing way.

By the early 1990s, old episodes of *Late Night* aired on A&E, so fans could watch two hours of the show every day. One ad featured Letterman saying, "It is not so much a television show as a nightly plea for help." His assistant, Laurie Diamond, said, "Whenever I see that, I think he's just telling us the truth here. At that desk, he's working out this angst that most of us work out on the couch."

Three months after the *New York Post* story, Carson made it official that he was retiring, starting a month of speculation that led, at least at first, to NBC's choosing Jay Leno. NBC executives Warren Littlefield and John Agoglia flew to New York to tell Letterman. "When I told him, he was shocked," Littlefield said. "He said, 'I'm not that young. I want *The Tonight Show.'* That was the most direct and honest and the most contact I had with him. He looked me in the eye."

Letterman didn't say as much in public, but his anger was evident on the show. In a conversation with Parsont that month, he was in an irritable mood. Instead of undermining her boyfriend, he said she could do much better than him. Then, when he saw in the background a woman's bare leg, his focus shifted again. When Parsont got in his way, he said bitterly, "There aren't many benefits of doing this job, and you just fouled one up."

One week later, a photo of Warren Littlefield appeared on the set. This was Letterman's idea. Paul Shaffer drew attention to it: "Who is that picture over there?" Hal Gurnee cut right to a close-up of Littlefield, while Letterman played innocent. "It's NBC president of entertainment Warren Littlefield." After more banter, Letterman said, with mock warmth, "It makes me feel like home."

That Leno was getting the *Tonight Show* job was now official, and Letterman expressed displeasure the way he usually did: indirectly, sarcastically, with a half-articulated edge.

He introduced this photo with little context or explanation, and certainly didn't mention the late-night news that was occupying the newspapers. This turned *Late Night* into a better reality show: now his running battle with his bosses was a fight with stakes. Would he leave the network? Would he stay and undermine *The Tonight Show*? Tune in and find out.

Letterman vented at Meg, acted irritated by his mom, and expressed muffled fury at his boss. Who couldn't relate? It made for excellent television, even if it was an entirely different version of the show from the experimental early years or the formally audacious shows of the middle of the decade. In this *Late Night*, Letterman didn't need punch lines. When he brought attention to the photo of Littlefield or mentioned network weasels, the crowd cheered. It became a storyline straight out of professional wrestling. But this wasn't a fake narrative. Letterman was expressing the real hurt he felt at being passed over for the job that he thought he deserved.

"I decided that I didn't like Warren Littlefield because I didn't get *The Tonight Show*," Letterman said, looking back at his behavior on the show. "I blamed the whole thing on him. Rather than accept responsibility myself, I decided, 'I'll blame somebody else.' That's it." Letterman emitted one of his loud laughs that fizzle out, a hollow expression of bitter mirth. "At the time, I was up to my nose in 'God dammit!'" he added, making an angry, righteous face.

Letterman's fury at Littlefield and the network was exacerbated by talking about it on the show. His off-camera disputes moved into the comedy on the show, and the distinction between his real grievances and the ones he aired on television seemed to blur. Anyone who watched Letterman regularly knew that his dispute with NBC wouldn't get patched up easily.

The mood in the office darkened. The network's jockeying to keep Letterman, and then his maneuverings to possibly get the job back from Leno, continued for the next year and a half, which caused a cloud around the office. "It definitely felt like there was a seismic shift and things were moving," Smithberg said. "There was stress throughout the food chain."

At the end of August, Letterman went on *The Tonight Show*, and as soon as he sat down, Carson asked him bluntly, "Just how pissed off are you?" Letterman said he wasn't, but of course that was the kind of diplomatic thing you would say on *The Tonight Show*.

Letterman was furious at his manager, Jack Rollins, for not doing more to position him for the job. When *The Tonight Show* announced that Leno got the job, Letterman had called Rollins, who told him,

"You don't really want that show. It's just a bunch of blue-haired la-dies." Rollins saw Letterman the way many of his fans did: as an innovative performer who preferred to be doing daring comedy rather than work under the inevitable constraints of appealing to a much larger audience on *The Tonight Show.*

What he didn't understand was that Letterman didn't see himself that way. He had bigger ambitions. He wanted to replace Johnny Car-son. "I held Jack responsible," Letterman said, once again appearing contrite. "But that might not have been fair."

In the late 1970s and early '80s, Rollins had provided credibility for Letterman as he started out in television, but by the time of the late-night war, he was getting older and was not as plugged in as he once was.

Letterman subsequently fired Rollins and hired Michael Ovitz, a co-founder of CAA and one of the most powerful men in show busi-ness. Ovitz was aggressive and imaginative, and he knew everyone in show business. He sold his clients on his having the best intelligence in Hollywood. Ovitz had heard that CBS was interested in expanding into late night, and ABC and Fox were curious about making changes. "We knew we had a lot of buyers," he said. "So when Dave came in, I had already reviewed his contract and had a complete strategy."

Littlefield said that, from the start, Letterman didn't focus on money or terms. What he wanted was to get *The Tonight Show,* which, despite the Leno announcement, was still in play, as some at NBC were having second thoughts. In a recent interview, Ovitz said Letterman would have taken less money to replace Carson, and that if he were primarily motivated by money, he would have made movies with Disney and renegotiated his NBC contract in the mid-1980s, as Jack Rollins had wanted him to. But that's not to say that money didn't matter to Letterman. "There's that old thing: How do you spell respect in Hollywood? With dollar signs," Steve O'Donnell said.

Ovitz set up meetings with many networks and helped facili-tate a bidding war, but he always viewed CBS as the best outcome.

"From day one, in the back of my head—and I never revealed this to anyone—I always felt it was CBS's to lose," he said. "They had a network, a lot of money, huge promotional development, a savvy guy with Howard Stringer. I knew they would pay the most money." Ovitz added that because Letterman wanted *The Tonight Show*, and there was a tradition of late night at the network, he had less leverage with NBC. "NBC—he wanted the show—would have been the most lean return for him, because they knew they had him. I also always felt Warren Littlefield was leaning to Jay over Dave," he said.

NBC head Warren Littlefield remembered it differently, saying that, because of Letterman's history of brilliant broadcasting, the *Tonight Show* job was his to lose, but that the negotiation with Ovitz made it impossible to make a deal. "Ovitz wanted significant salary, ownership of the show, and ownership of the following show," he said. "It was extremely aggressive in its demands. So we had to take a moment and ask ourselves, 'Does this actually make sense? Why should we give up ownership? Why should we do any of these things?' Had there been some compromise, we wouldn't have been able to take a strong position and ask if this makes sense. But there wasn't. My analysis is: Mike Ovitz overplayed his hand."

As news of this high-stakes negotiation leaked to the press, Letterman was making changes in the artistic direction of the show. His head writer, Steve O'Donnell, could sense that he was no longer in the good graces of the brass, even though he never heard that directly from Letterman. He simply heard less from him. One night in 1992, it was an hour before taping and they were still trying to figure out a comedy act. O'Donnell suggested they do a remote where they would go outside and try to find a baby. "That was the final blow for Letterman," Morton said.

But as with Sand, Letterman didn't fire O'Donnell so much as slowly phase him out. "Someone suggested Dave was trying to get

[me] to quit," O'Donnell said. But O'Donnell stayed on for three more years, graciously leaving the head writer job while staying on the writing staff. His replacement as head writer was Rob Burnett, who would prove to be the critical writer during the move to CBS.

Burnett had started as an intern, but he moved up quickly to the talent department, then was an assistant writer, a writer, and finally the head writer, before becoming producer. He would remain with Letterman until his retirement, becoming a favorite of the host and a confidant, earning a reputation on staff for being smart, funny, and ambitious. When Burnett first worked for the talent department, his boss went on vacation, and Burnett took the opportunity to rearrange her desk, build a filing cabinet, and organize all her shoes under her desk. "It was a one-hundred-percent case of sucking up, but it's also what I should have been doing," Burnett said. "I was unabashed about it."

He developed a relationship with Letterman, buying him a series of hot sauces for his birthday, one for every year, and delivering them to his house. "He did things like, on Dave's fortieth birthday, he got lacrosse balls and wrote numbers for each year. That was a little unctuous," the writer Dave Rygalski said.

Make no mistake: Burnett was a funny, nimble, and gifted comic writer who had a wide skill set that would come in handy on a bigger platform. "Steve O'Donnell had the original show dreaminess and oddness, the inexplicable beauty," Steve Young explained. "Rob Burnett certainly partook of that and loved it, but was a much more mainstream, eleven-thirty, 'We're going to get stuff that a wide audience is going to get and enjoy. And we're not going to be overly quirky.' He's more of a professional managerial sort, and it's what Dave wanted."

The network fight to keep Letterman heated up throughout 1992, with NBC trying to hold on to him for *Late Night* and then returning to the possibility of *The Tonight Show*. As Michael Ovitz shopped him around to other networks, Letterman's stock rose quickly. As it became clear he was in demand, Letterman started to become more open to new ideas. In the last year before Letterman moved to CBS, *Late Night* embraced more new scripted comedy, introducing new characters and expanding the opening remarks from three jokes to four. Kathleen Ankers, the longtime designer of the show, played Peggy the Foul-Mouthed Chambermaid, a proper English lady who cursed Letterman even more than the Guy Under the Seats had. And then there was Dwight the Troubled Teen, who acted out and ran offstage.

Then there was the page with the fake British accent, which was as straightforward as it sounded. "Let me hear you say 'snooker,' Letterman said to close the bit. One of the more popular sketches began with an idea from Steve Young to have a strongman going around the city breaking things. Rob Burnett liked the idea, brought it to Letterman, and together they refined it into "The Strong Man, the Fat Guy, the Genius," a remote where the characters with these names roamed around the city with Letterman. The strong guy looked for things to break. The smart guy would answer any question. And the fat guy would eat anything.

After a huge amount of backroom drama, Letterman eventually decided to move to CBS to start a new talk show, for a staggering salary widely reported to be $16 million a year, as well as ownership of the show and of the program in the following time slot. Once he signed in January, he started making shows with an eye toward a bigger stage. He did more press than he had in years, visiting affiliates. On the air, his show remained focused on his own life. In his final show at NBC, his monologue did not riff on anything topical and completely ignored the news. The premises were all built on his fractured relationship with NBC, the history of the woman who broke into his house, and some absurd joke about the sexual tension between Letterman and NBC newsman Garrick Utley.

All of the jokes on the final show require knowledge of the soap opera of David Letterman's life. His monologue had once been about newsmakers and stars. But by 1993, Letterman was one of the biggest stars in America, and he had a firm hold on his own public narrative. He ended the show with a clip of himself riding off on a horse, the hero leaving alone.

NBC's Rick Ludwin attended the show for the finale, even though his relationship with the host had become strained. "I went," he said, "just so he wouldn't say on the air that no one from NBC was there."

PART V

THE VERY BIG SHOW

1993–2015

The hookers in Times Square are now offering something they call their CBS special. For an extra twenty bucks, they'll guarantee you'll finish last.

—David Letterman, the *Late Show*, September 22, 1995

THE AGONY OF VICTORY

t was a duel between stark opposites: the difficult artist versus the blue-collar everyman, the ironic absurdist against the punch-line specialist, the acerbic smart aleck facing off with Mr. Nice.

This was how the media portrayed the rivalry between David Letterman and Jay Leno. However simplified the contrast may have been, it did make for great drama. As much as the shows themselves, this competition put late-night talk at the center of popular culture. But the late-night war, as it was called, would not be won or lost in the press. Ratings (and the hundreds of millions of advertising dollars that come with them) are what matter in network television, and when the *Late Show with David Letterman* premiered on August 30, 1993, opposite *The Tonight Show with Jay Leno*, the comedians were in competition for the same audiences looking to be entertained at 11:30 p.m.

The Tonight Show, the signature late-night talk show for nearly half a century, had always led the pack, boosted by the power of the NBC lineup and a series of likable comics at the helm. David Letterman ended this remarkable run.

The CBS *Late Show* proved to be a hit right from the start. Bill Murray was Letterman's first guest, just as he had been on *Late Night with David Letterman*, and not long after he rushed onstage, he told Letterman he had some advice. He explained how Chevy Chase (who would start an infamously terrible talk show on the Fox network one week after *Late Show* premiered) had told him it's important to get your name out there. He took out a can of spray paint and spelled DAVE on Letterman's desk.

Two weeks after Letterman started his new show, Conan O'Brien, a former *Simpsons* writer plucked from obscurity by Lorne Michaels, started his hosting tenure at *Late Night* with a video that portrayed him preparing for his new job, walking through the streets of New York as strangers repeatedly compared him to Letterman (Tom Brokaw warned, "You better be as good as Letterman") until finally he arrived at his office and decided to hang himself. The intimidating prospect of following David Letterman was the subject of a joke even on the network that he'd spurned. O'Brien would eventually establish his own distinct style. Six months after his premiere on CBS, Letterman returned to his old studios to appear on *Late Night*. O'Brien asked him if he was surprised by how much attention leaving *Late Night* and moving networks had received. "I had no idea that it was that important," Letterman said, then couldn't resist a shot at his old employers. "And NBC had no idea that it was that important."

Not only did Letterman regularly beat *The Tonight Show* in the ratings, but his victory was even greater in the press. Two months after the premiere of the *Late Show, People* ran an article declaring Letterman the "rightful heir" to Johnny Carson, adding that, because of him, "subversion has become convention." The next month,

Tom Shales, the influential television critic from the *Washington Post*, wrote in *Playboy* that Letterman was "the new lord of late night and heir apparent to the title of National Comedian."

In February of the next year, the *New York Times* ran a story with this headline: "How Letterman (and CBS) Won." The late-night war appeared to have ended in a rout. Letterman's opponents responded by imitating him (Leno started doing phone calls from his desk and more remote bits with him on the street) or disappearing. Fox canceled *The Chevy Chase Show* after less than a month, and *The Arsenio Hall Show*, which was dropped by many CBS affiliates once the *Late Show* premiered, went off the air in May.

Even when things went wrong at the *Late Show*, David Letterman came out on top. Madonna appeared as a guest at the end of March, in a disruptive mood, and in her interview she decided to curse as much as possible, saying "fuck" fourteen times, which posed a challenge to the network censors. Letterman was upset and uncomfortable. But it helped that the *Late Show* notched its highest ratings since its premiere.

Rob Burnett, the head writer, said he noticed the unstoppable popularity of the show when they aired a remote piece with Letterman going door to door with pizzas, which neither of them was particularly confident about. "It did not work," Burnett said. "People weren't home. Dave didn't click. It just fell apart." And yet they aired it anyway, with shots of Letterman knocking on doors and no one answering. "The audience was so with him," Burnett recalled, "that you could get away with a lot."

The most meaningful sign of success may have come on May 13, when the *Late Show* traveled to Los Angeles for the new show's first road trip, which received much fanfare and promotion. In one episode, after his opening remarks, standing at his desk, Letterman introduced "the host of *The Tonight Show*"—and here he took a slight pause, as if to make the point that Leno was *not* the real host—"for thirty years: Johnny Carson."

Carson had stayed out of the public eye since he left *The Tonight Show* and never appeared with Leno, so this was a booking coup. But instead of him, it was Calvert DeForest who walked out, told a joke, and returned offstage. Now that the audience thought the whole thing was a joke, Carson entered. Looking a little stouter than usual, he walked onstage, handed Letterman the Top Ten List, and sat down behind the desk. The crowd roared for a minute, Carson chuckled, and then he walked offstage. Letterman looked in awe. Without saying a word, Carson had made it clear which late-night host he preferred and provided a satisfying coda to the drama of the late-night war: David Letterman was the favorite son. Carson never appeared on television again, though he did periodically send Letterman jokes for his show.

It had been almost exactly nine years since Carson appeared on *Late Night* for the first time, both appearances symbolic signs of success.

By every conceivable metric, David Letterman was the most important talk-show host in the country. He had done what no one had accomplished: beaten *The Tonight Show* in the ratings. And he had done it on his own terms. Yet his misery remained. No one who worked with him saw any evidence that Letterman was enjoying his triumph or found any relief from his nagging worries and sense of impending doom. There was always another show he could mess up. "He always complained, from the very beginning," Hal Gurnee said. "Well, it got worse and worse when he got to CBS. Any flaw, minor flaw, he exaggerated." Paul Shaffer said that winning in the ratings was the goal, but it made him uneasy, too. "He was most uncomfortable at number one," he said.

For his whole life, Letterman maintained a ferocious fear of failure, but that didn't mean success made him happy. He fixated on guests botching their stories, or himself looking too old, or flubbing the setup to a joke. "He was always interested in the audience, but never satisfied with them," said Steve O'Donnell, who stayed on as a writer until 1995. "It was always too many college students, not enough college students. They laugh but don't whoop. They whooped, not applauded."

At the end of 1994, he did two interviews with major magazines—*Esquire* and *Rolling Stone*—both of which presented him as anxious and pessimistic, if not outright despairing, despite leading in the ratings. They included many scenes of his gloom, including one at a commercial break when he said to his producer, Robert Morton, "This is an audience who's watching somebody who's lost."

It didn't matter if his ratings were high or low or if he got *The Tonight Show* or not. "Everyone is born with an emotional thermostat," said longtime writer Steve Young. "You can nudge it up and down, but it will always revert to its natural setting. His was that he was never truly comfortable unless he was seething with unhappiness at something."

In his last years at *Late Night*, Letterman had always been blunt about his feelings and exposed more of himself, turning it into comedy. He continued in this vein on CBS, but it was more difficult to indulge his oddball streak on the *Late Show*. In part this was due to the earlier time slot and the pressure of appealing to a larger audience, but it also had to do with leaving the studio for the Ed Sullivan Theater. Letterman now had a huge new 461-seat home that was much more unforgiving to jokes that bombed than his intimate studio had been. This had a significant impact on the show. The band became larger, and Shaffer played loud music when guests appeared.

Now when Letterman walked onstage, he would roam around, wide-eyed and jittery, while the band jacked up the energy. At *Late Night*, Letterman walked toward the camera, gave it a sideways glance, and played directly to the viewers at home. He was a master at using the camera, but now he was more pointedly performing for the live audience. Yet he didn't abandon his quirks. They just got bigger.

His characteristic tic became a raspy, booming laugh that was always a little too loud to be genuine. He unleashed this guffaw when a joke bombed. But it never seemed to be only a dig at himself. Letterman had long been clever at employing subtle gestures that indicated disapproval: the repeating of a phrase, a lingering pause, a shift in his tone of voice. This laugh was not subtle. It was the kind of noise that matched the expanded orchestra (no longer the "world's most dangerous band"). His laugh was so extreme that it could seem a defiant expression of his own strangeness, a desperate refusal to smooth out his edges. Other times, it seemed a shouting yelp of triumph from a comic who had finally reached the height of success.

Within a few years, Rob Burnett would run Letterman's production company, Worldwide Pants, which Letterman hoped would outlive the talk show. Burnett had achieved a unique position. He not only had the host's trust and friendship, but he also appeared to be able to manage his dark moods. "Rob and I became very close when we moved to CBS," said Letterman, who made very few new friends. "Rob was the golden boy," Steve Young said. "For a while, Dave hailed him as a genius."

Burnett's writing partner, Jon Beckerman, had sway in the writers' room. "Rob and Jon would go in the back room and basically write everything. If the other ten of us happened to write something good, then maybe we could get a joke on the show," Young explained, saying that the writers rarely saw Letterman. "It felt like we were being kept around out of a sense of duty and politeness and no one really cared what we brought to the show, because it had already been decided in the back room."

It wasn't only writers, and whether fair or not, some saw Burnett as responsible for the growing distance between Letterman and his staff.

"Rob would exclude everyone," said Barbara Gaines, who became an associate producer when the show moved to CBS. "He alienated everyone from Dave. It used to be that Dave knew everyone's name and was in everyone's office." Letterman had in fact been growing distant from the staff for years. But Burnett and Letterman had personal chemistry. "He hooked right into Dave's psyche," Gaines said.

In the month before the *Late Show* went on the air, it was impossible to watch CBS without seeing the promo announcing, "Same Dave. Better time. Different channel." It ran so often that Letterman said in *Time* magazine that he was officially embarrassed. But was it the same Dave? And which one? Was it the Indiana weatherman with an absurdist streak from his first era, the freewheeling showman from the second, or the confessional neurotic of the last few years at NBC?

Letterman did change. If anything, he became even more of the focus, with Paul Shaffer talking less than he had on the old show. His mother returned as a correspondent. But the old clubhouse feel was gone. There was less room for baffling comedy that didn't get a response from the crowd. "I think the biggest change in the show was caused by the theater," Burnett said. "That's the most tangible difference. When you are in that theater, and 461 people are sitting there, it's a lot different than doing it in 6A, which was 186 people."

Letterman favored jokes with scale and spectacle. His stunts became more elaborate. Instead of dropping a watermelon from a roof, he had a professional bowler toss a ball down the street into a television set. The show opened not with a dark shot snaking through a bar, but with a view of the New York skyline. Letterman told Hal Gurnee to make New York look like a postcard for the opening. "The first year and a half at CBS was fun," said Steve Young. "Every night a circus." Letterman could no longer sarcastically refer to his show as an extravaganza, because it now actually looked like one.

Letterman still poked fun at everything around him, but now his target was not the shabbiness of his show; it was its waste of money and effort. When he introduced graphics that celebrated the Top Ten List with flying colorful letters, he pointed and quipped, "That's a million dollars right there." He would still try to make sarcastic remarks about himself ("the most powerful man in broadcasting"), but now they sounded more like Howard Stern's huckster boasts than self-deprecating insults.

CBS was much more lavish with money than NBC. And among the writers, the emphasis was on scale. With this in mind, Dave Hanson pitched ringing a gong used at the Cathedral of Saint John the Divine for the show, and it got accepted. He emphasized the size in the pitch. Letterman no longer seemed like a guy who'd broken into the studio to put on a show or a misbehaving employee. He became a rich star playing with his toys.

Burnett worried that the show worked too hard to have a sense of event. "At a certain point, we veered into energy over comedy," he admitted. In various high-concept jokes that had some of the old Steve Allen style, the *Late Show* became home to 101 Dalmatians and crowds of construction workers.

Letterman had never focused on the opening monologue in the same way that Jay Leno did. It was part of the show, but not necessarily the most important one. The original *Late Night with David Letterman* included only a joke or two at the start, then grew to three or four jokes that sometimes poked fun at the news, but often not at all. But on the *Late Show*, Letterman began with a much more traditional set. The monologue became its own division, with the former stand-up comic Bill Scheft in charge. Instead of three or four, Letterman now told eight jokes a night. It later doubled to sixteen. The punch lines were more topical and direct, the setups elaborate so that everyone understood. Letterman dedicated a huge number of jokes to the figure-skating firestorm that erupted after Tonya Harding ordered someone to hurt Nancy Kerrigan. Bill Clinton was a favorite target, his love of fast food becoming Letterman's go-to insult. (The last joke in "Clinton's Top Ten New Year's Resolutions," on a January show, was "Summit with Ronald McDonald.")

Jokes about jokes became increasingly scarce. The show ceased doing sketches that depended on style instead of punch lines. Burnett found that oddball jokes without hard punch lines would not get passed. He needed jokes that would get laughs from a broad cross section of people, not ones that would baffle. Letterman always wanted laughs, of course, but he could be talked into strange concepts, ones that could lead to awkward silence. On the bigger stage, he was focused on reaching the broadest possible audience, but just as important was making that larger crowd in the theater laugh. During the 1993 summer preparation between shows, Letterman and Rob Burnett worked feverishly to build up a backlog of seventeen remote pieces for when the show premiered. This set a standard that they couldn't sustain. "I think we hurt ourselves in the long haul," Letterman said.

Letterman quickly moved from one bit to another and almost never went outside the theater to talk to people. His interviews became longer, but there was less spontaneity or room for chance. Guests who could really sell a joke to the back row became more important.

Martin Short had long been a popular guest, who would do impressions and tell jokes. In the first week at CBS, Short sang a Broadway show tune, in honor of the new theater. The next time he was on the show, Letterman asked him to do another, along with two segments at the desk. This became the norm for every one of his appearances—a sit-down interview, plus a song-and-dance number. By the time the *Late Show* finished its run, Short had done twenty-five flashy song-and-dance numbers, with singers and show girls and elaborate lighting. Letterman wanted Short to do more than just do impressions and tell stories. He wanted a big show.

The battle for star guests became fierce. Some, like Howard Stern and Bill Murray, were clearly Letterman guests and stayed off other shows. "I did feel a proprietary obligation to Dave, a loyalty," Steve Martin said about the late-night war. "I also found my material went over better on Letterman. His audience felt like New Yorkers and out-of-towners. Leno's felt like out-of-towners."

The *Late Show* had lost much of the improvisational feel of *Late Night*. In the last few years at NBC, Letterman had become increasingly scripted, but there were still bits where he would improvise, like his banter with Meg Parsont. The *Late Show* brought Parsont back in a remote, but this time they built a fake office space and pretended that Meg still worked across the street. The entire spirit of the conversation had changed. The scenes with Letterman and Parsont had played off the voyeuristic pleasure of staring into the window of the person across the street. This new sketch was so obviously contrived and elaborate that it lacked authenticity. "It didn't work," Parsont said. "People wanted the real thing. I never heard from Dave again."

Another change was in booking. Cult performers like Harvey Pekar and Brother Theodore were out, in favor of the biggest celebrities they could find. On Letterman's birthday in 1995, Drew Barrymore jumped on his desk and flashed her breasts. Letterman's mouth hung open and his eyes grew wide, in a cartoonish expression of gratitude. Even his ogling had taken on a broader aspect.

On *Late Night*, Letterman rarely invited politicians on the show, and after the first year he steered clear of political figures or activists entirely. But one of the first coups of the *Late Show* was landing Vice President Al Gore, who suffered through some tepid jokes about his stiffness and then, in an effort to make fun of government waste, put on goggles and picked up a hammer to crush an ashtray. (Apparently the federal government had strict standards about ashtrays.)

Letterman treated his guests with a more restrained touch, becoming more complimentary, like every other talk-show host. On camera, his willful disinterest was replaced with something more engaged. Guests like Cher and Crispin Glover, who had made news by challenging and surprising Letterman, returned to the *Late Show* as tamed celebrities with friendlier attitudes and preapproved stories. His reputation for brutalizing stars diminished. It didn't fit anymore. What was once a show poking fun at show business had embraced it with open arms. "People used to say we were doing a parody of a talk show," Letterman said. "I would bristle at that. Clearly, it was making fun of show business. But later, on CBS, we completely rolled over and became a foil for show business, and were happy to do so." He still stewed over actors who brought little to the show, but he tried to hold it in check.

On a spring episode in 1994, Rich Hall followed a particularly awkward and testy guest appearance by Andie MacDowell, who told some banal Hollywood stories before trying and failing three times to toss a lasso on a camera to help promote a western she was starring in. After telling a few jokes from the guest's chair, Hall chatted with Letterman during the commercial, and the host asked him if he had seen MacDowell. Hall said he had, and then was startled when he heard Letterman say, "How would you like to be married to that cunt?" This baffled Hall. Sure, she had eaten up time with the lasso, but why would he say that, or mention marriage? "I thought: Where did that come from?" Hall said. "Where's even the logic in it?"

Larry "Bud" Melman (who was addressed on the *Late Show* as Calvert DeForest, because NBC claimed intellectual rights to his character's name) had a diminished role. Letterman found new ordinary people from the neighborhood to play off of. In a remote on one of his first shows, Letterman visited the Bangladeshi owners of a gift shop, named Mujibur and Sirajul. Rupert Jee, who ran the shop Hello Deli, took on an even more prominent role on the *Late Show.* They were in the tradition of his old remotes that poked fun at strangers and immigrant names. Letterman never seemed happier than when he was saying Sirajul.

Whereas Letterman had long hosted comics who pushed the limits of good taste, he suddenly became cautious. In October of the show's first season, he booked the polemical political comic Bill Hicks, who had performed on *Late Night with David Letterman* many times and was well known in comedy circles for uncompromising and extremely funny rants about politics and religion. He began with a joke about the singer Billy Ray Cyrus and moved on to abortion and religion. "A lot of Christians wear crosses around their necks," Hicks said in one setup. "Nice sentiment, but do you think when Jesus comes back, he's really going to want to look at a cross?"

Once he performed it onstage, Letterman told producer Robert Morton that there was a problem. "He came to me and said, 'We can't air that. It's too early in our run and we can't offend Catholics' or whatever," Robert Morton said. "He saw it as a twelve-thirty set, not an eleven-thirty one." The Hicks set was cut, and replaced by one by *Late Show* writer Bill Scheft that had been taped on one of the test shows before its premiere. Morton made the call to Hicks, telling him that he had "touched on too many hot spots."

Looking back on this now, Morton said, "I took the hit for that one."

Hicks died the next February, and sixteen years later, Letterman would have Hicks's mother on the show and apologize to her, then air the original stand-up set.

Letterman always positioned himself as a bemused and intelligent observer laughing at the idiocy of the world. But what had been slowly creeping into his act by the end of his old show and emerged dramatically on the new one was a new character: the Dumb Guy.

The Dumb Guy had a deep, grunting voice that sounded almost southern, and he lingered on vowel sounds. Letterman would often impersonate him in the middle of his opening remarks. His face went slack, and he turned into a character whose stupidity was as pure as that of Beavis and Butt-Head, the animated delinquents of MTV. Letterman had become enamored with the hit cartoon during his hiatus, imitating them on the show and eventually appearing in their movie.

Letterman had always enjoyed comedy about stupidity. It was right there in the name of his beloved Stupid Pet Tricks and part of the premise behind dropping things off roofs. But those bits were re-fracted through a sarcastic sensibility that made stupidity seem kind of smart. It was an unlikely trick, but it formed the foundation of his cult fan base. His dumb comedy hinged on the assumption that he was smart, but when he moved to the *Late Show*, that started to erode. Letterman's broader dumb guy impression didn't have any satirical point, nor was it a conceptual gag. The stupidity, as opposed to his perspective, was the point.

By this point Letterman had such a clearly defined attitude that he could get away with putting all kinds of lame things on the air with-out looking bad. Failure was his subject, but it didn't define him. He maintained that distinction for years with the tone of his voice and the right kind of smirk. As he got laughs from playing dopey, he may have expanded his appeal, but he shifted his style to do it.

"That was when the show turned for me," recalled Scott Auker-man, one of the many comedians inspired by David Letterman. "For me, Letterman was about him being smarter than anyone in the room and proving it with every minute of his show, doing something you've never seen before, a joke you've never heard before, interviewing peo-ple and constantly proving he's quicker," Aukerman said. "It was a bummer when he started championing dumb humor."

Letterman started *Late Night* with a few unofficial rules for him-self: no dancing, no funny hats, no acting. He violated them all, but particularly at CBS. Letterman sang parts of Broadway songs in set-ups to jokes. He even put on a dress for a bit with Dennis Rodman. Burnett had to convince him to do it, and he agreed to it only after a long discussion about the kind of dress. The night it aired, Burnett turned on *The Tonight Show* and Leno was also in a dress. When Letterman started going for broad, pandering laughs, he was playing on Leno's field.

In the transition to the *Late Show*, David Letterman also lost his greatest comedic antagonist: NBC. He still made jokes about his old network, of course, especially in his first few weeks, when he reminded viewers of his old hostility by calling executives at the network reptiles or weasels. He poked fun at the terrible CBS lineup, but it didn't have the same kind of rebellious punch, largely because his relationship with his bosses had changed. He was no longer the overlooked star. The executives at CBS had given him everything he wanted. There was not much to grumble about. In an early show, Letterman gently poked fun at CBS president Leslie Moonves: "What kind of man is named Leslie?"

"Moonves called me up," producer Robert Morton recalled, "and said, 'Could you tell him not to make fun of my name? My mom doesn't like it.' I told Dave and he stopped."

Hal Gurnee had championed the move to the Ed Sullivan Theater, but once there, he saw the advantages of the old cramped studio. Letterman missed the constraints and the physical presence that came with being inside the corporate offices. "When GE took over, it just reinforced his whole kind of contempt for the suited people who take themselves seriously, and so he was good at that," Gurnee said. "I think we kind of missed that, because there was nobody at CBS to play that role. He could get mad at the upper echelons for not having the right lead-ins and all, but there was nobody there on a constant basis to remind us that we were doing things we shouldn't be doing. And I think that that studio was good for that."

At CBS, Letterman couldn't play the underdog in the same way anymore. As Robert Morton told the staff at the time, the old show used mistakes and mishaps as grist for comedy. If something went wrong, they would joke about it. Now he was beating Jay Leno soundly in the ratings every day. He was making more money than Leno and putting on a big, splashy show inside an old Broadway theater. "In the old show, we always celebrated failure," Morton said. "Now we celebrated success."

THE OSCAR MYTH

Since her breakup with David Letterman, Merrill Markoe had written books, television shows, and a magazine column. She also returned to stand-up comedy. Her feverish productivity didn't slow, but she drew the line at writing for late night again, turning down offers from *The Tonight Show* and *The Larry Sanders Show*—even a fictional talk show was too much for her. But when the *Late Show* spent a week in Los Angeles in 1994, Markoe suddenly found herself surrounded by old memories.

Every time Markoe drove up La Brea Avenue, she saw a billboard with Letterman's gap-toothed grin. She stared blankly at an ad on the back of a bus on the freeway. Another day, she turned on the television and saw a *Hard Copy* report on the women in Letterman's life. There she was: "the ex-girlfriend." She nudged her dog: "Lewis, look who is on TV."

Merrill Markoe had been David Letterman's critical collaborator for the most formative years of his television career, creating so many essential parts of the show. As much as anyone, she helped invent the aesthetic of David Letterman. Now, at the height of his success, she was treated as just another ex-girlfriend. "It made me really angry," she explained. "Really, really, really, really angry. Four reallys."

Markoe then did what comics do with anger: transformed it into something funny. In a column for *Buzz* magazine, she wrote a short story called "Ed Is Coming to Town!," a lightly fictionalized account of what it's like to be inundated with the marketing and publicity of a famous ex-boyfriend. It was written in a sighing deadpan complemented by low-boiling exasperation. Markoe got a note from Letterman soon after publication, expressing regret. It was signed, "Best wishes, Ed."

That fall, as Markoe set out on a promotional tour for her new book of essays, *How to Be Hap-Hap-Happy Like Me!*, she got a call from a staffer at the *Late Show*, saying they wanted to book her as a guest. Markoe was nervous about going back. She didn't even watch Letterman's show anymore. But it was the best promotion she could possibly receive. How could she turn this down? Markoe agreed to appear, and when she arrived at the theater, she says she found little connection to the show, which took place in a different building that was filled with many faces she didn't recognize. Waiting backstage, she saw Letterman behind his desk. He waved.

"Instead of dissolving into emotion," she said, "a brand-new voice came into my head. It said: 'This is not a reunion. It's a book promotion.' And I went out onstage and promoted."

After walking onstage, Markoe talked to Letterman about the dismissive way she was treated by the press, noting wryly how a tabloid story from the *New York Post* had described her as "ex gal pal." Letterman, who earlier in the show said he was nervous to see Markoe, responded by treating it as more of a salvo at him, making a joke about this being "the first round," comparing the meeting to a boxing match. He was using his own anxiety to add to the drama as well. When he went to commercial, he riffed on the title of the *Post* story, poking fun at it gently: "We'll come right back," he said with an ironic lilt in his voice, "with Mr. Funny and his ex–gal pal."

They were both playing their parts in a familiar show business transaction—the guest telling a funny story, the host riffing on it, alluding to their history while also keeping it lightly amusing and superficial. What stood out for Markoe was how choreographed the interview had become, plotted out beforehand with his staff. "It was like a one-act play," she said. She stuck to the script she had gone over with his staff and hyped her book. For the length of a television segment, they were a great team again.

She appeared on *Late Show* three more times that decade, and the conversations with Letterman on air were always thick with tension. He threw teasing jabs and she responded with jovial threats to read old diary entries on air, even taking one out of her pocket at one point as a potential counterattack. These exchanges were riveting. Years of history together made every pointed comment seem charged and meaningful. When Markoe was promoting her spoof of romantic advice books *Merrill Markoe's Guide to Love*, she asked the host: "Who better to talk about love than me?"

Letterman mumbled: "Yeah, well," then stopped himself, turned to face the camera, and raised an eyebrow, letting the silence sit there for a startling amount of time. The audience cheered and neither of them said a word for twenty seconds, bringing the interview to an awkward halt. Markoe broke the impasse, asking: "Did you have a question?" She made her last appearance the next year, in 1998.

Merrill Markoe would hear from the *Late Show* only one more time, and it was a far more disorienting experience. A decade later, Barbara Gaines, who had started out answering phones on the morning show and had worked her way up to being a producer, left Markoe a message to gauge her interest in doing remote pieces for the Winter Olympics in Italy. This got her attention. Doing her own segments could be fun.

When Markoe called Gaines back, she realized that Letterman wasn't interested in her being on camera. He wanted her to write for a segment. Gaines asked Markoe, "Have you seen a segment we do called Stephanie the Intern?"

Markoe had not. Gaines explained that it was a regular segment where an intern named Stephanie Birkitt talks to Letterman, and in this case she would file reports from the Olympics, just as his mother had done, to much success. Gaines described Birkitt as a fish-out-of-water character. "Dave thought you could write her segments," she said. Markoe asked about the pay. Gaines said the budget was tight, and the talks of her returning fizzled out.

Several years later, in 2009, news broke of a sex scandal on the *Late Show*. David Letterman had been threatened with blackmail by the boyfriend of a staffer with whom he was having an affair. The staffer was Stephanie Birkitt. When Merrill Markoe heard this news, her mind flashed back to the talk with Gaines. David Letterman wanted her to write jokes for the intern he was having an affair with behind the back of his wife, the former staffer whose affair helped end her relationship with him? Markoe's mind reeled. "I felt like Bugs Bunny the time that Daffy Duck woke him up by putting the lid of a pot on his head and beating it with a spoon," she explained. "I could feel my eyes rolling in different directions, and my head vibrating back and forth like a tuning fork."

Markoe spent some time considering the proper response, and on her blog she wrote this joke: "As you can imagine this is a very emotional moment for me because Dave promised me many times that I was the only woman he would ever cheat on."

By the end of 1994, there were signs that the ratings success of the *Late Show* rested on a shaky foundation. *The Tonight Show* was narrowing the gap. CBS's losing the rights to broadcast the NFL had led to a realignment of affiliates. NBC had developed more popular lead-in shows, such as *ER*. Nor did it help that Letterman had decided not to joke about the biggest story of the year: the O. J. Simpson murder trial.

Letterman told his staff that he found nothing funny about the Simpson story. When Howard Stern appeared on the show, wearing a T-shirt with Simpson's mug shot on it, he asked Letterman why he hadn't made any jokes about the biggest story in the country. Letterman's retort: "Double homicides just don't crack me up the way they used to."

Leno, by contrast, had several lines of actors dress up like the judge, Lance Ito, calling them the Dancing Itos. The *Late Show* still consistently won in the ratings, but that would change in 1995. The most popular narrative is that the first turning point was when Letterman hosted the Academy Awards that spring.

Letterman had spent his career seeming like the kind of guy who would never host the Oscars. In fact, he refused to even say "Oscar" on his show; he would only say "Academy Awards." "It was almost like he thought it sounded too insider baseball or show business," Gerard Mulligan said. The *Times* reported that Letterman hosting the show was the "subject of as much pre-Oscar talk as the nominees themselves."

On the day of the broadcast, Letterman was pessimistic and feeling nervous about the opening monologue. He thought it wasn't funny enough. Some *Late Show* staffers were backstage helping him write jokes, and Letterman, in his tuxedo, worried that he needed something to punch up the opening. Looking at a seating chart of the guests, Rob Burnett got an idea for the first joke. Letterman lit up immediately.

At the start of the ceremony, Letterman walked onto the stage and told the crowd there was something he really wanted to do, looking like a kid who'd discovered a new toy. He walked toward Oprah Winfrey and paused near the lip of the stage. "Oprah," he said, as if he was introducing her to a friend. She smiled but did not laugh. He walked to the other side of the stage, near Uma Thurman. "Uma," he said. "Uma, Oprah." Then he chuckled, saying he felt better and adding, "Have you kids met Keanu?"

The crowd chuckled, but not heartily. It was the kind of goofy wordplay that Letterman delighted in, finding humor in the sound of words as opposed to hard punch lines. It had his trademark silliness (where is the joke exactly?) mixed with a hint of mockery of the entire event. Letterman often called his audience "kids" in a semi-satirical voice of a stodgy 1950s authority figure, but to those who didn't know his verbal tics, it could appear strangely dismissive. The way Letterman framed the joke made it about him, something silly he wanted to do. Oscar hosts typically welcomed the audience, expanded their range of references, but Letterman treated the Oscars like a bigger, more formal episode of his show. He even read a Top Ten List.

Letterman already had a chilly relationship with Oprah Winfrey, dating back to the 1980s, when he compared her to Mrs. Butterworth, the portly figure on the syrup bottle. When he brought his show to Chicago, Winfrey wanted to play along by wheeling out a giant Mrs. Butterworth doll. Letterman refused. Instead, she came on and was received by a snarky host and a loud crowd, one member of which yelled, "Rip her, Dave!" Winfrey decided not to return to the show. Letterman later turned her refusal to come on his show into a running joke but would eventually apologize to her on the air.

At the Oscars, singling her out did not come off as a friendly gesture. It didn't seem like an attack, either. It was odd and tense and exactly the kind of awkward moment David Letterman played for laughs on his show. After the ceremony was over, he and Burnett flew to London to shoot remotes for a week of episodes they were going to be taping in May. When they left the country, they felt that the night had been a success. Bill Scheft, who expressed some reservations about leading with the "Oprah, Uma" joke but was overruled, recalled Burnett saying at the end of the show that this was going to be so much easier when they did it the next year. "He also told me, 'Save the reviews,'" Scheft said.

The initial reviews were not terrible, although some critics certainly skewered Letterman. "The biggest surprise of Monday's Academy Awards telecast on ABC was the growing insignificance of David Letterman as the evening droned on," wrote John O'Connor in the *New York Times*, in perhaps the harshest assessment. Joyce Millman of the *San Francisco Examiner* raved, saying, "It is Dave's world. We only live in it." Tom Shales at the *Washington Post* didn't like the show but said the blame did not rest with the host.

Putting aside the critics, there was reason to think that Letterman had done well. The Oscars received extremely high ratings, the second best in its history. When Letterman returned to New York after a week, he began his April 3 show with no sign that he thought his performance had been the train wreck it would come to be considered. He began his show saying, "Okay, try it one more time: Oprah, Uma, Oprah, Uma." But after the show, he revealed some new insecurity, asking Bill Scheft, "Did I fuck it up?"

Over the next month, Letterman made several more jokes in the monologue about the Oscars. The perspective was less that he was terrible than that he had loathed doing it. In one, he mentioned that the heavyweight boxer George Foreman had said he was looking forward to fighting the champion, Mike Tyson. "Yeah, right," Letterman responded. "And I'm still looking forward to hosting the Academy Awards."

Letterman's comic tone grew darker after the actor Hugh Grant went on *The Tonight Show* in July. Grant, the stammering leading man from the romantic comedy *Four Weddings and a Funeral,* was dating model Elizabeth Hurley and had a new movie, *Nine Months,* to promote. But then he was arrested with a prostitute named Divine Brown, his startled but still rakish mug shot reproduced in tabloids around the world. Instead of dodging the issue, Grant did damage control, confessing his sins to Jay Leno, who began the interview with an uncharacteristically blunt question: "What the hell were you thinking?"

The Hugh Grant interview reached eight million viewers, a huge boost from a typical episode of *The Tonight Show,* and the *Late Show* lost the week in the ratings for the first time since it premiered. War- ren Littlefield started building up this moment as the turning point in a new narrative of the late-night war. "It all started with a pair of lips," he told *Vanity Fair* about the changing fortunes of NBC late night.

While NBC promoted *The Tonight Show* as resurgent, Letterman beat himself up more, making jokes about his hosting of the Oscars, month after month. It wasn't until after the *Late Show* started losing in the ratings that the premise of his Oscar jokes shifted. "The Acad- emy Awards received seven Emmy nominations" was the setup of a joke in late July. "In a related story, Chechnya was nominated for most livable city." In October, Letterman asked, "Do you realize that O. J. is getting less criticism than I got after the Academy Awards?" More than a year after the Oscars, Letterman was still regularly making these jokes. About the video of police caught hitting two suspected illegal immigrants, he said in April 1996, "That's the worst beating someone's taken in L.A. since I hosted the Academy Awards."

While some reviews were negative, there was no consensus that he had been a catastrophe; this perception formed only after Letter- man himself pushed it on his audience for more than a year. His re- flexive self-loathing turned into jokes that then became self-fulfilling, creating an impression of failure that reached more people than any review. In the past, he had turned his relentless negativity into funny entertainment, the theater of his tortured personality, but this time he only sabotaged himself. "He owned the failure too much," Robert Morton said.

To say that Letterman fell in the ratings because of the Oscars or Hugh Grant is a gross oversimplification, and the next two decades, when he rarely led *The Tonight Show* in the ratings, proved that the reasons that David Letterman had fallen behind could not hinge on one or two shows. After Leno passed him, however, Letterman became obsessed with regaining his position, pushing the network to do more to promote the show. He had regular shouting fights with Les Moonves. "The fight was: 'You've got to support the show more,'" Letterman explained. "'You've got to give me more promos. You have to do this, you have to do that.' It took me a long time to realize that, while those things would be nice, the real problem is more people liked Jay than liked me."

Success during the late-night war was measured one way: ratings. But decades later, it's worth asking: What difference do a few Nielsen points make? Does it really matter if half a million more people watched Jay Leno, in part because he did more O. J. jokes? There are Leno fans, but few argue that he put on a show that was more culturally or comically significant than Letterman's. When the question was recently posed to Warren Littlefield why ratings meant so much in the late-night rivalry, even he seemed flummoxed. The question must have nagged at Littlefield, because he later tried to clarify, pointing out that the additional ad revenue from higher ratings prevented layoffs and saved jobs. That's surely true, but, as portrayed in the press or understood by fans, the stakes of the late-night war were not employment numbers for television executives and staff. It was fought for comedic and cultural bragging rights as well. On those fronts, there is no question which host leaves behind the biggest legacy.

The artistic significance of the shift in ratings in 1995, when Jay Leno took the lead, is that it changed Letterman onscreen. He had become invested in this rivalry, and once he started losing, his mood darkened and his performance got downright strange. He increasingly fidgeted, shouted his jokes, and repeated punch lines over and over, particularly if they didn't get much of a laugh.

Part of what made David Letterman such a riveting performer was the restrictions that he labored under, whether they were explicit, such as the rules that *The Tonight Show* imposed, or just talk-show conventions. Letterman always seemed to be holding back his anger but still managed to communicate it through asides and sighs and expressions. His audience learned to decipher his ironic language, and it was part of what made him so fascinating to watch. He was hinting at something, but what exactly? On the *Late Show*, he had more freedom and clout, and the result was that what was once subtext now became more overt.

He started doing a character on the show called Creepy Dave, where a version of himself wearing a varsity jacket would linger behind the window near the host. With the help of technology, two different versions of David Letterman would appear onscreen at the same time—the host in the suit and the odd fellow staring in at him. He'd occasionally say, "What's up?" Creepy Dave was a strange character, and that Letterman approved this bit reflected how much he had internalized the idea that his brand was his own strangeness. Peter Lassally, who produced *The Tonight Show*, said he found Creepy Dave truly creepy. "It's that stare—something very unpleasant. Dave tells him to get out, but Creepy Dave won't go. It could be Dave's conscience, I don't know."

There were even comedy bits that seemed to reflect his irritation with the audience. In one sketch, Letterman got distracted during his monologue by an audience member (a plant) who looked disinterested, so he dragged him out of his chair and threatened to shake him out of his lethargy. Then, in a cartoonish display of violence, he proceeded to inject him with a needle, feed him NoDoz, hit him with tennis balls, throw him off a balcony, and get Connie Chung to punch him in the gut.

Letterman occasionally had success playing a jerk on *Late Night*. But his persona was far more broad and ingratiating. So when his comedy took a sadistic turn, it was jarring. By picking on a sleepy audience member, he looked like a bully.

It also played into the hands of Jay Leno, who made every attempt to seem like a close friend to his audience, even rebuilding his set so he would be within grabbing distance. He would open the show by slapping hands with people in the front row. "I remember Dave had a joke where he had a guy in the audience ask if he could shake his hands. He said sure," Leno recalled. "Then he walked behind a Plexiglas glass and shook. It was funny but also telling. I'm the opposite. I'm the populist comic."

By late 1995, Rob Burnett had left the show to start work on *The Bonnie Hunt Show*, produced by Worldwide Pants, but he noticed that the ratings were hurting Letterman's performance. "Dave was pushing," he said. "He was very unhappy on the air, but not in a good way. Not 'I'm an outsider,' in a funny way. He seemed uncomfortable." Burnett called Letterman to say he was making a mistake on the air.

I said to him, "People don't understand why you're behaving the way you're behaving. You have a lot going on in your head. Leno passed us in the ratings, I understand it. People want to see you be Johnny Carson." We had a candid conversation. "For you to be screaming and flailing, it turns people away. They don't think of you the way you think of you." I said to him, "You put your hands in your pocket and tell jokes." He went through a period in '95 pushing very hard, and he was very uncomfortable and he felt people didn't like him.

Letterman's high-pitched laugh transformed into a yell, a furious, joyless guffaw. It sounded like a dark parody of a man having a good time, almost as if enjoying a joke itself were absurd. After one lame Bob Dole joke, he croaked out a laugh, then another, until finally he bent over in mock pain. Letterman had always repeated lines from jokes, but in the past he had done it with playfulness. Now he would grab onto a phrase that had an interesting sound, but his repetition seemed more like a manifestation of self-mocking. Letterman finished off jokes by adjusting his tie and cracking his neck. He rarely looked happy.

Norm MacDonald did a sharp parody of Letterman on *Saturday Night Live* that captured this period in all its strangeness. In past impressions of the host, *SNL* had satirized Letterman's glibness or sarcasm, but this parody was more like Chris Elliott's impression of Marlon Brando: a star who had become so isolated and famous that he had lost touch with any semblance of normal human behavior. It captured his croaking laugh, his overbearing delight in words that no one else thought were funny, and his Dumb Guy character, who in this case kept asking, "You got any gum?"

Not surprisingly, Letterman became increasingly ornery as the ratings started to slide. Burnett recalled doing a remote in 1996 in which Letterman kept driving through a Taco Bell drive-through. Letterman didn't want to do it, in part because they had already done something similar in a McDonald's drive-through on *Late Night*. He sulked through the shoot. "He was being petulant, almost trying to prove it was a bad idea," Burnett said. "What do you want to say now? We'll do these jokes. What now? And eventually he got into it. And it ends up being one of the best pieces we ever did. There was a lot of that."

By the spring of 1996, the show was in last place in its time slot, trailing not only Leno but *Nightline*. One night, it had been preempted by a golf tournament, so it started later than usual. Letterman introduced himself as the "most powerful man in professional golf," before telling a joke about the woman who alleged that Mike Tyson had raped her, a struggle that had gone on for ten minutes. "She lasted nine minutes longer than Peter McNeeley," he said, referring to the man knocked out in Tyson's most recent bout. It was an ugly joke. The rest of his monologue featured an Elizabeth Taylor joke that bombed ("Maybe not," he said, recognizing its failure) and several Unabomber jokes—one was about his name, and another about his Mexican pen pal. "How many of you have a Mexican pen pal?" he asked. Then his eyes widened and he let out that laugh.

In the next segment, he did CBS Mailbag, the *Late Show*'s version of Viewer Mail. The first letter asked him how to lose weight. Letterman, who could be obsessive about his diet, shouted, "Stop eating!" A weak joke with another mean edge. Then, reading the next letter, he snapped. A man had written to ask if Letterman would marry his mom. Dave stumbled in reading the letter, which distracted him visibly. The planned joke was that he would say he was going to send a life-size David Letterman doll to the man's mother, and then he would bring out the doll, pull a string, and it would say abusive things like "Get me a beer, and step on it."

After making the jokes, Letterman put the dummy down on his guest's chair and walked back to his desk, then an idea popped into his head. He turned around, faced the dummy, and threw a right-hand punch at its head. The audience laughed. Then he threw another cross. More laughter. Letterman got into a boxer's pose and threw five more punches before mentioning that the dummy looked like Conan O'Brien. He threw nine more punches and, turning his back to the audience, started slapping it repeatedly. The laughter got quieter. What was wrong with Dave?

After a commercial, the dummy was still there. Introducing a bit about a contest, Letterman mispronounced Grand Rapids, stopped, turned to the dummy, and slapped it ten times. No one laughed.

In the *Washington Post*, Tom Shales wrote, "Letterman no longer seems to just have an edge; he is an edge, and who wants a big edge coming at you at 11:30 every night?"

I n his funniest years on television, Letterman played off others. He applied his comic attitude to the absurdity of George Meyer or the visual inventiveness of Hal Gurnee or the literate silliness of Merrill Markoe. But there were fewer writers around him with clout. "The problem was that guys who worked for us would leave for shows in California," Letterman said, adding that by the time he changed shows it had gotten worse. "Then guys didn't even want to go to talk shows and just headed straight to California."

Letterman made attempts to fix the problem, including recruiting the respected stand-up comic Louis C.K. from *Late Night with Conan O'Brien* to write for him. He stayed only a few months. In late 1995, the *Late Show* brought Joe Toplyn, who had been working at *The Tonight Show*, back as head writer. "By the third day, Dave realized that he couldn't stand to be in the same room with Joe," Steve Young said, telling a story confirmed by several other employees. "So he was no longer to have access with Dave. He could run things and send scripts in, but he could not see him. Jon Beckerman filled the role of head writer in all but name."

Loyal staff members started to leave. Director Hal Gurnee quit. "I wanted to travel, and also I'd been in the business a long time," he said. "To be honest, we weren't completely breaking new ground at that point."

When he said goodbye to Hal Gurnee in a monologue from his

desk to end the show, Letterman praised him for making him look better and funnier, then paused: "Well, no one could make me funnier." Even in his farewell to Gurnee, Letterman brought the joke back to one about his own failings.

Bill Wendell, the announcer who had been with the show since the beginning, also left in 1995. In a departing interview, he said he should have stayed at NBC instead of leaving the network with the show. "We used to do skits, go over and talk with Letterman—all of that is gone," he said, comparing the old and new shows. "I'll leave it to others to say whether it's better or not."

To some, the biggest change was Rob Burnett starting *The Bonnie Hunt Show*. This was part of Letterman's project of building his production company. When Burnett started work on a new pilot, that was when trouble started. "What I had not counted on is [Worldwide Pants] would take Rob out of the daily functioning of the show," Letterman said. "I really missed that. I had a longer history with Rob. We really made each other laugh."

Burnett was one of the few writers on staff by this point who could push Letterman to try something out of his comfort zone. "Dave became depressed," said a longtime staffer about this departure. "Whatever everyone else does, it won't be as good as what Rob did."

Robert Morton was fired in March 1996. He had been working with Letterman since the beginning of *Late Night*. What was startling was the harsh way the host characterized this dismissal in the press. "We had a little infection, and the limb had to come off," Letterman told *Rolling Stone*.

Morton was not just the longtime producer. He was also a familiar and reliable comic foil on camera. If he could be banished so quickly, anyone could.

Morton pointed to a conversation with Michael Ovitz, who had left CAA and gone to Disney. Ovitz asked him about Letterman. Morton responded that Letterman missed Ovitz. "So we hatched a plan for Disney to buy Worldwide Pants," Morton said. "That hurt me. It was threatening to people in Letterman's camp."

Perhaps. Letterman explained Morton's dismissal as a simple result of his devotion to Burnett. "Rob came to me and said, 'Look, if you make me the producer, everything will be better,'" Letterman said to me. "I thought, 'Great, let's do that.' So I fired Morty." Letterman added, "It's a sad thing. I liked Morty. It was the pressure from *The Tonight Show.*"

Burnett returned to the *Late Show*, but with a promotion. He went to work as an executive producer.

In the short amount of time since the *Late Show* started fading in the ratings, Letterman had lost many of his key collaborators and wasn't speaking to others. By the end of the 1990s he would become distant with even some of his closest and most loyal employees. Barbara Gaines had a quieter and briefer falling-out, after getting upset about not being invited to London to work on the shows they shot there right after the Academy Awards. They had long had an amiable, needling, but also affectionate rapport, not only in the office but also on the show. But after not going to London, she wrote Letterman a letter expressing her unhappiness, and they didn't talk for three years, outside of perfunctory professional exchanges.

When Burnett returned to the show, his relationship with Letterman became strained. "Dave got hurt and burned by Rob, and everything changed after that," said one longtime staff member. "Dave felt like he found his guy. He's going to make his production company and his legacy. Dave felt Rob was then like, 'Okay, thanks, bye.' Dave became depressed. He lost his person. It left a void."

In the next decade, Burnett started producing the sitcom *Ed* for Worldwide Pants. "He was happy about *Ed* originally," Burnett said about Letterman. "Then it got difficult. *Ed* was full-time. I was committed to it. We were committed to it as a company. We had a falling-out and it ebbed and flowed. The fourth year of *Ed*, I tried to run from the *Late Show*. It didn't work. *Ed* went off the air." Burnett never left the *Late Show*, but his relationship with Letterman became distant, to the point that they barely spoke to each other.

Even the mellow Paul Shaffer, always exceptional at managing the moods of the host, said the one time he lost his temper with Letterman was during this period. Letterman had been poking fun at Shaffer for decades, and Shaffer had always taken it in stride. Some days, they only saw each other backstage, for a few minutes, but on the air they got along.

"When we moved to CBS, there was more pressure. I felt it, too." Shaffer said, recalling a time when Letterman was upset that Todd Rundgren was sitting in with the band but wouldn't be playing more than one of his own songs because the band hadn't had time to rehearse more than one. On the show, he kept needling Shaffer about this, asking how many songs he would play, adding that after the show he would have to go up to his office and play Todd Rundgren songs on his stereo to hear them. Shaffer became furious and, for the first and last time that he could remember, lashed out at Letterman on the air: "Cat flies in to do us a favor and you just want what you want," he said.

It was not exactly a rant, but for Shaffer, who always took the abuse but never doled out aggression, this was an eruption. "I exploded and yelled at him on the show" was how Shaffer described it. This unusual display of anger became a running joke on the staff, and the tape was brought out and played every now and again. Shaffer, though, was embarrassed, and his comment was cut from the show that aired. "The next day, I called [Dave] and Rob up and apologized," Shaffer said. "Dave said he loved the moment. 'You can sit on my hair and I won't care.'"

In the late 1990s, Letterman didn't approach his guests with the same prickly sarcasm as he had in the previous decade. He invited stars who made him uncomfortable, such as Sandra Bernhard, less often. She appeared on the CBS show only twice, the last time in 1998, the same year that Shaffer lost his temper. Bernhard and Letterman had none of their old chemistry. She brought her usual flamboyance and energy, mentioning a bit she had done on the show a decade earlier, but he did not seem charmed or ruffled, just stern. Then, at the commercial, he turned to her and said, "Are you still trashing me in the press?"

"I felt like I walked onto a land mine," Bernhard said. She said she had no idea what he was talking about. She had appeared in *The Late Shift*, the TV movie adaptation of Bill Carter's book, which Letterman did not like. But she left the show that day with no idea why he was upset. She was never invited back again. "It's one of the most devastating things in my career," Bernhard said. "Besides the fact it was great to do his show, I really loved him. I admired him and thought he was original. It felt like my little brother rejected me."

In the final years of the 1990s, Letterman ran through a series of head writers, with none lasting long. The experience of Tim Long, a twenty-six-year-old who took over as head writer in 1997, provided a prime example of the challenges of the job. Long couldn't figure out how to make Letterman happy, or even how to handle his rejections and moods. "You know those guys who are so self-deprecating that you don't want to be around them anymore?" Long said. "The relentlessness of Dave's attitude wore me down."

Struggling with the constant rejection and general dissatisfaction of the host, Long started to gain weight and chew on Coke cans, his anxiety rising. "He became pasty and bloated," Steve Young said. "He stopped bathing. He was eating bits of cans. He was a cautionary tale on not being head writer. Being in the dressing room with Dave for too long, you get poisoned."

Long said that he did learn about how to manage Letterman from watching Burnett. He recalled sitting with the two men after a show when the host said it had been the worst episode he'd ever taped. "I felt really bad," Long said. "Burnett said, 'No, Dave. The one last Tuesday was the worst.' And Dave laughed."

Long also speculated that the Letterman he had fallen in love with watching *Late Night* as a kid had changed. He was more cautious now. He not only didn't want to shoot taped segments, but he was also more concerned about coming off as unlikable. After Long proposed a joke during a bit about hobbyists, Letterman told him to consider their humanity. "He didn't want to be mean," he said.

But mostly he found Letterman's attention span for comedy shrinking. "Dave had a tendency to lose faith in things," Long said. "If the first few jokes in a Top Ten didn't work, he would lose faith in the whole thing. He always put the show in a negative light, and we would pitch things to appeal to this attitude, that the show was terrible. "Dave came to not love comedy," Long reflected. "It stopped fascinating him."

Long fled the show after a year, taking a job with *The Simpsons*, where he would tease his former co-workers by sending them photos of himself happy at work. In retrospect, Long acknowledged that he had been too young for the job and took Letterman's reactions too personally. But his broader analysis echoed that of many who worked there in the late 1990s. David Javerbaum, a writer who went on to become an executive producer at *The Daily Show*, described a miserable atmosphere in the office created by the host who was a "detached, aloof figure who would stay there for, like, thirteen hours a day for no reason."

Part of the problem was that there were few people of stature left on the writing staff who could really push the host. "The legacy of that show, it was really shaped by what Dave *wouldn't* do," Long said.

Rob Burnett saw both the old and new eras and described the change this way: "What happened is that Dave systematically eliminated everything about the show that he didn't want to do. Things that Merrill and Steve and I could force him into doing. He stopped being forced. I don't think Dave ever liked doing remotes, but he had to do it. Dave was done collaborating."

Letterman always seemed a solo act of sorts, but his greatest years were marked by creative tension between him and his staff. Not only did they push him to be more ambitious, but in some regards they had a better understanding of what he did well. Letterman may not have liked doing remote pieces or felt at ease with Sandra Bernhard, but those videos were hilarious, and that tension with Bernhard made them fascinating to watch. He hated being surprised on the show, but it was often at its best when he was reacting to something unexpected in the moment.

Letterman earned the clout to do exactly what he wanted. Just as Johnny Carson had done with NBC, Letterman negotiated a contract with CBS that gave him the power to produce the show that followed his. In a bit of career symmetry, he picked Tom Snyder, the man he'd replaced at NBC in the 12:30 a.m. time slot, as the first host of *The Late Late Show.* Snyder's interview program, which had no studio audience or band, harked back to an earlier era of talk shows. After Snyder stepped down in March 1999, CBS replaced him with another broadcaster, former ESPN sportscaster and *The Daily Show* host Craig Kilborn, whose knowing style was a watered-down version of early Letterman. Letterman asked his former head writer Steve O'Donnell to help Kilborn run the show. O'Donnell was not impressed with Kilborn and said no.

"Dave seemed disappointed, and he called me up to set up a dinner with Kilborn, which I went to," O'Donnell said. "And my antipathy deepened. I was used to a smart, funny, quick person who could form humorous sentences spontaneously, not a preening cliché-monger."

What had a bigger impact on the future of the *Late Show* was not Kilborn's performance but the opportunity that his moving to network television opened up at *The Daily Show*. While the network programs regularly reached six million viewers, Comedy Central's shows, available in fewer than half of American households in the early 1990s, had an audience in the hundreds of thousands. But it was growing.

Jon Stewart, who had been a substitute host for Tom Snyder at *The Late Late Show*, took over at *The Daily Show* in January 1999, and within a few years he had built a new late-night comedy empire. The bones of the show were derivative, featuring satiric commentary at a desk, à la Weekend Update, and craftily edited remote pieces like those from *Late Night*. But it was the political conviction of Stewart that was new. He proved that the old middle-of-the-road evenhandedness that had marked late-night television starting with *The Tonight Show* was no longer necessary. While Stewart was a huge fan of Letterman, he ushered in a new politically engaged brand of late-night comedy that was stylistically the opposite of the ironic detachment that *Late Night* had mainstreamed so successfully.

The Daily Show, and subsequently *The Colbert Report*, captured young audiences, received rave reviews, and regularly earned Emmys. Like *Late Night* once had, Comedy Central's shows transcended their form and captured the zeitgeist. They reinvented television comedy and proved that righteous conviction with an overt political slant could wear well over a long period. They also showed that comedy could move into the journalism lane. Jon Stewart had silly and wiseguy streaks, but he was far more willing to be blunt and sincere on camera, making political comedy that dispensed with the caution and false balance of previous late-night hosts. This was something new, and its impact would be felt throughout all of late night, including by Letterman, who would become more politically outspoken on the show in the following decade.

That decade began with a health scare that changed his life. In

January 2000, an angiogram revealed that Letterman had five clogged heart vessels. He was fifty-two years old. His father had died of heart disease when he was fifty-seven. Letterman immediately underwent quintuple bypass surgery. After decades of worrying about various imagined sicknesses that could kill him, he was finally confronted with one that could. Steve O'Donnell joked that Letterman was such a hypochondriac that the bypass surgery was "one of his most satisfying experiences."

It was a major turning point for Letterman. "The heart surgery put an end to the hypochondria," Letterman said. "It gave me faith in doctors. It also made me realize that there are people in this world you can absolutely trust."

And it made Letterman reinvent the way he made his show.

HINKY

One week before his final episode hosting *The Tonight Show*, in 1992, Johnny Carson welcomed David Letterman on his show for the last time. After telling several funny stories and paying gracious homage to Carson, Letterman moved down the couch to make way for the next guest, Bob Hope. At ninety, Hope appeared frail and tentative, and had difficulty keeping up his end of the conversation. He even had trouble hearing the host. Carson handled him with grace and patience, but after the show, at dinner with Letterman, he expressed disbelief that Hope had not retired.

"Johnny was up in arms about 'When is Bob Hope going to quit?'" Letterman remembered, adding that Carson said he left the show when he did because he wanted to go out on top. "Well," Letterman added, a skeptical tone emerging, "that's a nice answer."

David Letterman did not leave late-night television on top. In his final fifteen years on the air, he never returned to first place in the ratings. Nor was he the critical favorite that he had been in the 1980s. The political satire on Comedy Central received more attention in the media, and in his final years, tech-savvy hosts like Jimmy Fallon outpaced him in reaching young audiences.

To be sure, Letterman remained a compelling storyteller and turned into the finest conversationalist in late-night comedy. He had a few deliriously bold experiments—like when he did a show with no audience after Hurricane Sandy hit New York—and as he aged, he became a kind of éminence grise of late-night television, a figure revered for his past irreverence. Letterman was at his best as a voice during moments of national importance, most famously after September 11.

His show rarely aimed for the cutting edge, and he was slow to adjust to technological shifts. Despite the encouragement of his staff, he never used social media. It's no surprise that a comedian who made so much wonderful comedy satirizing empty technological innovation refused to embrace the Internet. Letterman became so committed to his habits that his staff never stopped using a typewriter to put questions or jokes on the blue cards he had on his desk. Younger comedians like Jimmy Kimmel, Billy Eichner, and Conan O'Brien, who had grown up watching and adoring Letterman, did man-on-the-street pieces in his style. They also made comedy out of formal experiments. (O'Brien did a stop-motion animation show, which was an idea that Letterman had once considered but eventually turned down.) The style of comedy that Letterman had pioneered was being done—just not by him.

M any who worked on the show say this is a function of the host getting older and no longer wanting to put on a Velcro suit to get a laugh. But to understand what really happened to David Letterman in these final years, you need to look at how the process of making the show evolved.

After heart surgery, which kept him away from television for only thirty-four days, Letterman changed his habits. He cut out chocolates, moved to decaf, and began taking antidepressants. Most critically, he stopped going to rehearsal. "I was tired of it," Letterman said. "I wanted to save energy for the show, but also, there wasn't much I hadn't done before."

This fundamentally changed the way the show was put together and made producing comedy of any complexity more difficult. In rehearsals, Letterman had always added jokes, cut others, tossed around ideas. It was where he refined his comedy. That ended.

In 2000, brothers Justin and Eric Stangel took over as head writers, and they would stay for fourteen years, longer than any other head writers in the history of *Late Night* or the *Late Show*. Justin Stangel would stand in for Letterman at rehearsals, which were filmed on a VHS tape. If there was a comedy bit that required blocking, the Stangels—and producers Barbara Gaines and Jude Brennan—showed Letterman the tape half an hour before the show, often the only chance they had to see him.

When Letterman rejected jokes, they needed to be replaced in the thirty minutes before the show was scheduled to tape. This was not only a creative problem but also a logistical one. If Letterman cut four Top Ten jokes, his staff couldn't just substitute a few on a laptop computer. The entire list needed to be redone on a typewriter. Scripts were always being tinkered with up to the last second, so the head writers typically prepared for two shows instead of one, which, when it came to comedy, put an emphasis on volume. Eric Stangel described his and his brother's roles as completely different from those of all the previous head writers:

All the others met with David in the morning. They had rehearsal. They had pre-show. They had the dressing room to get everything right. They had the host telling them directly what he wanted. We had the head writer job the longest, and for most of that we had a host who didn't participate until half an hour before the show.

Letterman always worked with material created by others, but in his final years he didn't participate in the making of the comedy so much as show up to do it. He still produced some brilliant shows, but the structure made it more difficult to take risks. In some ways, the *Late Show* became built to fail.

"If there was something elaborate, they would show me," Letterman said, adding that otherwise the meeting to talk about the material was perfunctory. Paul Shaffer recalled seeing Letterman in the makeup room every day, reading the material for the first time only minutes before going on the air. "It would amaze me, but that's what the show was at that point," Shaffer said.

Letterman had been doing a nightly talk show for so long that he could get by fine without rehearsal. But knowing that anything complex would be too hard to pull off inevitably changed what seemed possible for writers and production. It became hard to fix problems. There was a recurring bit where the receptionist on the show played a crazed version of San Francisco 49ers coach Mike Singletary, yelling, screaming, doing push-ups. Letterman would check in with him periodically. He was a slightly unhinged, aggressive character in the spirit of Chris Elliott.

The *Late Show* featured Letterman talking to this receptionist more than twenty times, and the script would often be changed close to airtime, when Letterman would make a suggestion. Since he had little time to prepare, the receptionist often forgot his lines. Letterman demanded to know how this could be fixed. Eric Stangel responded, "We don't make last-second changes." But so much of the show seemed to happen last-second.

LETTERMAN

Since they rarely saw him working on the show, writers and producers often spent their time guessing what Letterman wanted. "We
were often caught in a vortex of pitching things to different people
who were anticipating what Dave would like," said Justin Stangel.

"And then sometimes you're pitching to people," his brother Eric
said, "and that decision is on you, and you don't know what Dave
thinks—the answer will most likely be no, out of fear. Say we wanted
to send Biff to Trump with the flowers, like we did with NBC. That
costs a camera and someone has to sign off on it. If we spend all this
money, and Dave says ten minutes before the show, 'I'm not doing
that,' we just wasted money, and no one is going to want to be responsible."

Over many years, Letterman built himself a cocoon where just
about the only people he trusted were producers who had worked
with him for decades, like Barbara Gaines, who had been with him
since the morning show. "Dave would always say, 'If it made you
laugh, let's do it,'" Gaines said. "After decades, I didn't laugh as much
at the printed stuff. I laughed at Dave."

A sense of mystery surrounded Letterman even within the office.
The decision-making process of the show turned baroque. In meetings about the comedy, Letterman would tell a writer that he would
accept a piece, then, when that person left the room, Letterman would
ask Gaines to cut it. Gaines said he did this because Letterman didn't
want to upset writers. "With him and Rob [Burnett], they bantered
back and forth. They talked to each other," she said. "He didn't have
that relationship with the ones who followed."

Letterman remained an occasionally acerbic interviewer. In a way
that no one else on television would or could, he surgically skewered
celebrities like Paris Hilton, parrying her deflections about her time
in jail with the single-minded focus of an investigative journalist. And
in keeping with the broader trend of a more politicized late night, he
engaged pundits more directly, which could result in an entertaining

debate with other large personalities, like Bill O'Reilly and Donald Trump. When a conversation interested him, he was also far more patient in exploring it than anyone else on late night, which could make his show in the later years an unusually refreshing change of pace.

"I started thinking the more important part to me was talking to people than the comedy," Letterman said. "I knew I couldn't compete with *SNL* or Jay's monologue. I found that what I really looked forward to was talking to people. I don't know if I was worn out or if that was an easy way out."

Some on staff viewed this as the natural evolution of a maturing artist. Merrill Markoe saw it differently. "I think Dave was inexorably turning more into himself," she said. "Dave always really wanted to be doing that show he is doing, where he could ad-lib and not have to rehearse other people's carefully written stuff."

D uring this time, Letterman began to speak openly about suffering from depression. In interviews, he said antidepressants had saved his life. On the show, he talked frankly with Howard Stern about his social awkwardness. "There are certain kinds of people who lament the fact they don't have close friends but don't do anything to create close friendships," he told Stern on the *Late Show*. "I'm kind of like that."

As you might expect from a celebrity who had been stalked, Letterman became protective of his privacy, hesitant to expand his circle of friends. Rich Hall recalled that once during a commercial, he was talking to Letterman about Montana, where they both had homes. Hall was returning there that night but had not booked a plane ticket. After a friendly exchange in which he asked Letterman which flight he normally took, Hall realized from the answer that Letterman had a private jet. When Hall suggested that he could ride with him that night and then take a taxi after they landed, the scene that followed was a textbook case of a talk-show host shifting gears from off camera to on with alacrity.

"He shook his head," silently refusing the request, Hall recalled. "Then we were right back from commercial and it was 'Hey, Rich, always great to see you.' He just wanted to ride on the jet alone."

At the same time, Letterman could be charming and even socially deft. Steve Martin had been to dinner parties with Letterman where he was outgoing. "He thinks no one wants to meet him, when the truth is the opposite—everyone does," Martin said. "He thinks he's not good in social situations. But I've been with him [in them] and he's delightful."

Letterman's life revolved around his show up until it ended, and he socialized with the staff so infrequently that the few times he did are the stuff of legend around the office. Jena Friedman, who worked as a writer for one year, said she met Letterman on the first day. "He said, 'This is a shitty place to work, but it will look good on your résumé.' And then he offered me a lollipop."

Rick Scheckman worked with Letterman for almost the entire run of both late-night shows, handling the video archives, and said that he never had an extended personal conversation with the host. "I've seen Steve O'Donnell get much too close to him and lose his mind," he said. "I've seen it happen to Rob. There comes a moment when he turns on you."

Steve Young, a writer who had been with the show since 1990, recalled not getting anything on the air and being convinced he was about to be fired when Rob Burnett told him that he was going to get his contract renewed. But first Burnett asked how he was doing. "I gave him an earful: that the show turned into this weird, thuggish, sour, celebrity-reference-chasing pile of steaming garbage that I don't feel enthusiastic about," Young said. "I don't understand it anymore."

etterman was in his Montana home when the planes hit the World Trade Center. He returned to New York and became the first late-night talk-show host to return to the air. His monologue was markedly different from and more significant than the rest. Several journalists announced that the terrorist attack represented the end of irony. This was premature, but it's telling that Letterman, the standard-bearer of ironic distance, would prove to be the entertainer with the most sober, earnest response to the terrorist attack. Part of the reason was that his reputation made its intensity so unexpected.

Letterman spoke off the cuff, examining the unspeakable tragedy that had occurred in his city. He told the audience that he had some jokes and was going to try them out, preparing them. Then Letterman didn't attempt to find meaning in the attack or sort through the politics. He explained the confusion people felt by dramatizing his own thought process making sense of the attacks. "If we are going to continue to do shows," he said dramatically, "I just need to hear myself talk for a couple of minutes."

What followed was not a cogent, linear argument, but a penetrating display of self-analysis that doubled as an explication of the national mood. It felt like a eulogy, a grappling with grief. After explaining the sadness in the city, he turned the fear and anxiety inside his head into a cerebral drama. Letterman has a gift for explaining his mind-set, delving into different worries and turning them into comedy. This time, he was employing the same tactic but for more serious purposes. When he articulated his own self-awareness, it could be fascinating. In this case, it was cathartic.

In explaining his confused state of mind, he didn't offer cheap comfort. He reflected back what his audience was feeling—that we were all anxious and lost and in pain, and in describing his own thinking with his customary self-awareness, he showed off his considerable skills as a broadcaster. He did something more difficult than express coherent ideas. He articulated baffling fear and unprocessed melancholy in a way that didn't diminish their gravity but put them into focus, and perhaps made it easier for others to deal with.

Letterman's most effusive tribute was for the way his guest that night, Mayor Rudy Giuliani, had handled the chaos in downtown New York. This was where Letterman was most passionate. "It's very simple: There is only one requirement for any of us, and that is to be courageous," Letterman said. "Courage, as you might know, defines all other human behavior."

His speech struck a chord not just because of its content but also because of who he was, a guy who not only kept his distance from engagement but used sarcasm as a shield. His history as an ironist gave him a kind of credibility when he spoke sincerely and from the heart and made his earnestness more powerful. Letterman had become the rare comedian with gravitas. What was evident from his shivering, dry-mouthed delivery was that he did this monologue shaken, even frightened. As soon as he finished his monologue and went to commercial, his producer Jude Brennan burst into tears and ran toward the desk to hug him. She was hardly the only one crying. Characteristically, Letterman had that familiar sinking feeling, the sense that he had messed up again. For him, the national neurosis and panic was not limited to extreme terrorist attacks. It was ordinary. Reflecting on his mood, he confessed, "I felt like we needed to do it over." But few agreed; Letterman's performance received some of the most effusive praise of his career.

Two years later, Letterman was once again emotional on the air, but this time he was talking joyfully about the birth of his son, Harry, named after his late father. "I could never imagine being a part of something that turned out this beautiful," he said on the show. Several staff members said that when Letterman became a father, it was the one time he appeared completely happy. "It made me understand what love is," Letterman said years later, reflecting on the moment.

"You are in love with your wife. You love your friends. But the real deal doesn't happen until you have a kid."

Around that time, Letterman removed the gap between his front teeth. It had become a signature, a staple of almost every profile written about him for decades. He had tried using inserts in his teeth early in his career but he didn't like them, and even told the press that he would never get his teeth fixed. By the time he became a father, his mind had changed. "I didn't want my son to be embarrassed by my teeth," he said, recalling the time his father writhed in pain after having his teeth removed.

Six years later, Letterman told his audience he was about to announce something important, something that they would tell their kids about. Then he read a news report that Bruce Willis had gotten married. After the crowd applauded, he announced that he, too, had gotten married, to his longtime girlfriend Regina Lasko.

As with his first marriage, the wedding was officiated by a justice of the peace. Fighting back tears, he sniffled while describing the wedding in the least sentimental terms possible. "I had avoided getting married pretty good for like twenty-three years," he began, starting one of his windy stories at the desk that became standards in his later period. On the way to the courthouse, his car had gotten stuck in the mud and he had to walk the two miles back home into what he described as a fifty-mile-per-hour wind. "The whole way, I'm thinking, 'See, smartass? See? You try to get married and this is what happens.'"

When his old fraternity brother Jeff Lewis saw this show, he thought back to when Letterman and Michelle Cook told him the story of his first marriage, where Letterman kept cracking jokes. Lewis saw it as a manifestation of his unease with commitment: "When I heard him about the car getting stuck," he said, "I thought, 'There he goes again.'"

Peter Kaplan, the late journalist and editor who wrote one of the first major national profiles of David Letterman in *Esquire*, months before he started on *Late Night*, had long been one of the comedian's most perceptive observers. He understood that Letterman's gifts were both as a talker and as well as a fascinating personality. "Just a funny guy is David L.," he had written in 1981, when Letterman only hosted a morning show, "just a firm hand who keeps his hostility in check, unsheathing, like Carson, a measured fury, and this restraint is what entitles him to the right to endure in a television age."

In 2009, Kaplan made the best argument for the artistic value of Letterman's late period in a long cover story in *New York* magazine. He wrote the piece at a moment when the late-night battle had shifted back in Letterman's favor. Conan O'Brien had taken over *The Tonight Show* from Jay Leno, and only seven shows into his tenure, Letterman beat him in the ratings. In an unusual and ill-fated experiment, Jay Leno prepared to start a new daily talk show at 10 p.m. These were both disastrous enterprises that sent the two talented hosts on a collision course. O'Brien's ratings fell, and Leno underperformed. After a clumsy attempt to keep both hosts, O'Brien left his job after a year, becoming another talk-show hero angry at NBC who set up shop on another network (in this case TBS). Leno returned to *The Tonight Show*, damaged, the nice guy transformed in the public eye into the villain. Sitting at his desk, Letterman talked about this soap opera on his show gleefully.

Kaplan argued that after losing the late-night war with Leno, Letterman had matured, giving up his detachment and ironic pose for something more earnest and politically committed. He had endured, and even become more willing to be open about his hostility, and now he'd moved "from a distinctive oddity of American comedy to something that came strangely close to greatness."

Kaplan cited "three spasms of event" that triggered the shift: Letterman's response to his heart surgery, his speech after September 11, and his increased outspokenness in the 2008 election, with sharp attacks on Sarah Palin and John McCain. In 2008, Letterman abandoned his political caution and came out as a partisan, skewering McCain for not showing up on his show. When asked about his increased political talk, Letterman gave a simple explanation: "Too much MSNBC."

The talk-show landscape had also changed. Jon Stewart's *Daily Show* made the fake balance of the network talk shows look timid. Letterman was upset at the disaster of the Iraq War and felt that being silent was dishonest or perhaps worse. In deciding whether or not to speak out, Letterman explained, his thought process had been: "You got a show and you don't have an opinion: What does that make you?"

Making the best case for his final years, Kaplan argued that Letterman had finally leveled with his audience and showed us his true, confused self. "Finally, Letterman had merged Steve Allen's absurdity, Jack Paar's neurotic confessionalism, and Carson's topicality," he wrote.

What Kaplan could not have anticipated was that one month after his story was published, a fourth spasm would hit the show—perhaps its biggest yet.

S itting at his desk, David Letterman cleared his throat. "I have a little story that I would like to tell you," he said, adding a folksy flourish right out of a kindergarten class: "Do you feel like a story?" Then he began describing the details of what sounded like an ordinary morning three weeks earlier. He woke up early and got into his car. Letterman explained that he was surprised to find a package there. The audience laughed, even though he hadn't made a joke. In the package was a letter. This was how he described its message: "I know that you do some terrible, terrible things. And I can prove that you do these terrible things."

The audience laughed again. Letterman had been telling comic fictions with conviction for so long that it was hard to tell if this was real. His tone sounded more like that of a producer pitching a hostage movie to a studio than a guy making a contemplative confession. Then he described the threat from the man who had written the letter, which made the situation even more ridiculous. He'd told Letterman that he would write a screenplay filled with the terrible things he did unless he got money. Gliding right past what those terrible things were, Letterman stopped and gesticulated. "That's a little—and this is the word I actually used—that's a little *hinky*," he said.

It was a quintessential Letterman word, obscure and silly-sounding. Then he stated clearly how scared this made him. "I am just a towering mass of Lutheran midwestern guilt," Letterman said in a rare onscreen reference to his religious background. The crowd cheered. As in his response to the September 11 attacks, Letterman spoke directly at the camera and invited the audience to look at the world from his anxious perspective.

The story had been going on for minutes, and yet it remained unclear what it was really about—those terrible things, what were they? Then Letterman dived into the weeds of the case. He called his attorney. A meeting was set up. Then the district attorney got involved and they planned another meeting. Throughout, Letterman kept telling jokes. He said he had planned the second meeting to make sure this guy was serious. "We all have a bad day," he said in mock sarcasm. "And stuff like this slips through the cracks," he added, pausing before speaking in a refined ironic voice: "You've inadvertently blackmailed someone."

Letterman said that earlier that day he had testified to a grand jury about "all the creepy things that I had done." Seven minutes into his yarn, Letterman had still revealed nothing specific about what he had done, and the audience laughed. He paused, looking baffled, and asked, "Now, why is that funny?" He smiled. It was funny because he told the story in the eccentric, suspenseful way he usually did when telling an anecdote. But this was clearly different. "Now, what was all the creepy stuff?" Letterman asked, letting the question hang.

"The creepy stuff was that I have had sex with women who worked for me on this show." Not "woman," but "women." He followed that with this question: "Would it be embarrassing if it were made public? Perhaps it would," he said, and paused before delivering a punch line with perfect timing: "Especially for the women."

The crowd cheered. David Letterman had just confessed to cheating on his wife multiple times, with women who worked for him, an imbalance of power that was, at the very least, troubling. And his audience actually applauded. Whatever its moral content, one thing was clear: this was one of the greatest performances of David Letterman's life.

"The goal was to be truthful," Letterman said, reflecting on this monologue. "My world was crumbling underneath me. I had to tell the truth, which is what I did."

He did tell the truth, but it was a finely edited version, as all the best television stories must be. He left out a lot: he did not name the staffer or explain that the man who wrote the letter was seeing her. Nor did he apologize or say anything about his wife. In his story, Letterman was the victim, which he clearly was in terms of the blackmail plot. But he downplayed his transgressions. Compare his speech with those of the many politicians forced by blackmail to confess to adultery and its brazen showmanship comes into focus. Letterman may have sounded modest, but he showed little contrition. He did, at any rate, win over his audience, for that night.

The next day, Letterman's infidelity was the biggest media story in the country. Over the course of the two shows, Robert Halderman, the blackmailer, appeared all over the tabloids, as did Stephanie Birkitt, who had been sleeping with Letterman while seeing Halderman. By Monday, the next day he was to tape a show, media had crowded around the Ed Sullivan Theater. The *New York Times* reported that his wife, Regina Lasko, "might make a statement of support." That did not happen.

Steve Young was scheduled to meet with Letterman to go over the monologue. The atmosphere in the room was bleak. Not knowing what to say, Young settled for something simple: "How was your weekend?" Letterman responded, "I'm in hell. I will always be in hell until the day after, when I will go to hell."

At his desk on the show that night, Letterman returned to the subject of his blackmail, but this time he put the focus on himself and his wife, whom he had married earlier that year. Letterman said she "had been horribly hurt by my behavior," and he had his work cut out for him at home, before saying that he also needed to stand up to criminals: "So I feel like I did the right thing."

But this time he didn't look like he had done the right thing. He was shaken. "It was akin to having killed your family in a car crash. It was like that to me," Letterman said, recalling his desperation. "I was afraid my family was gone."

To *Late Show* fans, Birkitt, a thirty-four-year-old New Hampshire native who graduated from Wake Forest in 1997, was not an unknown. She had appeared in short cameos around 260 times. An intern who had been promoted to one of Letterman's assistants, Birkitt became a member of the cast of supporting players. Though she had been part of a remote in 1996, Letterman started bringing her onto the show regularly as a comic foil in 2000, asking her to do mundane tasks or stunts. Early on, he called her to request that she tape-record an episode of the MTV show *Jackass*. The next week, he returned to this bit, asking her to tape an episode of the reality show *Temptation Island*. He also called her to discuss the weekend or to ask about a blind date.

They had a spiky, appealing chemistry. Birkitt, whom Letterman sometimes called Smitty, was a slightly awkward onscreen presence, more of an amateur than a polished performer. But she was no pushover. There was something knowing about the way she agreed to perform whatever stunts Letterman would ask her to do, a lingering sarcasm that those who grew up watching David Letterman internalized.

In terms of her onscreen character, Birkitt was essentially a later version of Meg Parsont: a charming, relatable romantic comedy partner for the host. The difference is that in Parsont's case, Letterman had been flirting with a woman he barely knew. Their charged exchanges were merely for the show. But over the years, the lines between Letterman's real life and the show continued to blur. He put more of himself and his life on the air. In this case, we can assume he had some fear of being discovered cheating on his wife with a staffer, and yet he put her on the show. It was a startling example of his private and public selves merging. That he asked his former girlfriend Merrill Markoe to write lines for his current one, Birkitt, could be seen through a pop psychology lens or merely a practical one. Birkitt was no comic and could use some jokes.

Not long after his heart surgery, Letterman did a bit with his doctor and Birkitt that came to a halt when he forced her to do an imitation of the way her old boyfriend danced. Letterman insisted on it. He just watched her dance next to the doctor who had saved his life and laughed, saying, "I enjoyed that, golly." He regularly asked her about dating. And in one show in 2003, Birkitt dressed up as Little Bo Peep. (It was an odd echo of a show in the 1980s in which Shelley Long surprised Letterman by coming on the show dressed as Little Bo Peep.) Letterman asked her why she was in that costume. "Because you made me," she responded.

Watching that show in the office before the scandal, one of the writers cracked a joke: "We should have Stephanie come out visibly pregnant and have Dave say, 'Why do you look like that?' 'Because you made me.'" Everyone laughed, even though the affair had been a well-kept secret.

After the second confessional show, Letterman stopped joking about the affair, but the press hounded him, digging up details from his past. Others stories emerged in tabloids of other affairs such as with the intern Holly Hester, an NYU student, and innuendo involving Laurie Diamond.

Most *Late Show* staffers said they had no idea that he was having an affair with Birkitt. Some suspected as much, and a few said they knew what Letterman was doing. There had been rumors among some on staff about Letterman's flirtations for years. "This is something that I can't verify, but when Dave was catting around, his preference was for NBC pages and interns," said Randy Cohen. But by the time of the scandal, Letterman had been so remote from the staff for so long that few really knew what was happening in his personal life.

Letterman survived, and in the ratings he even benefited from the scandal at first. Steve Martin told him on the show, "It shows you are human. We weren't sure before." But not everyone saw it the same way. Nell Scovell, the second female writer to be hired in the history of the show, wrote an essay for *Vanity Fair* criticizing the show for hiring so few female writers and describing it as having a "hostile work environment" that was "demeaning to women." Letterman became a punch line ("You know the best way to get Letterman to ignore you?" Jay Leno asked on his show. "Marry him.") and a subject of criticism in the press. Many of his oldest friends were shocked, including his friends from Indiana. "I lost a lot of respect for him," said Jeff Eshowsky, his grade school friend. "It bothered me tremendously. It was against my core values."

On television, David Letterman had long presented himself as something of an oddball: cranky, restless, often angry and quick to stir up trouble. He was also fine with coming off as a little bit of a jerk. "I'm no day at the beach," he would tell magazine interviewers probing his romantic past. Letterman never sold himself as a role model or a moral beacon. And yet, with the host in his later years leaning much more on his personal appeal, this scandal threatened to damage his connection with the audience. It called into question what people knew about him, and exposed a certain boys' club sexism that had been lurking under the surface.

As he got older, Letterman increasingly played the horny creep, making sexual commitment out to be a trap and treating interviews with actresses as opportunities to aggressively flirt, fawn, and ogle. He performed the role of the slobbering fool, pushing adoration of attractive female guests to levels that no other late-night host would approach—with the exception of Howard Stern, whose appearances on the *Late Show* had the feel of kindred spirits sharing a secret. Objectifying beautiful women for laughs had become a major part of the show.

When Letterman returned after heart surgery, he walked onto the Ed Sullivan Theater stage flanked by two young, pretty women dressed as nurses. They hugged him and lingered while the crowd gave him a standing ovation. Letterman delivered a joke about how he had new respect for Bill Clinton, whose affair with Monica Lewinsky was a go-to joke for Letterman for years. "I spent half an hour with Hillary," he said, referring to then–First Lady Hillary Clinton, who had been a guest not long before his emergency heart surgery. "Look what happened to me."

As the crowd hooted in approval, Jerry Seinfeld walked onstage and asked what Letterman was doing there, faking an adversarial relationship. It ended with Letterman telling him off: "So why don't you go on home to your wife."

Letterman was most crudely sexual in his interviews. If he complimented a woman's legs—as he did with Jennifer Aniston, Gwen Stefani, and many others—the camera panned down to them. Julia

Roberts and Letterman always played their interviews with a maximum of sexual tension. She kissed him on the air and he repeatedly gushed about her. That Letterman had become old enough to be the father of many of these women didn't change his approach. Blake Lively, at the age of twenty, almost four decades younger than the host, told Letterman in 2009 that she had a crush on him and proposed a three-way with Julia Roberts. He brought up his wife and said to Lively, "I'll tell you something off the record: we're not getting along."

There is, of course, a long history of this trope being played for comedy. Back in Indiana, Letterman watched a local star talk-show host named Paul Dixon who broadcast from Cincinnati. He was a goofball who leered through binoculars at the women in the front row, who, as was the show's tradition, would wear skirts above the knee. Dixon played the creepy voyeur for a largely female audience. He got away with it by mixing in his sexuality with overt silliness. He gave away salamis to his audience members. (Letterman would later give away hams.) "It was the stupidest show, and he would just say, 'This is the stupidest show!'" Letterman said about seeing Dixon in 1969. "I thought: That's really what I want to do."

Letterman didn't use binoculars, but he did occasionally greet female guests with a lingering hug, routinely flattered their looks ("You look great. You look like a million bucks"), and sought out sexual double entendres. The female guests laughed, flirted back a little, and played along gamely. These exchanges seem contrived, riffing on a hackneyed playbook. "He started to seem like a pervy old man," said Eric Stangel. "I don't think he ever really got past it."

The most important romantic relationships in Letterman's life have been with women who worked on the show. He started *Late Night with David Letterman* with his girlfriend, then married one of his employees, before cheating on her with another. He was blackmailed because of his fame from the show. And when his life was sent into turmoil by this scandal, he sank into depression, which he dealt with by relying more on the show.

After the scandal, Letterman changed the daily routine of the show again. This switch didn't have the impact that abandoning rehearsal had, but it was even more strange and telling.

After his on-air confession, Letterman decided that after every episode he would have a postmortem meeting with his top staff. It would be in Barbara Gaines's office and it would often go on for hours. His longtime employee and now producer Jude Brennan and the Stangel brothers were there, too. What made this unusual was that no one at the postmortem was allowed to actually talk about the show. This meant that it wasn't really a postmortem at all but a way for Letterman to cope with and avoid his personal life.

"I can't go home," Letterman told his staff. "I am the most hated man in America." And so everyone sat there and talked about television shows or a documentary about Hitler's final days, by which Letterman had become fascinated. Sometimes he would take a call, and everyone would be quiet while he talked. The staffers had to stay, even though no work was being done. "It was like a hostage situation," said one staff member.

Letterman didn't want to go home. He was scared, ashamed, and racked with self-loathing and worry. The only place he felt safe was on the show.

I was looking for a refuge, and I would go into this office, and there was Barbara, Jude, the Stangels, and we would just talk. Whether they knew it or not, they were being used to support me. I didn't want to go outside. Outside I was scared. Scared as I've ever been in my life. The show was endlessly helpful. I'd be thinking about it and thinking about it. Alan Kalter would introduce me and I'd stop thinking about it.

It's a sign of how dysfunctional the office of the *Late Show* had become that Letterman spent more time distracting himself with his head writers than working with them on the comedy. They couldn't have access to him to rehearse, but they were required to spend hours making small talk.

Letterman turned his anxieties into comedy for the show, and now the show was a vehicle to help him deal with his anxieties. Long after the scandal faded, the postmortem remained, even after Letterman no longer feared losing his family. "It became a habit," he said. The Stephanie Birkitt scandal informed a smaller firestorm that erupted around his show, this time as a result of a 2012 story I wrote for the *New York Times* on Eddie Brill, the *Late Show*'s longtime booker of stand-up comics. It was designed as a portrait of a gatekeeper. Brill had been picking the comics to perform sets on the show since 2001, and his taste favored broadly accessible observational male stand-ups.

In our conversation, Brill talked about what he looked for in a comic, frequently returning to the question of whether or not a stand-up is "honest." This premium on honest performers excluded a wide swath of comics—or, at least, a dogmatically defined version of "honesty" did. For instance, Brill said he wouldn't book Tig Notaro, who back then was known for formally experimental comedy. (Soon after, she would do some of the most confessional and revealing stand-up in years—in material about her cancer.) When I asked Brill why there were so few female stand-up acts on the show (of the twenty-four in 2011, only one was a woman), he explained the disparity this way: "There are a lot less female comics who are authentic. I see a lot of female comics who to please an audience will act like men."

When published, this comment drew widespread criticism, and Brill was removed from his job as booker within the week. He stayed on as a warm-up comic for a few years. Eddie Brill's comments articulated a stereotype that had been around television a long time, inherited from previous generations, including *The Tonight Show*. When that show's longtime producer Fred de Cordova was pressed on booking women as guests, he grew defensive: "I've heard it said that Johnny is intimidated by witty, intellectual women. Well, just who are these women?" He seemed to suggest that this humor doesn't translate onscreen: "We've so often been fooled by witty cocktail talkers who simply don't transfer to television."

The fallout from the Eddie Brill story may have revealed as much as the quote did. Brill denied making the statement, and in a later comment regarding comedian Amy Schumer, who was quoted in the piece saying the show seemed to prefer middle-aged men, Brill dismissed her as a "comedian's girlfriend." Schumer had dated Anthony Jeselnik, and reducing her to just a girlfriend, not unlike what had been done to Merrill Markoe, revealed the pervasive sexist attitudes that had long held female comics back. The comedian's girlfriend would go on to become the most successful comic in America.

On her show *Inside Amy Schumer*, she made the definitive spoof of the gender dynamics of late-night talk, playing an actress named Amy Lake Blively, pandering to a Letterman-like host played by Bill Hader by posing and flirting while going out of her way to seem like a nerdy male fantasy, expressing her love of sci-fi and sports while showing off her legs. The host played the leering juvenile, mocking his own wife and getting laughs from references to his erection. Knowing that she had to turn herself into an object of lust, Blively obliged. Schumer's perceptive sketch carried this insight: for women to succeed on Letterman's show, it often seemed that they needed to play a narrow, sexualized role.

The Eddie Brill controversy was more complicated than a sexist remark. According to several on staff, the comment wasn't the only thing in the article that got Brill in trouble. He ran stand-up workshops for aspiring comics, which some thought presented a conflict of interest, considering his role on the show. He also booked his friends, as well as himself. Some on staff had already been concerned about these issues. "They didn't know he did it the extent he did it," said Eric Stangel. "They didn't know people paid to do his classes. That was the last nail in his coffin."

As it matured into one of the longest-running shows on television, the *Late Show* had become a large, sometimes insular office filled with fiefdoms that could seem isolated from one another, the lines of communication easily frayed. This was in part a result of Letterman's retreating from his own staff, but it was also just the peculiar way the conventions of the show evolved, which Steve O'Donnell compared to the growth of Christianity.

"You start out having these very sincere little attempts to do things that turn into traditions and rituals," he said. "As the generations go by, they get slightly distorted, formalized, until they become a kind of sacred entity unto themselves, until you actually arrive at this sort of rich and well-heeled institution that has George Clooney and car services and a sumptuous greeting room."

MORE FUN THAN HUMANS SHOULD BE
ALLOWED TO HAVE

Two months after Jay Leno left *The Tonight Show*, David Letterman said that he was retiring from the *Late Show*. "Once Jay left, I knew I had to get out," he said. "I was already the old guy."

He made the announcement from his desk, in a discursive monologue that suggested that the question of retirement had hung over him for years. Letterman explained that his answer had long been, "When this show stops being fun, I'll retire ten years later."

He then told a story about going fishing with his son, a pastime he had shared with his late father. On a recent excursion, Letterman had spotted a bird and taken a photo of it, leading him to speculate about what kind of bird it was. When he returned to work on Monday, he had remained focused on the question and put his staff to work figuring it out. One employee called a "bird place" in Washington,

D.C.; another checked with the Audubon Society. Letterman taped his show that night and went home, and when his wife asked him about his day at work, he told her about the pursuit of information about the bird—which, it turned out, was "an immature bald eagle," a detail that seems almost too perfectly apt. His wife had responded, "Great, but who was on the show?" Letterman told the audience that he told her he could not remember, then he smiled. An epiphany.

Letterman started his talk-show career adopting an attitude that telegraphed that he was beyond caring that much. ("It's just television," he would tell people.) In explaining why he was retiring, Letterman said it was when he realized that he didn't care enough. It was an unusually direct admission of what anyone who watched the show already knew: his detachment during all those years had, at least in part, been an act.

His story about the bird was also a bluntly candid confession of what had happened in his final years: the show had begun to serve him as much as he served it. With an almost apologetic look on his face, Letterman asked his audience a rhetorical question: "If you spend all day trying to ID birds, should you really be running a network television program?"

In the months before David Letterman retired, he received a send-off befitting a secular saint. Conan O'Brien called him "the north star" for comedians of his generation, and Jon Stewart, who would stop hosting *The Daily Show* the same year, to less fanfare, described him as an "epiphany." No talk-show host was more effusive than Jimmy Kimmel, who took the night off on the final episode of the *Late Show*. He said Letterman was more important to him than sleep, and referred to Dave as "my Jesus."

The outpouring of affection for David Letterman spoke to his singular stature as not just the late-night talk-show host who had been around longer than any other, but the one who commanded respect throughout the culture. Several months before his final show, Letterman spoke at a tribute to Don Rickles, at the Apollo Theater, in which Jerry Seinfeld, Robert De Niro, Tina Fey, Amy Poehler, Jon Stewart, Chris Rock, Johnny Depp, and Martin Scorsese all gave speeches about the comic. Letterman appeared last and was the only one to get a standing ovation.

In his final month, his show returned to the center of the cultural conversation, and every night was an event. Letterman hosted his final Stupid Pet Trick and returned for a rare man-on-the-street bit with Billy Eichner. In Jerry Seinfeld's final stand-up set on the show, he told the exact same jokes he had the first time he was on *Late Night*, in 1982. Muffling tears, Adam Sandler said goodbye in a moving song that called the host the "king of comedy" and "our best friend on TV." Steve Martin, who was as close to him as any, steered clear of sentiment and poked fun at him. Julia Roberts kissed Letterman on the air and confessed that she had been terrified when she first met him, because she had seen him "absolutely dismember" so many young actresses. "Stupid people annoy you," she said, to which he responded, "This answers my problem of self-loathing."

Norm MacDonald, the deadpan comic who had once parodied Letterman on *Saturday Night Live*, delivered perhaps the most memorable of many emotional tributes. After a stand-up set, he declared Letterman the best talk-show host of all time, before saying, "Mr. Letterman is not for the mawkish, and he has no truck for the sentimental. If something is true, it is not sentimental. And I say in truth, I love you." Bob Dylan appeared as the final musical guest, and when he finished singing the haunting "The Night We Called It a Day," Letterman shook his hand and thanked him. Dylan responded, "It's an honor."

To celebrate his thirty-three years on the air, some co-workers from the show threw a party for more than three hundred current and former staff members at the Friars Club. At the event, he talked to Robert Morton for the first time since he'd fired him and told him that it had been a mistake. Morton also had a conversation with his successor, Burnett. "Rob came up to me and said, 'I had nothing to do with your firing,'" Morton explained, before referring to his relationship with Barry Sand. "I said, 'Rob, I don't believe you, but I forgive you. What you did to me, I did to my predecessor.'"

Many of the original writers attended, but Merrill Markoe stayed home. The Stangel brothers, who had left the show the year before, also said they had no interest in attending or seeing Letterman. His final episode opened with cameo appearances by four U.S. presidents saying, "Our long national nightmare is over." This set the unsentimental tone. "I'm going to be honest with you," he said in his monologue. "It's beginning to look like I'm not going to get *The Tonight Show*."

The emotional peak of the show was a beautiful series of photos from the entire run, assembled with sensitivity and an eye for detail, that told the story of a beloved entertainer who had grown old in front of millions. In his final speech, Letterman did not cry or get emotional, but he responded to the adulation he had received. "We have done over six thousand shows, and I can tell you, a pretty high percentage of those shows absolutely sucked," he said.

He thanked Paul Shaffer and the audience, but he singled out his family. He had never liked having them in the audience for his shows, which he thought would be a distraction, but for the first time, his wife, Regina, and son, Harry, were there. "Just seriously: thank you for being my family," he said. "I love you both, and really nothing else matters, does it?"

In the year after he retired, Letterman made only a few public appearances, moderating a panel, accepting an award. But he rarely performed comedy for a live audience. One exception was when he flew down to San Antonio to appear in a long-running show put on by Martin Short and Steve Martin that included music, characters, and comedy bits for years.

Sitting backstage with Short, his old self-critical streak returned. He kept telling Short that he was going to bomb, that he didn't belong there. Short assured him he would do great, that the audience would be thrilled to see him. Then the show started, and during one of Short's costume changes, he came offstage and saw Letterman, in a suit, waiting with a question: "How many other people have done what I'm going to do?" he asked. Short said none. "That's because they shouldn't." Short responded: "Dave, if you go out there and kill, which you will, will you drop this shit?" Letterman said: "For an hour."

Then he went out and read a Top Ten List about Donald Trump. It killed.

The late-night talk show has always been an ephemeral art form. It's no accident that Steve Allen called one of his memoirs *Mark It and Strike It*—industry jargon for taking down the set—to indicate how fleeting his work could be. When Jack Paar arrived at Rockefeller Center, where he had once hosted *The Tonight Show*, to be a guest on *Late Night with David Letterman*, he complained that the security guards who met him downstairs didn't recognize him. Even Johnny Carson faded from memory, surviving in the public imagination primarily as an influential gatekeeper.

Unlike the finest work of other signal comedies of his era, like *The Simpsons* and *Seinfeld, Late Night with David Letterman* is not constantly running in syndication. His early innovative work has faded from memories and to large parts of his younger audience, is little known. For some, Letterman will always be the hip alternative to *The Tonight Show*, but for others, he represents a stodgier, older generation. His longevity is one of his greatest accomplishments, but it also may have obscured some of his artistic legacy. Meanwhile, the late-night landscape has entirely transformed. Letterman's cynicism about celebrity and his hostility toward show business are almost entirely absent. Hosts not only are sunnier, but they have none of his skepticism of technology or delight in language. And because of DVRs and the Internet, you no longer need to stay up to watch these shows: Late-night television isn't even for late night anymore.

Yet, look hard enough and you can see the influence of David Letterman everywhere. The Internet has become the home of stupid pet tricks and prankish stunts, and the baffling absurdist comedy of *Late Night* is now mainstream. When James Corden shoots an entire show in a stranger's house or when Jimmy Fallon conducts an interview on helium or when Conan O'Brien puts together a deftly edited video of himself interacting with strangers on the street, they are walking in Letterman's footsteps. The remote pieces that Merrill Markoe pioneered have become common on almost all the late-night shows, and while his biting, ironic voice has moved away from late-night talk, it has become pervasive in popular culture.

But the real importance of David Letterman is not only to be found in the way his shows have been copied or whom they have inspired. Some of his best work was funny and exciting precisely because it was too odd to imitate. At his best, Letterman had the integrity and ambition to reach for something more eccentric and personal—a national televised talk show that had the feel of downtown performance art. His comedy always seemed to be commenting on itself, eluding easy readings, and raising questions about its own veracity. While his persistent self-awareness appeared designed to avoid directness, Letterman became one of the most fully realized characters on television, a beloved cranky figure, idiosyncratic, even off-putting, and entirely his own.

Letterman gave all of himself to television—but he needed help. The first two great eras of *Late Night* were the products of collaboration. In the third one, which bled into the CBS show, the writers were marginalized and an entirely new show emerged that in some ways was the most daring, integrated, and honest one yet. Its strength was not in the writing but in its hilarious portrayal of this difficult, fascinating, and self-lacerating character who hated revealing himself in his work but couldn't help doing so. The greatest legacy of David Letterman was that he proved that hosting a late-night talk show could be an inspired and highly personal art.

Letterman, of course, downplays the importance. And in retirement, he says he pays no attention to late night and goes to sleep too early to watch any of the new hosts. But he does care about how he's remembered. "Only because of my son," he said, toward the end of an interview, his glasses pushed up to his forehead so he looked barely recognizable. "My wife will remarry a dentist. But you want your kids to know what you did."

David Letterman says he's not looking to emulate Johnny Carson in his post-show career. After Carson retired, Letterman spent some time with him, and the portrait he painted was of an unhappy man who refused to engage with his history at all. Letterman's takeaway, he suggested, was that you have to take responsibility for your own happiness, a sign that he has matured.

Letterman can seem like a man who has moved on with his life. Other times, he's still in the middle of the late-night war.

Toward the end of one interview, I asked Letterman what the most underrated quality in a talk-show host is, adding as an aside that Jay Leno had answered the same question in one word: "kindness."

Letterman's face remained still upon hearing this. Then he launched into a monologue about the importance of handling guests who aren't performing well, before making one of those pivots that he did so deftly every night on his show. "And," he said, holding the silence for several moments, "kindness."

Letterman paused again, still deadpan, no smiles, waiting for the perfect split second, eyes widening: "Did I not mention kindness? Let me mention . . . kindness."

ACKNOWLEDGMENTS

My original plan was to start this book by watching all 6,024 episodes that David Letterman hosted during his late-night career. This turned out to be an even crazier idea than I thought. Many shows were online, but plenty were not. *Late Show* was generous in opening up its archives, but many episodes were on fragile tape. I scaled back my ambitions, but still saw between two and three thousand hours of television, along with much of his early radio and television work in Indiana and Los Angeles. Many people were helpful in tracking this material down, none more so than Don Giller, the most die-hard of Letterman fans, whose collection of shows, which he recorded on VHS and is currently transferring to a digital format, is complete. Known among Letterman obsessives as the Donz, Giller, whose sharp sarcastic wit may be the best evidence of his dedicated fandom, not only helped me locate and see countless episodes but also frequently provided his singular expertise. He gave this book a trenchant edit and rigorous fact-check, and it's much better because of him.

No one has been more important to the book, from its conception to its publication, than my agent, Daniel Greenberg, whose savvy, high standards, and creativity came in handy throughout the process. My superb editors at Harper, including David Hirshey and Barry Harbaugh, who originally secured the book, and Jonathan Jao, sagely guided it to publication. And much gratitude goes to three brilliant friends, Ada Calhoun, Jessica Grose, and Nick Joseph, for feedback on early drafts; and to Max Weinstein, Kevin Barker, and Max O'Connell for help with research.

I owe a major debt to my editors at the *New York Times*, who for many years have made my work appear better than it is, and never get enough credit for their stellar work. Stephanie Goodman has been particularly important for this book, since she has consistently sharpened my thinking and writing on comedy since I started a biweekly column in 2011.

Far too many people to mention here offered important assistance on this book, but I want to single out Tom Keaney for being a straight shooter, Ella Hurrell, and Misha Collins for generously providing lodging in foreign lands; and my in-laws for necessary help with child care. I am also grateful to my mom and dad for their sense of humor and for helping me clarify the shape of the book. Thank you to Agnès for being the best; to Penny for wisely nixing my original title; and Alice, whose fake laugh is a constant source of inspiration.

NOTES

AI indicates "author interview." All such interviews were conducted between 2014 and 2016.

INTRODUCTION

ix   **"I could not lose her":** AI with David Letterman.

x   **"I was hitchhiking":** AI with Letterman, Sue Berninger, and Pat Wiehle.

xii   **"He's like our Bigfoot":** *Late Night with Seth Meyers*, May 12, 2016.

xiii **His greatness has:** Bill Zehme, "The Fall and Rise of David Letterman," *Esquire*, October 2, 2009; Josh Eelis, "David Letterman: Happy at Last," *Rolling Stone*, May 13, 2015.

xiii **"This show has always":** Deborah Paul, "From Here to Maturity," *Indianapolis Monthly*, July 1991, p. 105.

xvi   **"I feel like":** AI with Letterman.

3   **"From that point on":** AI with Letterman.

4   **"It was the first time":** Ibid.

4   **"You know, for some reason":** Ibid.

4   **"I remember him on the floor":** Ibid.

6   **"[Letterman] emulated him":** AI with Fred Stark.

6   **"That was part of his charm":** AI with Letterman, Stark, Deborah
     Paul, Bill Sellery, Jeff Eshowsky, and Rick Posson; Rosemarie Lennon,
     David Letterman: On Stage and Off (New York: Pinnacle, 1994).

7   **"It's a gelatinous substance":** AI with Jeff Lewis.

7   **"It was an instant confidence booster":** *The Magazine of Sigma Chi,*
     Spring 1988, p. 12.

7   **Today he mostly recalls:** AI with Letterman, Mike Little, Lewis, and
     Chuck Crumbo.

7   **"I am convinced":** Darrell E. Wible, "The Letterman Gang" (unpub-
     lished manuscript in archives at Ball State University, 2006), p. 45.

8   **And as for rock 'n' roll:** Wible, "The Letterman Gang."

8   **"When I first heard Dave":** AI with Chuck Crumbo, Tom Cochrun,
     Al Rent, Tom Watson, and John Gall.

8   **"I remember going":** AI with Letterman.

9   **"You know the de Lune sisters":** Bill Adler, *The Letterman Wit* (New
     York: Carroll & Graf, 1994), p. 23.

9   **"He was in the control booth":** AI with Letterman.

10 **"Dave didn't worry":** AI with Rent and Letterman.

10 **On their last day:** AI with Letterman and Crumbo; Wible, "The Let-
     terman Gang."

11 **Darrell Wible, a professor:** Wible, "The Letterman Gang."

12 **"I was playing exactly to my friends":** AI with Letterman.

12 **The Wagoner Hall revolt:** AI with Tom Watson.

13   **"It was thought"**: AI with John Gall.

13   **"I am informed"**: Wible, "The Letterman Gang."

13   **"We were kids"**: AI with Tom Watson.

15   **"Her goal in life"**: AI with Pat Wiehle.

15   **"I lived in terror"**: AI with Letterman.

15   **"I walked right"**: AI with Letterman, Sue Berninger, and Jeff Lewis.

15   **"When she got back"**: AI with Lewis.

16   **"The office manager"**: AI with Posson.

16   **"Everyone was like"**: AI with Letterman.

17   **"I was dying to be funny"**: Ibid.

17   **Being funny was fine**: AI with Lewis. Lewis said he asked Bill Werch, the head of Channel 13, what had happened. "He told me what David didn't understand is, we wanted a weatherman, not a comedian."

17   **"Letterman started saying jokes"**: AI with Cochrun and Letterman.

19   **"He wanted me to come"**: AI with Letterman.

19   **"I just felt"**: Ibid.

20   **"You have to give them Carmel"**: AI with Jeff Smulyan.

20   **"That was huge"**: AI with Letterman.

21   **"If Dorothy [Letterman]"**: AI with Cochrun.

21   **"I don't know if"**: AI with Letterman.

21   **"If it doesn't work out"**: AI with Cochrun.

CHAPTER 2:

WHEN DAVID MET MERRILL

23   **"It got attention at parties"**: AI with Merrill Markoe.

24   **"My mom didn't work"**: Ibid.

24   **"Whether you call it"**: AI with Gerard Mulligan.

24   **"It was the first show"**: AI with Markoe.

25   **"The title poked fun"** : Alan Sepinwall and Matt Zoller Seitz, *TV (The Book)* (New York: Grand Central, 2016).

25   **"He was the kind of person":** AI with Markoe and David Letterman.

25   **"She looked—the term":** AI with Letterman.

26   **"I remember noticing":** AI with Jay Leno; William Knoedelseder, *I'm Dying Up Here: Heartbreak and High Times in Stand-up Comedy's Golden Era* (New York: PublicAffairs, 2009); Yael Kohan, *We Killed: The Rise of Women in American Comedy: A Very Oral History* (New York: Sarah Crichton Books, 2012); Richard Zoglin, *Comedy at the Edge: How Stand-up in the 1970s Changed America* (New York: Bloomsbury, 2009).

27   **"I went up to him":** AI with Leno.

27   **"Rollins and Joffe":** AI with Robert Morton.

27   **"They used to say Charles":** AI with Stu Smiley.

27   **Buddy Morra, Charles H. Joffe:** AI with Larry Brezner and Buddy Morra.

28   **Comedy scouts from *The Tonight Show*:** Knoedelseder, *I'm Dying Up Here*, p. 107.

28   **"My wife was working":** AI with Letterman.

28   **Walker had a team:** Jimmie Walker, *Dyn-o-mite!* (New York: Da Capo Press, 2012).

28   **"He said that his first wife":** AI with Steve O'Donnell.

28   **"It would be so middle class":** AI with Hal Gurnee.

28   **Letterman later described:** *The Barbara Walters Special*, January 29, 1992.

29   **"I wasn't the bridge":** AI with Markoe.

29   **"That he thought you":** Excerpt from Merrill Markoe's diary.

29   **"He pretended nonchalance":** Ibid.

30   **"This was before everyone":** AI with Letterman and Markoe.

30   **"The first thing":** AI with Markoe.

30   **"Ahh, good, the last":** Ibid.

31   **"They were absurd":** AI with Mulligan.

32   **"Why are no talk-show hosts Jewish?":** AI with Albert Brooks.

32   **"He was edgy":** AI with Morra.

33 **"She had very sharp"**: AI with Rich Hall.

33 **"She was a great"**: AI with Letterman.

33 **"But it was still like"**: AI with Sandra Bernhard.

33 **So when Johnny Carson:** Timothy White, "Johnny Carson: The Rolling Stone Interview," *Rolling Stone,* March 22, 1979.

34 **"I was having a hard time"**: AI with Markoe.

35 **"I have mixed emotions"**: *90 Minutes Live,* February 24, 1978.

35 **"Well, from this moment"**: AI with Letterman and Jo Anne Worley.

36 **"You were the first"**: *Late Night with David Letterman,* March 30, 1990.

36 **Feldman later talked:** AI with Dave Feldman.

36 **Looking back, Markoe:** AI with Markoe.

37 **"I became his secret agent"**: Ibid.

37 **"The hard part"**: Bill Barol, "Staying Up Late with Letterman," *Newsweek,* February 3, 1986.

38 **"I will never do that again"**: AI with Wil Shriner.

38 **"I've never seen an actor"**: Will Harris, "Surely You Can't Be Serious: An Oral History of *Airplane!*" *The A.V. Club,* April 17, 2015.

41 **"I recall getting a call"**: AI with Deborah Miller.

41 **This irritated Carson:** AI with Fred Silverman; Henry Bushkin, *Johnny Carson* (New York: Houghton Mifflin Harcourt, 2013).

42 **"He was a little caustic"**: AI with Silverman.

42 **"There are only so many"**: David Browne, "How David Letterman Reinvented TV," *Rolling Stone,* September 29, 2011.

43 **"I liked Godfrey"**: AI with Letterman.

43 **"He said, 'Arthur Godfrey?!'"**: AI with Silverman.

44 **was the first:** Matt Schudel, "Billy Taylor, Revered Musician, Broadcaster and Spokesman for Jazz, Dies at 89," *Washington Post,* December 30, 2010.

44 **"I could have gotten an-all black band"**: AI with Frank Owens.

45 **"My first clue of what"**: Markoe's diary.

45 **"You know what's wrong"**: AI with Ed Subitzky.

59   **"How do I know"**: AI with Barry Sand and Markoe.

59   **"What did we know"**: AI with Markoe.

60   **"They were game show people"**: AI with Sand.

60   **"It was total chaos"**: Ibid.

60   **"Edie was more vocal"**: AI with Dency Nelson.

61   **"One of the reasons"**: AI with Hal Gurnee; AI with Letterman and Smiley.

63   **"What he perceived"**: AI with Gurnee.

66   **"Merv called one day"**: AI with Deborah Miller.

66   **"It was the most somber"**: AI with Sand.

67   **"If it wasn't for you"**: AI with Markoe.

CHAPTER 4:

NOT TONIGHT

70   **"What are you doing here?"**: AI with Leno, Shriner, Letterman, and Markoe.

70   **"Rich Hall and I"**: AI with Markoe.

70   **"She told me how crazy"**: AI with Markoe and Hall.

71   **Miller wanted to hide:** Ibid.

71   **Weeks later, Letterman and Markoe:** AI with Markoe.

72   **"It was a defensive move"**: AI with Silverman.

72   **"It's crap and it's annoying"**: Deborah Paul, "Hitting the Big Time," *Indianapolis Monthly*, December 1981.

73   **"Oh yeah"**: AI with Letterman.

73   **"To me, nothing"**: Paul, "Hitting the Big Time."

73   **"years of indoctrination"**: AI with Letterman.

73   **"Oh, well, I thought"**: AI with Markoe.

74   ***Late Night* is like calling"**: AI with Letterman.

74   **"Maybe [Letterman] was uncomfortable"**: AI with Hall.

74   **"Frank [Owens] was really"**: AI with Sand.

74 **"They wanted to go with a personality":** AI with Owens.

75 **Sand proposed Paul Shaffer:** Letterman recalls that Merrill Markoe suggested Shaffer, but she denies it.

75 **"Barry Sand always":** AI with Paul Shaffer.

76 **"He was a computer":** AI with Martin Short.

76 **"Hanging out with them":** AI with Shaffer.

77 **"Dave never wanted":** Ibid.

77 **"The engineers said":** Ibid.

78 **"You are my music":** Ibid.

79 **"Paul's temperament is easygoing":** AI with Short.

79 **"You parody what you love":** AI with Shaffer.

80 **"We're looking for somebody":** AI with Stephen Winer.

81 **"For me, anytime":** AI with Karl Tiedemann.

81 **"We thought we":** AI with Letterman.

83 **"We baffled all of America!":** AI with Winer.

83 **"She had an endless enthusiasm":** AI with Randy Cohen.

84 **"I looked for language":** AI with Markoe.

85 **Some of the first reviews:** Howard Rosenberg, "Letterman: Better 'Late' Than Never," *Los Angeles Times*, February 8, 1982.

85 **The *New York Times*'s:** Tony Schwartz, "TV: David Letterman," *New York Times*, February 3, 1982.

85 **"He would become":** AI with Markoe.

86 **"If you have any":** Lewis Grossberger, "David Letterman: Resurrection After Midnight," *Rolling Stone*, June 10, 1982.

86 **"You can hurt":** AI with Sand.

86 **"We would joke":** AI with Barbara Gaines.

87 **"I could say":** AI with Leno.

87 **"Dave always laughed":** Ibid.

87 **"It was the hipper":** AI with Carol Leifer.

87 **"I structured it":** AI with Short.

88 **"He made fun":** AI with Paul Reubens.

88 **"I think it's important"**: Sam Merrill, "David Letterman: The Playboy Interview," *Playboy*, October 1984.

89 **"I found him sexy"**: AI with Sandra Bernhard.

89 **"But that was their thing"**: Ibid.

91 **"I never met anyone"**: AI with James Downey.

92 **"Just the fact"**: AI with Scott Aukerman.

93 **"For me, it was"**: AI with Letterman.

CHAPTER 5:

THE HARVARD TAKEOVER

95 **"I wasn't radical"**: AI with Tom Gammill.

96 **Many of their friends:** AI with Max Pross.

96 **"*Saturday Night Live*"**: Ibid.

96 **"It was nasty"**: AI with George Meyer.

96 **"We would sit"**: AI with Gammill.

97 **"They had a much broader"**: AI with Letterman.

97 **"Merrill was sly"**: AI with Meyer.

97 **"Tom and Max"**: AI with Andy Breckman.

97 **"They hated people"**: AI with Richard Morris.

98 **"I could see"**: AI with Breckman.

98 **"I remember thinking"**: AI with Gammill.

98 **"That was the big split"**: AI with Winer.

99 **"The impression I got"**: AI with Pross.

99 **"George was always"**: AI with Markoe.

99 **"It pleased the crowd"**: Ibid.

99 **"We are spending 10–12 hours"**: Markoe's diary.

100 **"It was a daylong fistfight"**: *The Phil Donahue Show*, January 25, 1986.

100 **"The last ten months"**: Markoe's diary.

100 **"*You* sleep with him"**: AI with Gammill.

100   **"I think we were both relieved":** AI with Letterman.

101   **How exactly would this work?:** AI with Breckman.

101   **"As a paranoid young man":** AI with Meyer.

101   **"More dial-it-services?":** AI with Breckman.

101   **"We've got to reeducate":** AI with Gammill.

102   **"We went from being these two young idiots":** AI with Pross.

102   **"He was the coolest guy I ever met":** AI with Gurnee.

102   **"Jim Downey would say":** AI with Meyer.

102   **"You guys can play":** AI with O'Donnell.

103   **"Words are very important":** AI with Downey.

103   **"You're not just some":** AI with Martin.

103   **"If you're ever":** AI with Downey.

103   **"Downey had his own schedule":** AI with Sand.

104   **What mattered to him:** AI with Downey.

104   **"Downey would sometimes":** AI with O'Donnell.

105   **"What I was trying to do":** AI with Meyer.

106   **"It started as one thing":** AI with Markoe.

107   **"After the show":** AI with Breckman.

108   **Imitating and subverting:** The writer Steve Winer recalled, "I used to say to Tom, 'All your pieces have this line in it: "So you see, Jimmy."'"

108   **Letterman called this:** Nell Scovell, "The Lost Laughs of Letterman," *New York*, May 5, 2015.

109   **"It was getting kind of":** AI with Meyer.

110   **"Dave would say something":** AI with Downey.

110   **"I hear Rollins":** Ibid.

111   **"Every person on the staff":** Ibid.

111   **"Letterman was not":** AI with Breckman.

111   **"Dave was hurt":** AI with Meyer.

112   **"So Dave gives me":** AI with Downey.

NOTES

112 "[*Late Night*] gave us the confidence": AI with Meyer.

113 "It's kind of like": AI with Tim Long.

114 "They broke so much ground": AI with Matt Wickline.

CHAPTER 6:

THE FOUNDING FATHERS OF LATE NIGHT

118 "It is not part": Steve Allen, *Mark It and Strike It* (New York: Holt, Rinehart and Winston, 1960), p. 242.

119 **Letterman saw Steve Allen's show:** Ben Alba, *Inventing Late Night: Steve Allen and the Original Tonight Show* (New York: Prometheus, 2005); Allen, *Mark It and Strike It*; Jack Paar, *I Kid You Not* (New York: Pocket Books, 1960); Jack Paar, *P.S. Jack Paar: An Entertainment* (New York: Doubleday, 1983); Jack Paar, *My Saber Is Bent* (New York: Pocket Books, 1961); Bernard M. Timberg, *Television Talk: A History of the TV Talk Show* (Austin: University of Texas Press, 2002); Alex Ross, "The Politics of Irony," *New Republic*, November 8, 1993; Kliph Nesteroff, *The Comedians* (New York: Grove Press, 2015); AI with Gurnee, Letterman, Martin, Winer, Fred Graver, and O'Donnell.

120 **In a definitive magazine profile:** Kenneth Tynan, "Fifteen Years of the Salto Mortale," *New Yorker*, February 20, 1978.

120 **His producer Fred de Cordova:** Ibid.

121 **"People my age":** AI with Winer.

121 **Cavett gave a forum:** Chris Ip, "When Late Night Went Political," *Columbia Journalism Review*, October 2014.

122 **"It's hard to criticize":** Judd Apatow, *Sick in the Head* (New York: Random House, 2015).

122 **"We should get together":** AI with Markoe.

123 **"It broke that illusion":** AI with Letterman.

123 **"He was at his best":** Ibid.

124 **"Of the newest personalities"**: Paar, *P.S. Jack Paar*, p. 27.

124 **"What the fuck"**: AI with Gurnee.

125 **"Jack gets pissed off"**: AI with Gurnee, Letterman, and Markoe.

125 **"I do remember"**: AI with O'Donnell.

125 **"That's just the kind"**: AI with Jeff Martin.

125 **"That seemed good"**: AI with Markoe.

125 **"In those days"**: Ibid.

126 **passed on Conan O'Brien:** Boyd Hale got the writer's job over Conan O'Brien in 1987.

126 **"The joke among the writers"**: AI with Randy Cohen.

126 **"I would sometimes"**: AI with O'Donnell.

127 **"Merrill said it once"**: AI with Mulligan.

127 **To our discredit:** Ed Bark, "A Vintage, Self-Analytical Letterman during a Rare One-On-One Sit-Down," Uncle Barky's Bytes, http://www.uncle barky.com/back_files/71ae7106cea4d88ed1ad34597ee863db-35.html.

128 **"a man in a suit"**: AI with Sand.

128 **"He's suavely repressed"**: James Wolcott, "Dead Letter," *New York*, May 30, 1983.

128 **"It affected me"**: AI with Letterman.

128 **"Part of the point"**: AI with Joe Toplyn.

129 **"The stunts and informality"**: AI with Leifer.

129 **"But Steve Allen"**: AI with Martin.

130 **"Dave was this punky"**: AI with Short.

130 ***Playboy* magazine announced:** Merrill, "David Letterman: The Playboy Interview."

131 **"I don't think"**: *Donahue*, January 25, 1986.

131 **"How bad is the new"**: AI with Downey.

CHAPTER 7:

THE WRITER UNDER THE STAIRS

134 **"What if there isn't?":** AI with Chris Elliott.

134 **"I remember George [Meyer]":** Ibid.

135 **"That shit's been happening":** AI with Elliott and Letterman.

135 **"I was the kind of guy":** Ibid.

135 **"I never had the chops":** Ibid.

136 **"They were amused":** Ibid.

136 **"There was a kind":** AI with O'Donnell.

136 **Elliott, along with:** AI with Elliott.

137 **"Chris had an awareness":** AI with Matt Wickline.

137 **"We thought there was something":** AI with O'Donnell.

140 **"You move the show":** AI with Cohen.

141 **"The narrative of these characters":** AI with Elliott.

141 **"It's the stuff I used":** Ibid.

142 **"It ripped me up":** AI with Graver.

142 **"I was stunned":** AI with Elliott.

143 **"Because Chris has":** AI with Graver.

144 **"Merrill saw that":** Ibid.

146 **"Was he inside the joke":** AI with Cohen.

146 **"We thought Pat Boone":** AI with Elliott.

CHAPTER 8:

THE LETTERMAN GENERATION

148 **"We are determined":** David Leavitt, "The New Lost Generation," *Esquire,* May 1985.

148 **"You wanted to impress him":** AI with Short.

149 **"Dave got through to me":** AI with Shaffer.

149 **"David said, 'You'":** Ibid.

150 **"I had a hard time with Paul":** AI with Cohen.

151 **"If a joke wouldn't work":** AI with Letterman.

153 **In his history:** Tony Hendra, *Going Too Far* (New York: Doubleday, 1987), p. 445.

153 **"He used to make fun":** AI with Markoe.

154 **68 percent of its audience:** Glenn Collins, "Can David Letterman Survive Success?" *New York Times*, July 27, 1988.

154 **"The joke was on television":** AI with O'Donnell.

154 **To Wallace, Letterman:** David Foster Wallace, *A Supposedly Fun Thing I'll Never Do Again: Essays and Arguments* (New York: Little, Brown, 1997); D. T. Max, *Every Love Story Is a Ghost Story* (New York: Penguin, 2013).

154 **"Few artists dare":** Stephen J. Burn, ed., *Conversations with David Foster Wallace* (Jackson: University Press of Mississippi, 2012), p. 48.

155 **That this show:** David Foster Wallace, "Late Night," *Playboy*, June 1988.

155 **"The great thing":** AI with Martin.

156 **"I went to L.A. over the holidays":** AI with Jon Maas.

158 **"Camp Lite uses irony":** Paul Rudnick and Kurt Andersen, "The Irony Epidemic," *Spy*, March 1989, p. 93.

158 **Alex Ross wrote:** Ross, "The Politics of Irony."

159 **"I thought he was":** AI with Letterman.

160 **"He's not a comic":** AI with O'Donnell and Rob Burnett.

161 **"I had a degree":** AI with Letterman.

162 **"The writers and clip guys":** AI with O'Donnell.

163 **Letterman, who wanted:** In a *Boston Herald* article by David Wecker ("Letterman Presents 'Guerrilla TV' at Its Best," from June 12, 1986), Letterman said, "I still feel comfortable with the level we reached, I can still see myself as kind of an underdog. Still scrapping, rather than being on top."

CHAPTER 9:

THE TWO DAVES

165 **"Dave gives credit":** AI with Barbara Gaines.

167 **"It started as conceptual":** AI with O'Donnell.

167 **"There are two Daves":** AI with Wickline.

168 **"Three is the funniest":** AI with Graver.

168 **"It felt like those":** AI with Markoe.

169 **A photo-by-photo version:** David Letterman, *Late Night with David Letterman: The Book*, ed. Merrill Markoe (New York: Villard, 1985).

169 **"He got angry":** AI with Markoe.

170 **"It was meant":** Ibid.

170 **"An early nugget":** AI with O'Donnell.

171 **In a *Rolling Stone* interview:** Lynn Hirschfeld, "Out in Left Field with David Letterman," *Rolling Stone*, June 20, 1985.

171 **"I don't think":** AI with Gurnee.

174 **"If the show":** AI with Cohen.

175 **"Before that, when you":** AI with Gurnee.

178 **Letterman told Meyer:** AI with Meyer.

178 **"A lot of what":** AI with Burnett.

179 **"We were very good friends":** AI with Wickline.

180 **"Dave nixed it":** AI with Elliott.

181 **"Good. It's my house":** AI with O'Donnell.

183 **"I remember thinking":** AI with Jeff Martin.

CHAPTER 10:

COMEDY IS NOT PRETTY!

188 **"The doctor told me":** AI with Markoe.

188 **"You could do a chapter":** AI with O'Donnell.

189 **"He called me":** AI with Letterman.

189 **"He thinks he's dying":** AI with Hillary Rollins.

189 **"The running joke":** AI with Steve Young.

190 **"Then Dave very carefully":** AI with Gurnee.

190 **"So you're going skating":** AI with Dave Hanson.

190 **"He wasn't a hearty":** AI with Sand.

191 *Max Headroom:* "John J. O'Connor, "Max Headroom as Host of an Interview Show," *New York Times*, August 6, 1987.

191 **"Who the hell":** AI with Sand.

192 **"It was misguided":** AI with Shaffer.

192 **"I didn't want":** AI with Sand.

192 **"It became something":** AI with Dency Nelson.

192 **"It got to the point":** AI with Letterman.

193 **"We had an answering machine":** AI with Markoe.

194 **"I felt personally betrayed":** AI with Cohen.

196 **"He's the only guy":** AI with Bill Scheft.

197 **"That was a common":** AI with Kevin Curran.

197 **"Before, the head writer":** AI with Jude Brennan.

199 **"That show bothered me":** AI with Bernhard.

200 **"The show invited":** Glenn Collins, "Seriously Now, Can Writerless Comics Cope?" *New York Times*, August 7, 1988.

200 **"All the writers":** AI with Madeleine Smithberg.

203 **"I heard years":** AI with Wickline.

203 **"I think it's true":** Richard Zoglin and David Letterman, "Interview: David Letterman: He's No Johnny Carson," *Time*, February 6, 1989.

203 **"He says he really misses me":** Markoe's diary.

203 **"I (ahem) intercepted":** AI with Markoe.

204 **In a *Rolling Stone* interview:** Fred Schruers, "Man of the Year: David Letterman," *Rolling Stone*, December 29, 1994.

204 **"When Merrill left":** AI with Cohen.

204 **"Without her, you and I":** AI with Letterman.

205 **"The show became":** AI with Martin.

CHAPTER 11:

MEG AND MOM

207 **On February 11, 1991:** Bill Hoffman and Timothy McDarrah, "There Goes Johnny: NBC Looking to Dump Carson for Jay Leno," *New York Post*, February 11, 1991.

207 **As Bill Carter detailed:** Bill Carter, *The Late Shift: Letterman, Leno, and the Network Battle for the Night* (New York: Hyperion, 1994), p. 48.

207 **Henry Bushkin and Dave Tebet:** AI with Letterman and Henry Bushkin.

208 **When he asked why:** AI with Warren Littlefield and Rick Ludwin; Carter, *The Late Shift*.

208 **"It was a little shocking":** AI with Littlefield.

208 **When told this today:** AI with Letterman.

208 **"Jack Paar would turn":** AI with Ludwin.

209 **"From the numbers":** AI with Sari DeCesare.

209 **Late-night talk shows:** Bill Carter, "Luring *Late Night*'s Letterman Is a Matter of Time and Money," *New York Times*, November 30, 1992.

209 **"I remember when Rick Dees":** AI with Smithberg.

210 **In a *GQ* story:** Jennet Conant, "David Letterman: Is He Still the King of Hip?" *GQ*, June 1990.

210 **"I've had this job":** Ibid.

211 **"If you want something":** AI with Letterman.

213 **"[Dave] called him":** AI with O'Donnell.

213 **"He loves his mother":** AI with Smithberg.

214 **"The only time":** AI with Steve Young.

214 **"I remember one time":** AI with Markoe.

216 **"He had us over":** AI with Martin.

217 **"He had the rights":** AI with Elliott.

217 **"The old-timers":** AI with Young.

220 **"There was a slightly":** AI with Meg Parsont.

221 **"In the beginning":** AI with Letterman.

221 **"That's super-complicated":** AI with O'Donnell.

CHAPTER 12:

THE AGONY OF VICTORY

236 **"He was most uncomfortable":** AI with Shaffer.

237 **"He was always interested":** AI with O'Donnell.

237 **"This is an audience":** Zehme, "Letterman Lets His Guard Down."

237 **"Everyone is born":** AI with Young.

238 **"Rob and I became":** AI with Letterman.

238 **"Rob was the golden boy":** AI with Young.

238 **"Rob and Jon":** Ibid.

239 **"Rob would exclude everyone":** AI with Gaines.

239 **It ran so often:** Richard Zoglin, "Dave: He's Tanned. He's Rested. He's Ready. Is America?" *Time*, August 30, 1993.

239 **"I think the biggest":** AI with Burnett.

239 **"The first year":** AI with Young.

240 **"At a certain point":** Ibid.

241 **"I think we hurt ourselves":** AI with Letterman.

242 **"I did feel":** AI with Martin.

242 **"It didn't work":** AI with Parsont.

243 **"People used to say":** AI with Letterman.

243 **"How would you":** AI with Hall.

244 **"I took the hit":** AI with Morton.

245 **"That was when the show":** AI with Aukerman.

246 **"Moonves called me up":** AI with Morton.

246 **"When GE took over":** AI with Gurnee.

247 **"In the old show":** AI with Morton.

CHAPTER 13:

THE OSCAR MYTH

249 **"the ex-girlfriend":** AI with Markoe.

250 **"It made me really angry":** AI with Markoe.

250 **It was written:** Merrill Markoe, *What the Dogs Have Taught Me* (New York: Villard, 2005), p. 112.

250 **"Instead of dissolving":** AI with Markoe.

251 **"It was like":** Ibid.

252 **"I felt like Bugs Bunny":** AI with Markoe and Gaines.

253 **"It was almost like":** AI with Mulligan.

253 **The *Times* reported:** William Grimes, "'Forrest Gump' Triumphs with 6 Academy Awards," *New York Times*, March 28, 1995.

255 **"He also told me":** AI with Scheft.

255 **The initial reviews:** John J. O'Connor, "The Winner Isn't David Letterman," *New York Times*, March 29, 1995; Joyce Millman, "'Late Show' Star Makes It Fun," *San Francisco Examiner*, March 28, 1995; Tom Shales, "And the Award for Longest Ceremony," *Washington Post*, March 28, 1995.

255 **But after the show:** AI with Scheft.

256 **"It all started":** Lloyd Grove, "Late-Night Sweats," *Vanity Fair*, October 1996.

257 **"He owned the failure":** AI with Morton.

257 **"The fight was":** AI with Letterman.

258 **Creepy Dave was a strange character:** Schruers, "It's Dave's World."

259 **"I remember Dave":** AI with Leno.

259 **"Dave was pushing":** AI with Burnett.

260 **"He was being petulant":** Ibid.

262 **"Letterman no longer":** Tom Shales, "Late Night's Late Riser," *Washington Post*, June 18, 1996.

262 **"The problem was that":** AI with Letterman.

262 **"By the third day":** AI with Young.

262 **"I wanted to travel":** AI with Gurnee.

263 **"We used to do skits":** N. F. Mendoza, "Letterman's Show Losing Its Voice," *Los Angeles Times*, August 18, 1995.

263 **"What I had not counted on":** AI with Letterman.

263 **"We had a little":** Schruers, "It's Dave's World."

263 **"So we hatched a plan":** AI with Morton.

264 **"Rob came to me":** AI with Letterman.

264 **"He was happy":** AI with Burnett.

265 **"I exploded and yelled":** AI with Shaffer.

266 **"I felt like":** AI with Bernhard.

266 **"You know those guys":** AI with Tim Long.

266 **"He became pasty":** AI with Young.

267 **"I felt really bad":** AI with Long.

267 **"a detatched, aloof figure":** Chris Smith, *The Daily Show (The Book): An Oral History as Told by Jon Stewart, the Correspondents and Guests* (New York: Grand Central, 2016).

267 **"The legacy of that show":** Ibid.

267 **"What happened is that":** AI with Burnett.

268 **"Dave seemed disappointed":** AI with O'Donnell.

270 **Steve O'Donnell joked:** Ibid.

270 **"The heart surgery":** AI with Letterman.

CHAPTER 14:

HINKY

271 **"Johnny was up in arms":** AI with Letterman.

273 **"I was tired of it":** Ibid.

273 **"All the others met":** AI with Eric Stangel.

274 **"If there was something":** AI with Shaffer and Letterman.

275 **"We were often":** AI with Justin Stangel and Eric Stangel.

275 **"Dave would always":** AI with Gaines.

275 **"With him and Rob":** Ibid.

276 **"I started thinking":** AI with Letterman.

276 **"I think Dave":** AI with Markoe.

276 **During this time:** David Bauder, "Letterman Tells Oprah About Affairs, Depression, Leno," *Boston Globe*, January 8, 2013.

277 **"He shook his head":** AI with Hall.

277 **"He thinks no one":** AI with Martin.

277 **"He said, 'This is'":** AI with Jena Friedman.

277 **"I've seen Steve O'Donnell":** AI with Rick Scheckman.

277 **"I gave him":** AI with Young and Burnett.

279 **"I felt like":** AI with Letterman.

279 **"I could never imagine":** Ibid.

280 **"When I heard":** AI with Lewis.

281 **Peter Kaplan, the late:** Peter Kaplan, "That Joke Had Everything," *Esquire*, December 1981.

281 **"Just a funny guy":** Ibid.

281 **He had endured:** Peter Kaplan, "Couch Warfare," *New York*, September 6, 2009.

282 **"Too much MSNBC":** AI with Letterman.

282 **"You got a show":** Ibid.

282 **Making the best case:** Kaplan, "Couch Warfare."

284 **"The goal was":** AI with Letterman.

285 **The *New York Times* reported:** Bill Carter and Brian Stelter, "Letterman Apologizes to His Wife and Staff," *New York Times*, October 5, 2009.

285 **"I'm in hell":** AI with Young.

285 **"It was akin":** AI with Letterman.

287 **"This is something":** AI with Cohen.

287 **Nell Scovell, the second female:** Nell Scovell, "Letterman and Me," *Vanity Fair*, November 2009.

287 **"I lost a lot":** AI with Jeff Eshowsky.

289 **"It was the stupidest show":** AI with Letterman.

289 **"He started to seem":** AI with Eric Stangel.

290 **"I was looking":** AI with Letterman.

291 **"It became a habit":** Ibid.

291 **"There are a lot less":** Jason Zinoman, "The Comedy Gatekeeper Who Makes Letterman Laugh," *New York Times*, January 11, 2012.

292 **"I've heard it said":** Tynan, "Fifteen Years of the Salto Mortale."

292 **Brill denied making the statement:** Drew Grant, "David Letterman's Booker in Hot Water After New York Times Controversy," *Observer*, January 16, 2012.

293 **"They didn't know":** AI with Eric Stangel.

293 **"You start out having":** AI with O'Donnell.

CHAPTER 15:

MORE FUN THAN HUMANS SHOULD BE ALLOWED TO HAVE

295 **"Once Jay left":** AI with Letterman.

297 **"It's an honor":** AI with Shaffer.

298 **"Rob came up to me":** AI with Morton.

298 **The emotional peak:** Barbara Gaines spearheaded this effort, with help from Randi Grossack and Mark Spada.

299 **"How many other people":** AI with Short.

301 **"Only because of my son":** AI with Letterman.

301 **Toward the end:** AI with Leno.

301 **Letterman paused again:** AI with Letterman.

INDEX

ABOUT THE AUTHOR

J ASON ZINOMAN writes the On Comedy column for the *New York Times*. He has also contributed to *Vanity Fair*, the *Guardian*, and *Slate*, and is the author of *Shock Value* and *Searching for Dave Chappelle*. He lives in Brooklyn, New York.